COMPLIANCE CAPITALISM

In this book, Sidney Dekker sets out to identify the market mechanisms that explain how less government paradoxically leads to greater compliance burdens. This book gives shape and substance to a suspicion that has become widespread among workers in almost every industry: we have to follow more rules than ever—and still, things can go spectacularly wrong.

Much has been privatized and deregulated, giving us what is sometimes known as 'new public management,' driven by neoliberal, market-favoring policies. But, paradoxically, we typically have more rules today, not fewer. It's not the government: it's us. This book is the first of a three-part series on the effects of 'neoliberalism,' which promotes the role of the private sector in the economy. *Compliance Capitalism* examines what aspects of the compliance economy, what mechanisms of bureaucratization, are directly linked to us having given free markets a greater reign over our political economy. The book steps through them, picking up the evidence and levers for change along the way.

Dekker's work has always challenged readers to embrace more humane, empowering ways to think about work and its quality and safety. In *Compliance Capitalism*, Dekker extends his reach once again, writing for all managers, board members, organization leaders, consultants, practitioners, researchers, lecturers, students, and investigators curious to understand the genuine nature of organizational and safety performance.

Sidney Dekker is Professor and Director of the Safety Science Innovation Lab at Griffith University in Brisbane, Australia, and Professor at the Faculty of Aerospace Engineering at Delft University in the Netherlands. He has been flying the Boeing 737 for an airline on the side. Sidney is a bestselling author of, most recently: *Foundations of Safety Science; The Safety Anarchist; The End of Heaven; Just Culture; Safety Differently; The Field Guide to Understanding 'Human Error'; Second Victim; Drift into Failure;* and *Patient Safety*. More about him is available at sidneydekker.com.

THE BUSINESS, MANAGEMENT AND SAFETY EFFECTS OF NEOLIBERALISM

This mini-series sets out to explore the far-reaching effects of neoliberalism. Neoliberalism supports and promotes the role of the private sector in the economy, and argues that markets and free trade are the only way to get the best price for the best quality. In this series, Sidney Dekker examines how neoliberalism actually affects business, management, and safety in practice.

Compliance Capitalism
How Free Markets Have Led to Unfree, Overregulated Workers
Sidney Dekker

For more information about this series, visit: www.routledge.com/The-Business-Management-and-Safety-Effects-of-Neoliberalism/book-series/BMSEN

COMPLIANCE CAPITALISM

How Free Markets Have Led to Unfree, Overregulated Workers

Sidney Dekker

Routledge
Taylor & Francis Group
LONDON AND NEW YORK

First published 2022
by Routledge
2 Park Square, Milton Park, Abingdon, Oxon OX14 4RN

and by Routledge
605 Third Avenue, New York, NY 10158

Routledge is an imprint of the Taylor & Francis Group, an Informa business

British Library Cataloguing-in-Publication Data
A catalogue record for this book is available from the British Library

Library of Congress Cataloging-in-Publication Data
Names: Dekker, Sidney, author.
Title: Compliance capitalism: how free markets have led to unfree, overregulated workers / Sidney Dekker.
Description: Abingdon, Oxon; New York, NY: Routledge, 2021. |
Series: The business, management and safety effects of neoliberalism |
Includes bibliographical references and index.
Subjects: LCSH: Deregulation. | Free markets. |
Industries–Self-regulation. | Employee rules. | Labor. | Bureaucracy.
Classification: LCC HD3612 .D45 2021 (print) |
LCC HD3612 (ebook) | DDC 331.25/6–dc23
LC record available at https://lccn.loc.gov/2021005062
LC ebook record available at https://lccn.loc.gov/2021005063

ISBN: 978-1-032-01236-0 (hbk)
ISBN: 978-1-032-01235-3 (pbk)
ISBN: 978-1-003-17780-7 (ebk)

Typeset in Joanna MT
by Newgen Publishing UK

L'homme est né libre, et partout il est dans les fers
(Humans are born free, but everywhere they are in chains)
Jean-Jacques Rousseau (1762)

CONTENTS

FOREWORD

RICHARD I. COOK, MD

When you read Dekker's latest book, now in your hands, you might find that he is right—and depressingly so. The picture he paints is sometimes so recognizable, and so dismal, that you could find yourself driven to despair. With compliance capitalism, there appears to be no limit to, nor escape from, the machinery that is draining expertise from society, destroying the fabric of the economy, and, additionally, promoting the rise of authoritarianism.

Historical antecedents abound. Administrative structures have long sought control over worker practice. Watchclocks are a good example. The portable watchclock was developed to provide an independent record of watchmen making their rounds. The watchman would carry the sealed clock on his route, and all the time the clockwork slowly drove a coiled paper strip where it could be marked by a coded key. This then provided a record in time. The company would chain different keys at locations on the watchman's route. Arriving at the location, the watchman would insert and twist the key, leaving a distinct mark. At the end of the shift, the watchman would turn the watchclock over to an administrator who would check to see that the marks were present at the appropriate times. Invented in the middle of the 1800s, the watchclock underwent rapid development in the first two decades of the 20th century. More than 30 patents from that era were held by the largest US manufacturer, the Detex Corporation.

By 1930 watchclocking was widely used to track watchmen, especially in large corporations. The processes became integrated into administration and finance. Some commercial insurance policies required that the company establish procedures to provide independent review of the watchclock recordings in order to maintain coverage of the facilities. Mechanical watchclocks were used as recently as the 2010s. Todays 'watchclocks' are electronic devices with radio frequency identification (RFID) tags and global positioning system (GPS) and a host of other functions. But the basic principle remains the same: assuring compliance through surveillance. The watchclock reminds us that there is a behind-the-scenes web of influences and commitments that antedate the computer and our current mess. It also shows how the advent of the computer and related technologies has allowed this web to become the straightjacket that it is today. Dekker describes that web, letting us see how the individual threads combine and support each other. Technological and political-economic developments have together given rise to two worlds. One is a formal world that consists of computerized databases and their contents. The other is an informal world that contains our experiences and actions. Dekker shows how our efforts to make the real world better have, instead, made a dazzlingly elaborate formal world that hides the real one from view.

These are not separate worlds, of course. The formal world and the informal one often touch and influence each other. When I conduct an anesthetic procedure, a formal record of that event is created and it remains as testimony. The anesthetic itself dissipates rather quickly; yet the formal record persists. The database entry for this formal anesthetic record is remarkably rich. It includes links to the patient record; elaborate pharmaceutical and supply accounting; other practitioners involved in the care; performance measurement systems; and – of course – to accounting, billing, and financial processes. It also includes data derived directly from the patient and related equipment: blood gas machine readings; the glucose meter on the anesthesia backstand; even the warming blanket I place over the patient registers its presence. It is quite intricate. This is an expensive assembly which requires a small army of support personnel, programmers, administrators, and repair people in the hospital—not to mention a rather astounding amount of money for the software, services, and computing. For many hospitals, information technology (IT) has become a huge and sometimes crippling cost.

When things are working well, these data flow inside a network made up of thousands of devices, all churning along in their continuous generation and consumption of data. All these data are captured and maintained in databases that represent the other world—the world of 'data doubles,' as Dekker will call them later in this book. For all this behind-the-scenes machinery to work, I have to take care that the formal record contains all sorts of evidence. I must certify that certain things have happened before the anesthetic begins, that various safety protocols have been followed, and even that I have myself been present at various times and done all the things I should have done and none of the things I should not have done. I am tracked and watched like the watchmen of the 19th century—but then on steroids.

The compliance pressure can be enormous. At one point I started counting the checkboxes and menu drop-downs needed to complete an 'ordinary' formal anesthetic record. I gave up when I came to 50. Thankfully, the computer has a templating mechanism that allows me to specify all the checkboxes and menu selections so that I can populate most of these entries in the database record for a given anesthetic by pressing a single button. Yet herein lies a paradox: most of these things can be done with the push of a single button. I need not read or select the specific items to create the formal record—indeed it would be almost impossible to do so in the time available. The machinery of compliance and attestation is so awkward and large that it has spawned its own remedy—its own 'workaround.' A review of the formal record will show that I have done all the steps but someone watching me would see me choose one item from a dropdown menu and proceed.

Indeed, a great deal of medical record documentation is now automated in exactly this way—however perverse. The requirement for so many pieces of information for each patient is met by use of automation that fills in many of these details. For example, rules specify that an attending physician must personally document aspects of the patient's condition on every day of the hospital stay. The automation makes this easier by allowing the physician to bring forward the entries from yesterday and 'paste' them into the current day. A minor sport in the modern hospital is examining patients and contrasting them to what the formal record records; the descriptions are often disparate. A patient might be described as being mechanically ventilated when she is actually extubated and breathing spontaneously, for example. Sometimes very strange things appear in records. I discovered an entry saying that crutches had been provided to a patient in the emergency department who was being admitted for abdominal bleeding. I suppose those crutches are still waiting patiently for someone to use them. But all the discrepancies between the two worlds are evanescent: eventually the patient leaves the hospital and only the formal record remains, becoming the canonical record of both worlds.

This is, of course, insane. We are making up records that attest and characterize to meet the demands of a large, mostly uncoordinated but insistent and intrusive apparatus of assurance. The records amount to bland, voluminous drivel that serve mainly as testimony to our compliance. Indeed the content of many patients' records are so byzantine that clinicians often have to resort to actually talking to the patients in order to figure out what has been happening with them. And this seems to be at least as much by design as by chance: records are preemptive defenses against potential future criticism. How is it, then, that meaningful, thoughtful, effective work is still done? Is it all because of covert work systems? Are all the 'good' doctors and nurses like the Lindesfarne monks, preserving the last bits of civilization in lead-sealed casks in the hope that future generations will recover them? You could be forgiven for thinking that those on the frontlines have simply been drawing on a residuum of professional ethos. Indeed, the premise that all the compliance is inefficient and unnecessary seems to depend very much on the reservoir of motivation, knowledge, and wisdom in the workers. Distributional inequalities aside, this might explain, in part, that a great deal is being produced and consumed despite all the compliance—by all accounts orders of magnitude more than half a century ago.

Perhaps the miasma of rules, the capitalism of compliance, is an inevitable cost of production. It might even be a key element that rationalizes work and participation. Indeed, an apologist for the current situation might aver that buying and selling risk using financial machinery is a good thing, because it frees up capital to address uncertainties. Of course they can get it wrong (just think of the 2008 financial crisis). And of course there are unscrupulous people who seek to profit from impure markets. But this is by no means novel or modern, or even necessarily western. Monty Python's skit about the efficiency experts trying to modernize medieval manufacturing comes to mind. Both ancient and modern China demonstrate the same commitment to compliance and bureaucracy (the Chinese might be said to have invented it) and crytpo-surveilo-Tayloristic management. Even the sheer collapse of society itself, seemingly just around the corner, isn't a new concern or preoccupation. In *Compliance Capitalism*, Dekker shines a light on one of the latest incarnations of this concern. It won't be until his later books in the trilogy that light will be shown on pathways out of this mess. Until then!

PREFACE

When I was in Graduate School at the Ohio State University in the 1990s, most of the students and faculty in our field were members of the Human Factors and Ergonomics Society (HFES). HFES, founded in 1957, is a US-based professional association for those committed to designing systems that work for humans. Mostly visible for their organization of conferences, scholarships and awards, I hadn't yet realized how one of the roles of such an association is to defend the interests of the profession in a shifting political and regulatory landscape. This blew into view upon the installation of George W. Bush, who followed Bill Clinton as US president at the end of the 1990s. The first substantive policy that Bush signed into law, in March 2001, was a repeal of the Occupational Safety and Health Administration's (OSHA's) ergonomics program standard. The congressional voting that had preceded this was surrounded by an intense HFES campaign, which was ultimately unsuccessful. The federal ergonomics standard had to go; the regulator had to pull its head in.

The repeal of a federal ergonomics standard wouldn't seem like the thing you'd get excited about. After all, the standard mostly involved paper bureaucracy and the kind of work that doesn't typically kill people or trigger devastating, highly visible accidents. But it became a perfect micro-case of deregulation that ends up causing market-inflicted overregulation. It became a case where a retreating government—under pressure from free-market proponents—drove the so-called 'responsibilization' of workers who now became tasked with assessing and regulating ergonomic standards by and for themselves, and who had to carry the blame if they didn't. It was a case of a politically marketable effort to reign in a putatively overreaching, intrusive government, to stop them from overburdening businesses with seemingly gratuitous paperwork. And it led to businesses imposing seemingly gratuitous paperwork on their workers instead (of course, without them giving up any of their productivity). Duly signed off, all this paperwork could then let businesses off the hook for workplace ergonomic injuries. It was a case where a retreating government made space for a new market in which private insurers and purveyors of occupational safety, and ergonomics consultants, could capitalize on liability fears and then sell products to businesses keen on avoiding trouble and costs associated with injury claims.

Before we go to one of the more popular private 'products' supplied by the market that ostensibly help companies manage their liabilities around workplace ergonomic injuries, let's look at what the state had in mind in the first place. What was the problem that OSHA was trying to tackle? And what did Bush actually repeal, which was then replaced by a market rapidly filling the gap, leaving the worker with more compliance paperwork and less protection? It would seem hard to believe today, but when I was in Grad School, personal computers had only just become the dominant thing on people's desks. OSHA, a division within the US Department of Labor, saw trouble looming. Long hours of computer work would lead to an explosion of musculoskeletal disorders (MSDs), particularly repetitive strain injuries (RSIs) to hands and wrists, spreading to arms and necks and backs and more. Explaining its proposed rulemaking, which OSHA had to submit under the 1995 Paperwork Reduction Act (an indication that the state already knew it created too much compliance paperwork), OSHA argued:

> These disorders cause persistent and severe pain, lost worktime, reduction or loss of the worker's normal functional capacity both in work tasks and in other of life's major activities, loss of productivity, and significant medical expenses. Where preventive action or early medical intervention is not provided, these disorders can result in permanent damage to musculoskeletal

> tissues, causing such disabilities as the inability to use one's hands to do even the small tasks of daily life (e.g., lifting a child), permanent scarring, and arthritis.
>
> (2000, p. 1)

For OSHA to come this far was a victory in itself. A coalition of organized labor, women's groups, and committees on occupational safety and health fought for two decades to secure the ergonomics standard. From ground level, after all, it hadn't been hard to see how RSIs had dramatically increased with the spread of repetitive motion and computer work in both blue-collar and white-collar sectors of the economy. After the 1994 Republican takeover of control of Congress, the Clinton administration had been forced to make numerous concessions to the ergonomics standard, and it was finally signed in the closing days of his presidency (Morgensen, 2003, pp. 5–6). What was left for OSHA to do about the problem of rising MSDs? The standard was made up of seven steps, which employers had to comply with. Companies needed to show leadership by encouraging employees to voluntary report MSDs and MSD hazards. Hazards had to be identified as early as possible to avoid any employee injury from getting worse, job hazard controls had to be put in place, and job factors needed to be evaluated to assess their contribution to MSD symptoms. Employees, supervisors, and administrators were required to get training to recognize and control MSDs and MSD hazards, and the company's ergonomic program had to be evaluated periodically. Relevant records needed to be kept. Workers on the way to developing MSDs should be given the option of being granted temporary work restrictions. OSHA also reserved the right:

> ...to prescribe, where appropriate, the type and frequency of medical examinations or other tests which shall be made available, by the employer or at his cost, to employees exposed to such hazards in order to effectively determine whether the health of such employees is adversely affected by exposure.
>
> (OSHA, 2000, p. 2)

OSHA proposed that MSD-injured employees should be compensated for up to 90 days with both pay and benefits. The standard was going to affect about 102 million workers at some 6 million work sites across the United

States, and was estimated to cost employers about $4.5 billion per year. To us today, much of this probably sounds familiar, and we probably shrug at some of it. But for a president keen on opening the first front in his war on unduly burdensome federal regulations,[1] the standard was a soft and juicy target. The OSHA standard, its opponents had argued, would cost employers a lot of money. It would pose overwhelming compliance pressures on employers because of cumbersome or vague provisions. And critics believed it wasn't going to address ergonomics hazards, instead mostly dealing with what needed to be done for workers *after* the injuries had already occurred (Saunders, 2001, pp. 29–31). Pulling government out and letting the market do its work voluntarily was going to change all that. The government was going to get out of the way: on 20 March 2001, Bush signed the repeal of the OSHA rules that had taken effect only a few weeks earlier, four days before he himself was sworn in. In the double-speak typical of such occasions, Bush' 20 March signing statement assured his people that:

> The safety and health of our Nation's workforce is a priority for my Administration. Together we will pursue a comprehensive approach to ergonomics that addresses the concerns surrounding the ergonomics rule repealed today. We will work with the Congress, the business community, and our Nation's workers to address the important issues.
>
> (Saunders, 2001, p. 33)

Of course, Congress proceeded to not do much of anything about the 'important issues' because it was now up to the market to address them through voluntary compliance. The business community's 'important issue' (don't cost us any money) became a honeypot for new market actors attracted to selling products that could deal with lingering fears of liability for ergonomic injury. And the Nation's workers got more compliance pressure and less protection. It gave 'corporate interests greater leverage to discipline the labor force, limit workers' rights, and further unravel the social safety net' (Morgensen, 2003, p. 6). The market keenly set to work to address the Bush administration's concerns about OSHA's standard.

About 10 years later I was giving a talk about compliance pressure and nonsensical company rules when one of the middle managers volunteered a great example. It was the 'how to sit at your desk checklist' that his company had just adopted. The provider of the checklist was an ergonomics consultancy, and it quickly dawned on the company that they could save on insurance premiums for worker's compensation if they adopted the checklist. He handed me a copy of the checklist after my talk. It was four pages long. Here are some extracts.

How to sit at your desk

Workers have to check YES or NO to the following questions (the original working-at-a-desk checklist runs for four pages):

CHAIR

1. Is the chair easily adjusted from a sitting position?
2. Is the backrest angle adjusted so that you are sitting upright while keying, and is it exerting a comfortable support on the back?
3. Does the lumbar support of the backrest sit in the small of your back (to find the small of your back, place your hands on your waist and slide your hands around to your spine? The maximum curve of the backrest should contract this area)?
4. Are your thighs well-supported by the chair except for a 3-4 finger space (approx.) behind the knee (you may need to adjust the backrest of your chair to achieve this)?
5. Is there adequate padding on the chair (you should be able to feel the supporting surface underneath the foam padding when sitting on the chair)?
6. If you have a chair mat, is it in good condition?

DESK

1. Is your chair high enough so that your elbows are just above the height of the desk (note: to determine elbow height relax your shoulders and bend your elbows to about 90 degrees).
2. Are your elbows by your sides and shoulders relaxed?
3. Are your knees at about hip level, i.e., thighs parallel to the floor (may be slightly higher or lower depending on comfort)?
4. Is there adequate leg room beneath your desk?
5. Do you require a foot rest?

SCREEN

1. When sitting and looking straight ahead, are you looking at the top one third of your screen?
2. Is your screen at a comfortable reading distance (i.e., approximately an arm's length away from your seated position)?
3. Can you easily adjust and position your screen?
4. Are all the characters on the display legible and the image stable (i.e., not flickering)?
5. Do light reflections on your screen cause you discomfort (you may need to adjust the angle of your screen)?
6. Do you wear bifocal glasses during computer work?
7. Do you have dual monitors at your workstation?

KEYBOARD

1. Is your keyboard positioned close to the front edge of your desk (approximately 60-70mm from the edge)?
2. Is the keyboard sitting directly in front of your body when in use?
3. Does it sit slightly raised up?
4. If the keyboard is tilted, are your wrists straight, not angled, when typing?
5. Are the keys clean and easy to read?

MOUSE/LAPTOP

1. Are your mouse and mouse pad directly beside the end of the keyboard, on your preferred side?
2. Do you use a laptop computer for extended periods of time at a desk?
3. Is the screen raised so that the top of the screen is at eye level?
4. Do you use an external keyboard and mouse?

DESK LAYOUT

1. Are all the items that you are likely to use often within easy reach?
2. Is there sufficient space for documents and drawings?

3. If most of your work requires typing from source documents, do you require a document holder?
4. If you use a document holder, is it properly located close to your monitor and adjustable?
5. Is your workstation set out to prevent undue twisting of your neck and back?

The checklist, the manager said to me, took about 20 minutes to fill out, even after you got pretty routinized at it. After filling it out, the worker had to take the completed checklist to his or her Safety Professional who had to sign it, and then to the Safety Manager who also had to sign it (these titles are actually capitalized on the checklist form, I'm not making this up). Each completed checklist was kept on record in the worker's personnel file. The company, in a bid to save money and increase efficiencies on its office staff, then decided to institute hot-desking. This meant that no worker had his or her 'own' desk anymore, but that workstations had to be grabbed in the morning on a first-come, first-serve basis. With each new workstation, however, a new ergonomics self-assessment had to be conducted and a checklist needed to be filled out. The checklist now took 20 minutes out of every workday, or 40 if you were unlucky enough to lose your desk space over a lunch break. I am sure that there were workers who snuck a stack of checklists home with them so that they could pre-fill them for the week or month to come (or have their kids do it just for the heck of it). That way, they could at least get on with their jobs after arriving at yet another random hot desk in the morning.

Remember how proponents of the repeal had argued that vague provisions would lead to undue compliance burdens on employers. These vague provisions were now exported, with the help of a private market actor, to the workers. As free agents, as self-regulating beings, they now had to make determinations about what constituted 'slightly raised up,' 'adequate leg room,' 'easily adjusted,' or 'good condition.' These were all pretty vague judgment calls, of course, unless you did ergonomics for a living. The point was never to make workers ergonomically comfortable or safe, the middle manager assured me, even though the checklist was cloaked in exactly that intention. But if that were the real aim, it would have required some professional help to the workers about what all these things meant, and how they should be determined, and what should be done if some of them didn't meet the 'vague' standard. No, the manager said, the point was to save money on insurance premiums and compensation claims. After all, if a worker had ticked the box that assured his or her Safety Professional and then Safety Manager that there was 'no undue twisting of neck and back,' then there was no basis for a claim about neck- or backpain induced at work.

The example of how to sit at your desk is the perfect coalescence of deregulation and free markets at work. Here, roughly, is the playbook:

- Get rid of the regulation, and get rid of the regulator if you can. Tell the state to stay away.
- Then give everything a price, or, rather, let the markets set a price for everything, including injury.
- Abolish the state's worker compensation scheme and outsource injury compensation to the private insurance market instead.
- Allow the burgeoning of a consultancy market where someone will come up with a 'how-to-sit-at-your-desk-checklist' and sell it to you by sowing fear about what it might cost if you don't buy it.
- Then responsibilize your workers to do their self-regulatory work by plodding through that checklist every time they go sit at a desk, and implicitly or explicitly warn them of making 'poor choices' when working at their stations.
- Then hold your workers accountable for compliance with your new rules through this arduous four-page long process that will allow you to pass the buck back to the worker when it turns out that they got RSI after all.

Welcome to freedom. This is an instructive example of how free markets lead to unfree, overregulated (and probably poorer and less healthy) workers. The repeal of the ergonomics standard was a case of less money and less work for the state, of less money and more work for the workers, and of more money and more work for private actors who quickly found their feet in a new market for do-it-yourself-ergonomic standards and assessments. With Bush repealing the federal standard, everything changed. And yet very little did, except who now did most of the paperwork, and who lost, and who won.

Out of complexity, a new order

A 'how to sit at your desk checklist' is just one example. Even if you don't have to complete such a checklist where you work, you probably have more rules to follow than, say, 20 years ago. I bet that 20 years ago, you didn't have a rule that says you have to fill in a seven-page risk assessment for a business trip to a neighboring city, in the same country, fewer than 200 kilometers away. Or a rule that stipulates that you need to chock the wheels of a parked company truck on both sides of the wheel—even if you have parked on a hill (though as far as we know, Newton is still correct on this one: gravity only pulls in one direction). And if you weren't yet working 20 years ago, then ask a colleague who was. Or try to imagine how it would have been back then. I can tell you, from my own organization, and from talking to lots of people about this, that—yes—we now indeed do have more such rules. They are made up somewhere, then written down, communicated, followed up, enforced, signed off, recorded, and stored. There's a bunch of people in my organization (and yours) busying themselves with these rules. A lot of *those* people have told me they don't like all those new rules either. Yet they tell me they are powerless to stop them.

But wait, you might argue, haven't we just gone through a couple of decades of deregulation and privatization? Wasn't government supposed to get out of the way, and let people regulate themselves and let markets do their magic? Wasn't getting rid of rules the whole point of privatization and deregulation? Yes, it was the point—one of the points, in any case. Many countries have embraced market-driven policies on production and trade, and for the distribution of their income and wealth. Deregulation and privatization were expected to rid our industries from excessive rule-making. They were supposed to liberate us from ossifying government ownership and control of viable and vital societal services. They were intended to lift from us the burdens of unnecessary legislative requirements, statutes, certification, licensing, and inspection activities. And all that without a loss in the quality and safety of the products and services delivered. In fact, deregulation and privatization consistently promised not only better products and services, but greater efficiency in creating and delivering them. Market-driven policies may have delivered on some productivity promises, but not consistently, not everywhere, and not for everyone.

When retreating government is the problem

In one of my previous books, *The Safety Anarchist*, I talk about the introduction of the State in regulation and control of people's lives. I asked age-old philosophical questions such as 'who has the right to rule.' I concluded that the insertion of the State into areas of people's health and safety—while driven by well-intentioned schemes to improve the human condition—could occasionally lead to really unsafe and unhealthy situations, and seemingly overregulated ones. Prohibition and eugenics were just some of the most egregious examples. Well, today it turns out that the State is actually not the biggest problem, neither by the volume of rules we have to follow, nor in the qualities of what that State still asks us to do and don't do. The problem, instead, is a retreating State. The paradox is this. More rules and compliance demands (many of them seemingly asinine and not intended to actually help the person complying) tend to show up:

- When governments get out of running things altogether
- When governments leave it to organizations to regulate themselves
- When governments try to make fewer rules
- When governments are trying to count, contain, and limit the rules they still have to make and measure the impact they have on people and businesses
- When governments in some cases even commit to trading at least one old rule for every new one they make.

How is it possible that free markets—and indeed deregulation—have exacerbated the experience of overregulation? How can free markets have led to unfree, overregulated workers? In a sense, we're now sitting on the results of a massive natural experiment—an experiment that was gradually rolled out across the world over a period of some 40 years. The fact that this experiment was a kind of gamble is intuitive: our political-economic arrangements are hugely complex, after all. And if you experiment with complexity, you can get surprising, counterintuitive results because complex systems connect things in non-linear ways. They have feedback loops we may not have known about. They have weird dependence on tiny initial conditions that can generate huge changes later on. There is emergence of behavior that we cannot explain by reference to the behavior of the parts. Complex systems are capable of adaptation and novelty. But—and this is critical—unpredictability doesn't imply the absence of order because the order is there. States letting go of the running and controlling of entire industries, and letting markets take over, have led to a new kind of order. That deregulation of a complex system doesn't create an unregulated system, but rather a newly self-regulated one, could have been predicted:

> If the traffic in London was left to itself, there would be little doubt that it would eventually become a self-regulating system (just like in Cairo and, sometimes, in Athens or Rome). The problem in such a case would not be so much disorganization as *undesirable* organization: the traffic patterns which would eventually emerge perhaps would not satisfy most people's criteria of efficiency and fairness, but patterns (namely organization of some sort) there would be ... for most people, however, that kind of world is organized for serving the wrong purposes, making use of unacceptable means; it is the wrong kind of order. In other words, as ethnomethodologists keep reminding us, social life is de facto organized: we, as sentient beings, have no choice but to organize our world and our actions in it. The interesting questions are how we do it; what do we do it for?
>
> (Tsoukas, 1998, p. 292)

Leaving a complex system to itself creates new kinds of order. The system re-organizes and self-regulates in new ways. For complexity theory, particularly when applied to social or socio-economic systems, this is an almost trivial observation. But saying that new kinds of patterns of organization were going to emerge is not the same as being able to explain or predict the details of such emergent behavior. In fact, the latter is impossible in complexity. But, if we follow Tsoukas' lead for a moment, we can now see, at least in the results, how free markets have not improved economic and social conditions for many people. Inequality has risen sharply. Precarious employment has too. In the United Kingdom (UK), 30% of children grow up in poverty, and one in five children goes hungry almost every day. Life expectancy in the United States has declined for three years in a row. And in deregulated, non-state-run enterprises, people have to meet more compliance demands than ever before, with trust in their professionalism eroded, and concern about short-term results and liability driving recording and reporting requirements up to unprecedented levels. A nurse in a non-state healthcare system like in the United States now can easily spend over 35% of a shift on documentation, administrative and compliance activities. So, an order has emerged, for sure. It is an order that has created new kinds of winners, and losers. It is an order, a way of organizing—to speak with Tsoukas—that probably doesn't meet most people's criteria of efficiency or fairness. The problem is not disorganization, but undesirable organization.

In the next chapters, I take a serious stab at examining and explaining the latter of these results—the paradox of less government, but more compliance. Notwithstanding the severe limits that complexity itself places on any such endeavor, I try to trace the macroeconomic, meso-economic, and micro-economic forces and effects that can account for the paradox. We need all three levels of understanding economics for this. Microeconomics is the study of economics at an individual, group, or enterprise level. It focuses on issues that affect individuals and companies—not just financial implications, but also in the experience of compliance pressure, job content, satisfaction, and a sense of control, of ownership and autonomy. Macroeconomics is the study of a national (or even global) economy as a whole and the policy directions and societal trends that help drive it. Meso-economics sits between them, tracing how governance structures and interorganizational order connect macro-economic and political forces to what individuals can and cannot do. You will find the intertwined and mutually reinforcing workings of altogether ten factors that make it so. Together, and in their interplay, these factors constitute compliance capitalism: the commercial colonization of the rule-making space left behind (or brought into being) by a retreating government. Together, these factors can help explain why we have more rules, not fewer—despite deregulation and privatization, or rather because of it. Here they are:

Macroeconomic factors—these factors are related to the decisions of governments and countries, as well as societal, political, and demographic trends underlying these decisions:

- Privatization and corporate, as opposed to state, governance
- Deregulation and performance-based regulation
- Market concentration
- A decline of participatory equality.

Meso-economic factors—these factors are related to the structures and interorganizational or industry arrangements under which the micro- and macroeconomic forces play out:

- Deprofessionalization
- The growth of compliance workforces
- Surveillance capitalism.

Micro-economic factors— these factors are related to the decisions of individuals and businesses about how prices are set, how money is made, saved and distributed, how 'success' is counted:

- Auditism
- Financialization and short-termism
- The monetization of compliance.

You will find these three sets of factors in chapters 3, 4, and 5, respectively. Then we also need to answer why governments have 'missed' this; why they've not noticed how attempts to declutter and debureaucratize have in many cases led to the opposite. Governments have been keen on measuring and demonstrating the effects of privatization and deregulation on the economy and productivity. So how could they not know that their efforts were creating effects directly counter to the goals they were pursuing? Over the last two decades or more, studies have been commissioned, inquiries set up, and measurement instruments introduced—all to demonstrate that these governments' so-called 'new public management' was yielding the deregulation and efficiency it promised. These themselves have yielded a relatively disappointing insight: on average deregulation and privatization haven't really delivered on their own promise. Reagan and Thatcher, to name two of the greatest proponents, actually didn't succeed at rolling in their respective governments' 'red tape' at all. On the contrary, by 1993, three years after the end of Thatcher's rule in the UK, and four years after that of Reagan in the United States, there was *more* government red tape in each country than before they began. That much, however, governments would have known, and indeed *do* know.

The issue at stake here is different, however. It is that there is a large portion of new rules, guidelines, policies, and compliance bureaucracy that doesn't come from government. It comes from the *retreat* of government, and the workings of markets themselves. On average, the portion of new rules that come from the marketplace is actually larger than the portion issuing from government. That portion comes from the organizations that operate in the market, from the many players spawned by and orbiting around newly deregulated, privatized industries. As you'll learn in much greater detail in this book, it turns out that running a previously public service in a market—now organized around pricing, shareholder value, contracting, accountability, and risk—creates far more rules than what were necessary under public governance. Up to 60% of all the rules we have added since the beginning of deregulation and privatization are made up by the market and self-imposed by those who operate in it (Saines et al., 2014).

So how can governments not know this? They don't because *we ourselves* slipped in those rules or let them proliferate as a by-product of the workings of the market itself. These rules flew into our workplaces under the radar of governments measuring the effects of their market-oriented policy-making. We have made up most of these rules ourselves. Government never asked for most of them. These additional rules have come from us, from the organizations we work in, or for, and from the markets in which these organizations nowadays operate. And government measures exactly 0% of those newly added rules. They don't show up on a government's scoreboard for the results of deregulation and privatization—because those typically contain only *their* rules, not the market's.

So, let's have a look at what you can expect in this book.

Chapter 1, "The freedom to make more rules," tells the story of one industry (railways), with one particular activity (surveying), tracking the story of privatization and deregulation and splitting up the industry from the inside-out. It sketches the policy priorities of 'neoliberalism': smaller government, a lighter-touch government, a reduced regulatory footprint, as well as more private actors in a market to own and run things. The chapter then offers some of the evidence for the problem the book sets out to better understand. Healthcare in the United States, for instance, suffers under an enormous compliance burden, but only 22% of the rules come from actual statutory and regulatory requirements. The system has made up the rest itself, in order to keep the 'market' for healthcare (such as it is) putatively running and accountable.

Chapter 2, "Free markets in theory; intensive managerial control in practice," takes you back to the ideas of the Frenchman Richard Cantillon and his Anglo successor, Adam Smith and how they wanted to offer different models for how to deal with very real problems of food—and other economic insecurities typical of 18th-century Europe. It weaves from there to Keynes, to Mont Pèlerin, and to the birth of 'neoliberalism' in the *Colloque Walter Lippmann* against the backdrop of Stalinist state terror and the rise of fascism in Italy and Germany—all of which relied on strongmen leaders and a totalizing role of the state in the economy and affairs of citizens. It traces how the alternative of unfettered free markets transmogrified from a fringe, oppositional political commitment to pretty much the *only* solution to economic problems from the 1970s onward. Of course, as has been argued endlessly, under certain conditions a free market with little or no government intervention will find its own equilibrium and fairness. This, however, can work only under the ideal conditions of *voluntary* exchanges by *independent* and *autonomous* actors. Many of our newly privatized, deregulated markets violate these conditions (just think of aged care), where immense amounts of compliance clutter come from the contorted, unchecked workings of the free market itself.

Chapter 3, "The macro: sell out and pull out," runs through the macroeconomic factors that help explain how free markets lead to unfree workers. Macroeconomic factors are related to the decisions of governments and countries, as well as societal, political, and demographic trends underlying these decisions. It describes how and why private–corporate governance actually requires a lot more rules and bureaucracy than a government would if it runs the same thing. Then it covers deregulation and particularly performance-based regulation, explaining how these give rise to overselling and over-demonstrating compliance with whatever statutes and regulations are left, and how fear of legal and insurance liabilities (abetted by market actors who might benefit from encouraging such fear) increases internal compliance clutter. The chapter also tracks the phenomenon of market concentration, or the consolidation of supposedly free, open, competitive markets into a few oversized actors (or even a monopoly). The larger an organization, the more bureaucracy and compliance clutter. It finishes with the decline in participatory equality, which has effectively removed workers from bargaining tables in many industries. This has been accompanied by a proliferation of outsourcing and precarious work, which in turn has created more compliance-capitalist opportunities that spawn additional paperwork and clutter.

Chapter 4, "The meso: mistrust and monitor," covers the meso-economic factors behind overregulation in privatized, deregulated industries. Meso-economic factors are related to the structures and interorganizational or industry arrangements under which macro- and micro-economic forces play out. The first development in the chapter that has co-occurred with the rise of neoliberalism is deprofessionalization. It shows how an erosion of mastery, a decline in commitment to a profession as a career, and the disappearing sense of a collegial community is undermining the self-monitoring and self-regulation that professions have always enjoyed as their 'freedom-in-a-frame,' replacing it instead with a whole host of external forms of surveillance and control—not from a government, but from elsewhere in employing or contracting organizations. Deprofessionalization has, unsurprisingly, been accompanied (if not accelerated) by the growth of compliance workforces, which has introduced additional people who now claim to have something to say about how the professional (or anybody else) does their work. Instead of relationships of trust, compliance workers (in human resources, office management, audit roles, project management, and so on) rely on reduced autonomy and individuality, and on relationships of control. Finally, the growth of surveillance capitalism—whose revenue model is to sell the perceived need (as well as solutions) for monitoring and control over professional and other workforces—has added to both the volume and 'bite' of compliance clutter. It has also eroded authenticity and trust, as workers become concerned with how their *data doubles* might look to the anonymous big brothers behind the lenses, screens, and keyboards.

Chapter 5, "The micro: audit and cash in," talks about the micro-economic factors in free markets that help produce compliance capitalism. It begins with auditism, a condition where the things being audited and methods for auditing them have become consistent only with themselves, almost entirely missing how work actually goes on, and what it takes (and doesn't take) to get things done when the auditors aren't there. These 'audit loops' are one perverted, compliance-capitalist result of more generalized accountability mechanisms that operate in a deprofessionalized markets, where neither the audits nor the auditors (need to) have much detailed substantive knowledge of the nuances and messy details of actual practice. Audits have risen to such prominence, however, because of financialization and its ally: short-termism. Financialization is a result of privatization, increasing the size and importance of a country's financial sector, the stock market and financial institutions. Financialization can explain, to a great extent, organizations' focus on the short term, and their preoccupation with all kinds of compliance indicators, measures, indices, benchmarks, and standards, because the financialized market in which they operate holds them accountable for those. Finally, the chapter delves into the creation of compliance capitalism through a revenue model for an infinite range of consultancies and contractors, and how newly privatized, deregulated industries have opened new markets where bureaucracy can be monetized.

Chapter 6, "How could governments have missed this?", explains how the growing compliance burden has managed to stay under most governments' radars. Governments—because of how they have measured the effects of their own deregulation and privatization—have pretty much missed this growth of internal compliance bureaucracy. Governments, keen to take credit for the cleansing effect of their deregulatory and privatizing policies, haven't been able to know about all these rules because they don't measure them. Regulatory Impact Assessments (RIAs) of various kinds have become the norm as an accompaniment to the consideration of new regulations, but those apply to the rules the government makes. They don't apply to the rules that industries or organizations or departments make because governments have stopped owning that industry, or stopped regulating it as they did before. This means that they, and we, have systematically missed the major source of overregulation that has been hiding in plain sight: the market itself.

Chapter 7, "A retreat into rules," suggests that free markets can't explain everything about our current unfree, overregulated state. There are things about why we are less free than before that we can't blame markets for. This chapter asks whether we are hapless bystanders, looking on as the invisible hand of the free market rolls out more and more rules over us, or whether we (or some of us) *like* rules, or derive something else from demanding and expecting compliance. That free markets have some role in abetting this is probable, as they may well have created the kinds of political, economic, and social conditions that make us more liable to retreating into rules. The dynamics this final chapter talks about are *Safetyism*, an increasing sensitivity and risk aversion which has led to a search for, and expectation of, protection by second or third parties from any kind of harm, whether physical, emotional, or psychological. In return for this protection, we welcome (or, in many cases, have little choice but to acquiesce in) the shrinking bandwidth around what is considered acceptable behavior. It then discusses *moral entrepreneurism*, the promotion of more rules, conformity, and obedience, driven by the belief that norms are slipping in today's societies and that 'accountability' is eroding, leaving people to assent to more authority and compliance. Finally, it returns to the classic idea of *escape from freedom*. Escaping from freedom alleviates burdensome choices and responsibility and reduces uncertainty and ambiguity. People have long been willing to trade freedoms for economic prosperity, which is where a compelling link to the promises (though not generally delivered realities) of neoliberalism becomes visible.

Beachtungsgesellschaft

In his 1986 *Risikogesellschaft*, which appeared as *Risk Society* in 1992, sociologist Ulrich Beck describes how we have ended up in a kind of 'second modernity.' Modernity roughly overlaps with 'the industrialized world,' though industrialization is not its only dimension of interest (Giddens, 1991). Modernity here refers to Western society since the late 19th and 20th centuries—dramatically transformed from what it was previously. Industrialization and urbanization gave us confidence in the power of rationality, planning, measurement, and science. Armed with them, we could ever better control our health, our livelihoods, our economies, our productivity, and the integrity of our systems. But it wasn't all good. In fact, it got worse because of everything we were doing to make life so good for ourselves. Beck's 'second modernity' happened because the first modernity started producing side-effects that ran directly counter to the beliefs and hopes we had for it. As Giddens put it:

> Modernity reduces the overall riskiness of certain areas and modes of life, yet at the same time introduces new risk parameters largely or completely unknown to previous eras. These parameters include high-consequence risks: risks deriving from the globalised character of the social

> systems of modernity. The late modern world … introduces risks which previous generations have not had to face.
>
> (1991, p. 4)

The side effects of modernity which introduces these new risks, Beck argued, are made by humans. No pleasure of plastic toys without the risk of an occasional oil rig explosion; no consumerist equality through mass tourism without the risk of an occasional air disaster; no dream house in a garden suburb without a builder sometimes falling off a roof, or choked freeways and air pollution; no electricity for all the appliances and devices in that house without the risk of a nuclear core melt-down further up the coast. With its chemical process plants to nuclear warheads, its large-scale industrial explosions to environmental destruction, modernity started turning on itself. Order and predictability were threatened, new insecurities blossomed. It turned out that modernity, instead of supplying certainty and assuring constant improvement, portended unprecedented health problems, new dangers, lives cut short in novel ways, and introduced a host of psychological, social, and physical uncertainties. Risk society is the result. It is a society preoccupied with living in the future rather than the present; its people and organizations busying themselves with divining and controlling and averting risk.

When Beck wrote *Risikogesellschaft*, modernity had permeated itself with new kinds of risks that were the by-products of its own success. A few decades later, modernity has embroidered into our societies a new and increasingly dense web of compliance. Perhaps our hope is that this helps us control the risks of modernity itself. In which case, we have gone from Risk Society to Compliance Society, or *Beachtungsgesellschaft* if you want it in German. And, you might ask, does it work? Is compliance capable of keeping the lid on risk? Compliance, of course, enlists the key devices of modernity in the quest to control the risks of modernity. To keep the lid on the risks of its own making, modernity deploys what it knows best: linear order, planning, standardization, measurement, calculability, predictability, rationalization, and bureaucratization, to name but a few. And that is precisely where the shoe pinches. Modernity has created all these risks as byproducts of its own success. And now we are throwing even more modernity at the problem so as to contain the risks created by modernity. You are forgiven if Einstein comes to mind here. Because we are trying to solve the problem at the same level at which we have created it. I'll leave the judgment of whether it works or not up to you, but I doubt you'll be too hopeful once you get past chapter 6.

Black Elephant

Because what we are dealing with here seems to be a bit of a *Black Elephant* (a term coined by Adam Sweidan, an investor and environmentalist based in London). It combines *Black Swan* (an unlikely, unexpected event with enormous ramifications) and *elephant in the room* (a problem visible to everyone, yet no one has found a way or mustered the will to address it). Now that we face an unprecedented compliance burden, in sharp contravention to the promises of economic liberalization, we might say, 'Wow, we didn't see that coming.' *That* was unforeseen when we started embracing these ideas decades ago. That would make it a *Black Swan*. And the initial enthusiasm (or perhaps even perceived political-economic imperative) for our embrace may have blinded us to the downsides. But as you will find out in this book, there was research predating our embrace of market-favoring economic policies that could have forewarned us. Intensive managerial control is to be expected when everything gets a price tag.

Fear of liability would seem an intuitive explanation for the expansion of rules for people to follow, even, or especially when operating in free markets. But the many intertwined mechanisms that drive additional rule-making are more subtle than that. The sheer workings of markets, propelled by a profit motive, not only form no protection against ever-expanding rules and bureaucracy, but also open new ways of monetizing rules and bureaucracy. If that actually introduces inefficiencies (which it does—in spades), then, well…, Adam Smith himself could have told us that markets wouldn't work efficiently in many of the areas in which we have now deployed them—because those areas fail to meet the basic conditions of informed buyers, multiple choices, or voluntary participants.

A growing compliance burden belongs to a class of effects of neoliberalism that may have received some marginal critique. But, as Styre dryly understates, it is otherwise 'largely absent from management research' (2014, p. 278). Way back in the 19th century, Marx wasn't as subtle. As he did in his time, he might today have railed against the *tyranny of unquestioned, self-serving ideas*. For Mark Lilla, the reason that these ideas have remained unquestioned isn't just the invisibility of our present condition itself, the taken-for-grantedness of the market-favoring political economies we inhabit. It is that we lack adequate concepts or even a vocabulary for describing the world we find ourselves in—this world at 'the end of history' or 'the end of ideology' that came with the conclusion of the Cold War in 1989. Since then, he suggests, we have been living in an illegible age where categories that were useful before no longer seem to apply. Perhaps it isn't that we haven't been willing to ask the question; it is that we haven't had a language that enables us to do so (Lilla, 2014). In either case, it is an *elephant in the room*. It is something we know is there now, even if we are a bit hazy about how it got there (which this book should help clear up at least to some extent).

At the same time, we're not acknowledging or dealing with it at the scale necessary. It is something that many people don't want to acknowledge or deal with, because they can't afford to. For them there is too much at stake—a political reputation to sustain, money to be made, a moral bureaucratic undertaking to defend, a compliance job to hang onto, a safety management system to sell, and so on. And let's face it, we may all in our own ways and roles, reap material and symbolic rewards for pretending the elephant isn't there. Lorenz (2012) suggests that people use an almost Orwellian language so that we can all leave the elephant standing there. This is the kind of language that redefines concepts such as quality, accountability, responsibility, professionalism, and even freedom. It tends to invert, if not pervert, them into the opposite of their original meanings. Quality gets to mean compliant—not straying outside a narrow bandwidth of acceptable performance. Accountable gets to mean compliant—you can show, or be accountable for, how you followed the rules. Responsible gets to mean compliant—taking ownership for nothing more or less than seeing that compliance expectations are met. Professional gets to mean compliant—somebody is a professional when they don't flout the rules. Freedom gets to mean compliant—not with what the government wants you to do, but what a free market demands you to do so that you are free to settle the accounts for your own successes and failures (or injuries). In Lorenz's reading, the deployment of such language means the elephant is resistant to moving along. Because we talk to each other about it as if this elephant is the morally right thing to have in our room. And who doesn't want to be seen as a responsible, accountable professional who delivers quality products or services? Who doesn't want freedom?

If you've read works by me before, you probably don't expect me to let the elephant be. You're right, I won't let it be. What I won't do in this book, however, is deliver a straight answer to the question whether markets are good or bad. Because there isn't a straight answer. It depends. In their consideration of the consequences of free markets, other books handle that question much better, and necessarily so. But to be sure, it's not all good. Just think of the sharp rise in inequality and localized economic decline that market-favoring policies have brought (Piketty, 2017; Rodrik, 2017), or a stifling of competition and innovation through conglomeration and oligopolarization of the market (Philipon, 2019). What I try to do here is find answers to the question why free markets lead to unfree workers. What aspects of compliance capitalism, what mechanisms of bureaucratization, can we find that are directly linked to us having given free markets a greater reign over our political economies?

In my search for a coherent answer, I have wanted to give some shape and substance to a suspicion that has become widespread among workers in almost every industry I and my research lab have worked with: *we have to follow more rules than ever—and still, things can go spectacularly wrong*. Many of those rules are as silly as the disasters are devastating (and typically have nothing to do with those rules or compliance). Many rules get in the way of us actually doing our work, of us being the professionals we would like to be, with the capacity to influence the quality and safety of our products and services, and the ability to steer away from breakdown. The growing number of rules can hurt our efficiency, our productivity, our quality, our bottom line, and indeed possibly even the safety and survival of the system we are working for. They impact our deference to expertise, our reliance on professional judgment. In the end, as I argued in *The Safety Anarchist*, it may well erode our pride of workmanship, a part of our humanity.

So, you will ask, what do we do instead? I know, I know—always the hunger for a solution. The long wait, throughout the whole book, for me to tell you what to do. Well, I am not going to tell you what to do. If that's all you want to know, then you'll simply have to wait a couple of books more. Then I might tell you what to do. This book, *Compliance Capitalism*, is the first of a three-part series on the effects of what its detractors now call *neoliberalism*. *Neoliberalism* supports and promotes the role of the private sector in the economy. It argues that markets and free trade are the only way to get the best price for the best quality. It encourages governments to pull back from stringent regulatory oversight and to pull out of things they shouldn't be running—like railways, electricity generation and distribution, drinking water supply, schooling, higher education, healthcare, etc. *Compliance Capitalism*, the one you are holding now, sets out to identify the market mechanisms that explain how less government paradoxically leads to more rules, thus undoing much of the promised benefits of letting the free market do its work. The second book in the series seeks to explain how market-driven governance of complex systems can amplify and accelerate the mechanisms of human-made disaster and drift into failure, and why this increased potential for system collapse lies beyond the reach of more rules and compliance. The third book in the series introduces the socioeconomic success and value system that distinguish Rhineland economies from Anglo ones. It explains how complexity can never be governed through hierarchy and compliance, but necessarily requires trust and horizontal coordination. It offers a vision of humanity richer than capitalism alone could ever fulfill—a kinder kind of capitalism.

So, the contours of a solution are out there. But for now, you'll have to go through this one if you really want to appreciate the message of the next two. And I'd like to hope that you have nothing to lose by thinking a bit more critically and deeply about our current predicament. It will be time well-invested. This sort of thinking has been trained since Socrates—fostering critical reflection, encouraging the questioning of your own unexamined beliefs and the hand-me-down received wisdoms from those around you. Such thinking can of course lead to you, or those around you, being nudged outside of your comfort zones. That is what happens on the way to understanding and innovation—you can only innovate if you are aware of, and willing to break through, constraints that everybody else takes as given. You'll find that it's actually not a deficit of ideas that is keeping us back. It is a deficit of courage to ask the necessary questions about our current state; the lack of a realization that we even *should* ask questions about what most people take for granted. The desire to skip to a solution, to start rolling out and implementing a list of recommendations, is as common as it is impatient. It doesn't work that way with something that is as large and pervasive as what we're dealing with here. To build something new, we need to first recognize and have some idea of the old, and how we could start dismantling it. As Nietzsche put it, 'if a temple is to be erected, a temple must be destroyed.' This aphorism, or micro-philosophy, should help destabilize our complacent or wishful thinking. Before we are able to see the world as it could be, it forces us to first confront the world as we know it now. First, though, we need to find it. So, let's go look for that *Black Elephant*.

Note

1 George W. Bush of course followed in the footsteps of previous administrations, beginning with Ronald Reagan, who declared in 1981 that 'Government regulations impose an enormous burden on large and small businesses in America, discourage productivity, and contribute substantially to our current economic woes.'

ACKNOWLEDGMENTS

A thank-you to Eric Wahren for starting my thinking about this issue all those years ago. And thanks to Henri Dekker and Darrell Horn for various proofreads, improvements, and corrections.

1

THE FREEDOM TO MAKE MORE RULES

In 1986—I was 16 and soon headed into my last year of high school—I got a summer job with the Netherlands Railways. The Railways at that time were a semi-government organization. For a number of weeks, I was assigned to various surveying teams. These went out to survey—measure in all kinds of ways, really—locations for the country's ever-expanding railway network, which included a bridge west of Gouda, a marshalling yard in Rotterdam, a bend where tracks were going to be doubled south of Amsterdam, etc. My job was mostly to saunter into the corners of the site and hold up a little mirror mounted on a yellow-and-red pole, so that various vertical and horizontal angles could be measured with a theodolite operated by a surveyor on the other end (safety shoes, it seemed, had not yet been invented, and I actually don't know what good they would have done). Train traffic wasn't halted when we were working, so one of us would be designated the safety person. His or her job was to keep watch and yell 'treintje!' (the Dutch love to use diminutives, particularly for things that are actually big and quite dangerous, like an oncoming train). We would then step out of the way and let the train (the '*little* train') pass.

Even though the Netherlands is not a large country, a fair amount of travel was involved in getting to these sites. Train tracks are pretty agnostic or oblivious about what they run through, as long as there is a good bed of track ballast to hold them up. That meant that we could be in everything ranging from a field with black-and-white cows in it, a densely populated urban residential area, an industrial estate, banks of a river or canal, a piece of forest, or a peat swamp. Getting there almost always took time. Previously, railway surveyors used trains themselves, taking a bicycle with them to get from the closest station to the place where measurements are needed to be taken. In 1986, these means of transport had been replaced by white vans, which had all the surveying equipment in the back. I typically arrived at the railway headquarters at eight in the morning (by train, with free duty travel), and figured out what team and location I'd been assigned to. By that time the boss' clock was ticking, so there was little point in rushing. At least, that is what the surveying teams showed me. First there was a cup of coffee, maybe two. Then we headed out to the site. It could take up to the middle or even end of the morning before we were set up to actually start doing some surveying.

Soccer balls and stick shifts

I remember one team in particular. As others, it was made up of two guys, who'd worked with each other quite a bit. I had been paired with these two for a couple of days, and it didn't take me long to figure out that the work of surveying was incidental to their days. On the first day, in some forgettable little town, I had gone to the assigned corner of the first site we had to work, and held up the mirror as instructed. We were not actually on or near a train track, so one of the guys had nothing to do. He sat by the side, smoking. The other was behind the theodolite. It would have been around 11 in the morning. After 20 minutes, the measuring was done. I honestly believed that we'd pack up and drive to the next site, even if still in the same pointless town. But that didn't happen. When the two guys had piled the equipment into the van, they ducked back out—one of them clutching a soccer ball under his arm. Soon a match had erupted between the two of them, leaving me stupefied on the sideline. An hour or so passed, with them increasingly frenetic and panting and eventually worn out. Then, of course, it was time for lunch. Because surveyors go to godforsaken places, they have to take their own lunch. I had as well. They sat in the van and ate theirs, and smoked some more. I sat on a log and ate mine—probably in three minutes (a boy of 16, right? Always hungry). Then there were 90 more minutes to go. Of lunch time, I mean. It was super tedious because I had nothing to do and the little town offered nothing in the way of distraction or diversion. Moreover, I was under the impression that I was still on the boss' clock and supposed to work, or at least be ready to report for more work.

There never was any more work that day. After the soccer match and extended lunch break, the guys called me over. We piled into the van, three abreast on the front seats, and started driving. We drove straight to railway headquarters, where we parked the van without any haste, went upstairs to where the surveyors had their offices and archives, and had more coffee. Then I clocked off and we all went home. The next few days with this team were pretty much the same. We'd been talking about driving cars for a few shifts, since I was 16 and learning how to do that (on private land, mostly airfields, since I was too young for lessons in the Netherlands back then). At some point, I decided to try to learn something new (and redeem my day that way) and asked whether it was possible to shift gears in a manual car without depressing the clutch. You probably see where this is going. 'Yes,' it was possible, I was told. As we'd pulled to a stop before a traffic light on the way back from a grueling measurement session (it must have been 40 minutes of work and lots of soccer), the surveyor who was driving said he'd demonstrate it. I was sitting, as usual, in the middle, wedged between the two guys. When the light turned green, he pulled the Netherlands Railways van up sharply in first gear. Then he let up on the accelerator and yanked the tall gear handle hard back into second gear without depressing the clutch with his left foot. The groaning crunch underneath me, of engineered parts being compelled to do things they weren't designed for, was painfully palpable. Yet the van (with a diesel engine) shuddered and soldiered on. The surveyor who was driving looked at me with an accomplished grin, the other one laughing and shaking his head. When we got back to headquarters at the 'end' of our day, we'd delivered half an hour of tool time, and an abused van.

This may not have been a typical crew, for sure. But you'd think that there would be a better way to work. A more efficient way, a way that would get the organization more tool time. That way, indeed, has long been known as outsourcing, and in this case privatization. Take the job to the market, ask for bids, get the best bid, and make them do the work. Let competition in, let private entities and entrepreneurs compete, and get the best job at the lowest price. The belief is that organizations like a state-owned railway shouldn't be in the business of surveying in any case. Perhaps they shouldn't even be building or maintaining track themselves, nor purchase or operate trains on it. That can all be best left to the market. Today, the Netherlands Railways doesn't employ surveyors, nor does it have surveyor vans that carry soccer balls or vans that get abused by guys shifting gears without clutching. The railway surveying department is gone; it was put out to market. Today contractors do this work. Maybe the guys were asking for it, you'd say. If the guys play soccer and have lunch all day and drive around abusing company vans, then outsourcing their work could feel justified. If they deliver so little tool time, so little value for money, the guys shouldn't be surprised that their jobs will be farmed out at some point. Maybe the whole organization was asking for it. Maybe it never had the incentive to match surveying needs with available manpower and capacities in a manner that produced anywhere near 'full deployment' of surveyors internally—at least not *vis-à-vis* the timelines they themselves applied to those jobs. So, you can be sympathetic to the belief that markets can do this 'better.'

A smaller government

And yet... A little over a decade after my Netherlands Railways summer job, I was a fresh Assistant Research Professor at a university in Sweden. I went to meet the director of the organization that had sponsored my position at the university, which turned out to be the civil aviation inspectorate. Things had developed quickly during my nine years of studying at various universities in Europe and the United States. A movement known as neoliberalism had taken hold, even in Sweden where I'd moved for this job—a country known for its socialist high taxes and well-run, ever-present, broadly accepted, all-encompassing government. Neoliberalism supports and promotes the role of the private sector in the economy. It argues that markets and free trade are ways to get the best price for the best quality. It encourages governments to pull back and out of things they shouldn't be concerned with, including the detailed regulation of industries. So, it was with the aviation safety regulator in Sweden. Aviation operators, the thought was, have a huge stake in flying safely, otherwise people won't want to fly with them at all. Markets in fact force them to be safe. The same went for those building airplanes (e.g., Saab in Sweden).

An important consequence of neoliberalization was that the aviation safety regulator had less money to work with. One of the tenets of neoliberalism, after all, is smaller government, a lighter-touch regulator, and a reduced regulatory footprint. These reductions and deregulations happened at a time when the computer revolution had fully hit cockpits and other areas of aviation, making the task of meaningfully inspecting and regulating vastly more complex. Expertise was hard to find and hard to keep. The solution was to shift to what became known as *systemtillsyn* or *system oversight*. Instead of the regulator checking (or sampling) that all parts of the aviation system were up to specifications and regulations, it now asked the market itself to convince the regulator that they had the systems and processes in place to adequately do such checking themselves. The regulator, in turn, was going to look at samples of those systems and processes to get the confidence that the operators indeed had ways to keep their risks under control.

The problems I was confronted with early on in my job as Assistant Professor seem pretty intuitive and obvious today. But of course, when you're in the middle of things, it is not as easy to look over the top of an emerging situation and see where it comes from or where it is headed. One problem was that the remaining inspectors, trained in the old-school examination of component parts, were at a loss on how to inspect or audit a 'system.' So, they simply treated the new 'system' as a collection of parts that could be inspected according to the old logic. An incident reporting system, for instance, with no incidents in it, or with 'too many' incidents in it, raised suspicions. Inspectors' thinking was still driven by decomposition assumptions that once worked for the engineered systems they were trained to inspect. In those, the functioning (or failure) of the whole can be explained by the functioning (or failure) of (one of) its parts. But that of course doesn't work for complex systems. Indeed, the inspectors' approach remained far from what would, yet another decade later, become known as *resilience*: the ability of a system to recognize, absorb, or adapt to harmful influences, including those that fall outside of its design base. The kinds of 'system inspections' that were being done in the 1990s offered very little insight into *resilience* capacities such as anticipating, monitoring, responding, and learning (Hollnagel, 2018). They weren't geared for them. Yet the market smelled an opportunity.

Two thousand years of reading

This was becoming obvious in the 1990s already. The director of the civil aviation regulator told me how aviation operators were throwing all kinds of things at his inspectors—things they *thought* the inspectorate wanted to see. The amount of ill-coordinated paperwork was overwhelming. Perhaps aviation operators thought (or were told by their legal counsel or consultants) that safe was better than sorry. So, they kept piling it on, in the hope that the regulator could make sense of it for whatever determination they needed to make. They couldn't, not really. We were all in a newly opened-up, pioneering landscape of neoliberal governance, and few people knew what they were looking for or even needed to be looking for. Those who benefited most were those who traded in anxiety. Sell clients a safety management system that is bigger than what they need, because then chances are that they at least have what they need. And once you'd sold it, then finding the right thing, or making sure of its upkeep, was somebody else's problem (or rather *your* new market opportunity). More was always better; more was always more. Lawyers, deployed ever more to advise company boards about their obligations, added to this anxiety and the considerable bureaucratic antidotes to it, added to the burden. There turned out to be plenty on tap. Company boards typically face liability under hundreds of laws and regulations—and most countries or states can't even say exactly how many (Saines et al., 2014). And so, more internal rules are made to try to manage the liabilities and reduce exposure and uncertainties through webs of bureaucratic accountability strung across the organization. Deregulation thus became overregulation—no matter where the rules came from. There were always more. Deregulation meant more rules, more paperwork, more administration, and more bureaucracy—not less.

TIME TO SLIM DOWN AVIATION'S EVER-EXPANDING RULE BOOK

Having been a professional pilot for 23 years now,

De Wannemacker (2020) laments, I'm sure that most will agree with me: rules, regulations and procedures in our job are only ever increasing. Many colleagues will recognise the weekly torrent of company notes, effortlessly sent to you by digital means. Certainly, some events like the 9/11 terror attacks, accidents where human error was involved, and now the COVID-19 pandemic merit additional regulation. But from my own experience, I reckon that in those 23 years, the number of rules, regulations and procedures governing my job has easily doubled. That doubling has taken place despite the fact that we are flying aircraft that have hardly evolved, on operations that haven't changed all that much either. That leads you to ask several questions. Is this mountain of rules justified? Do they add value? Looking at safety statistics, as far as Western countries are concerned, airline transport was safe 20 years ago and still is today.

If that's the case, do we need more regulation? I believe extra rules aren't always the answer and can be counterproductive. Don't get me wrong, rules are a necessity, but there is a limit to their effectiveness. Rules are born from experience, but also from imagination. Things can go wrong. We create rules to avoid a repeat. We also try to imagine what could go wrong, inventing rules that will hopefully avoid undesired events. We humans understandably try to create a zero-risk environment. We don't like risk. In the same way, aviation authorities and airline companies try to control every imaginable scenario, whether a normal or a non-normal situation, to create their own zero-risk paradise.

An ever-expanding rule book, especially for us as pilots, is considered the price we have to pay; the logical path to heaven. Consumers have the same attitude, always eager to point out things that didn't match up to the perfect experience. The press is on a constant hunt looking for when things become messy. We have to accept we will never live in a zero-risk world—even with unlimited rules. We should understand that human beings are not computer programs: you can't just drop in another line of code to fine-tune them. Instead, rules should provide a framework to help us cope with the complexities of everyday operations up to full-scale emergencies. But it is just that: a framework, not an endless user's guide the human memory will struggle with. Call me cynical, but it is very convenient for the authorities and airline management to transfer all responsibility to the flight crew for not doing exactly as described in book three, chapter 12, paragraph 21, subsection b.

Let's fix the balance. Get rid of the fat that has crept in our rules and procedures. Make them healthy again, designed to help us pilots. Have faith in human beings and their cognitive abilities. After all that's what we human beings are good at: we can observe, analyse, act and adapt in an ever-changing environment. This attitude is far more efficient than endlessly asking what the book says. It is a more satisfying and motivating working environment too. Pilots should be trained this way too. Make them resilient. Don't turn them into automatons, programmed to simply execute a set of rules. Train them to take healthy decisions, to cope with the complexities of daily operations, to get on top of hairy situations. The books are important, but they are a starting point. Don't think they will always give the answers. Over-reliance on them can be dangerous too, giving a false feeling of full control.

Now that aviation is in this unprecedented crisis, I fear we are yet to experience another significant expansion in rulemaking. Faced with the coronavirus, every country seems to be coming up with its own plan to make flying safe again from a medical point of view. Airlines in overdrive for another round of extra measures. As we all know from the past, new rules are born very easily but soon become etched in stone. Even when the crisis is over, we consider them 'indispensable' without stopping to think why.

Please don't cripple us with yet more regulation.

In the example above, much of the new rulemaking actually didn't come from the regulator. It came from the airline organization itself, and from the swirl of industry stakeholders (suppliers, contractors, clients, and insurers) around it. In fact, some aviation regulators have acknowledged that writing more rules is neither desirable nor feasible in many situations (Mark, 2020). Amalberti (2001) even spoke of the 'paradox' of almost totally safe transportation systems. Rule-writing has become a purely additive activity: nothing is taken away when a new rule is introduced. Yet that new rule always fails to show any impact in the already really low incident and accident rate. The marginal safety return of additional regulations has been tracking an asymptote to nothing. Regulators who have recognized this instead direct their efforts at collaboration, inspiration, or joint agreements born out of common interests with the industry they regulate. In the United States, for instance, the Commercial Aviation Safety Team (CAST), wrestling with an uncomfortably high accident rate from the 1990s, created an ambitious plan to reduce the risk in commercial aviation by 80%by 2007. To pursue this, CAST didn't propose new rules or regulations. Instead, it:

> ...developed and started implementing a comprehensive safety enhancement plan. By 2007, CAST was able to report that, by implementing the most promising safety enhancements, the fatality rate of commercial air travel in the United States was reduced by 83 percent. CAST keeps developing, evaluating and adding safety enhancements to its plan for the continued reduction of fatality risk by using, according to the Federal Aviation Administration (FAA), data-driven approaches to identify and address potential risk factors. The agency says the methodology includes voluntary commitments, consensus decision-making, data-driven risk management, and a focus on implementing the agreed upon safety enhancements. In a highly regulated industry like aviation, CAST's safety enhancements surprisingly didn't translate into additional regulations but instead focused on the use of new technologies, as well as training and procedures for pilots, mechanics and air traffic controllers... In all, CAST produced 229 safety enhancements in its first decade of operation.
>
> (Mark, 2020, pp. 41–42)

So, leave it to the regulator (and leave a solid role for the state), and you might actually get fewer regulations—no new regulations even (though, granted, it did include 'procedures for pilots,' but those may have served to replace or enhance already existing ones).

Aviation is not alone, of course, in experiencing greater compliance pressure despite (or because of) deregulation. Expanding compliance bureaucracies are agnostic about which field of practice they colonize. Jeffrey Braithwaite, a leading healthcare researcher at Macquarie University, recently asked how many policies apply to the work of a typical hospital ward nurse. He and his colleagues found some 600 policies under which a nurse can be held accountable. Rules penetrate into every little crevasse of their work: from hand hygiene to protocols for patient identification to medication preparation to avoiding sexual harassment to not blocking fire doors to stacking cups and dishes in the break room. But how many of these policies did the nurses actually know? The answer was surprising even to the researchers themselves. On average, nurses were able to recite fewer than three of the 600 policies that apply to their work. The rest was simply not relevant to their day-to-day existence. Or it was already embedded in their practices in ways that made the policies invisible or redundant. Patients mattered to the nurses, not policies. Getting work done mattered to them. Because there was always the next patient, always the next request or task.

But rules and policies keep coming. In 2019, the National Academies of Science, Engineering, and Medicine in the United States set out to identify:

> ...administrative barriers that add little or no value to clinical care, interrupt clinician workflow, frustrate patients and clinicians, or are otherwise wasteful of time and resources. To accomplish this, the participating organizations asked their clinicians and patients "If you could break or change any rule in service of a better care experience for patients or staff, what would it be?" Only 22 percent of the rules identified were actual statutory and regulatory requirements. The rest were either organization-specific requirements (62 percent) or organization behaviors with little or no legal or regulatory basis (16 percent).
>
> (Carayon & Cassel, 2019, p. 141)

Like in aviation, much of the bureaucratic compliance clutter was self-imposed. Carayon and colleagues have pointed out that organizations can find these self-imposed rules when they put their minds to it. We were able to confirm this in other industries (Jacobsen, 2019). Some of them have even mustered the courage to get rid of compliance clutter without violating any legal, regulatory, or statutory requirements. But many have yet to discover that much of the clutter they work through every day is of their own making, and often unnecessary. Every hospital and healthcare system has to maintain a significant bureaucracy (which, ironically, tends to contain a lot of nurses who no longer work on the wards) which imports or writes the rules, prints the posters, sends the reminders, monitors compliance, and keeps itself busy by adopting additional guidelines or developing more rules. By 2008, medical-surgical nurses were spending more than 35% of their time on documentation (Hendrich, Chow, Skierczynski, & Lu, 2008). An intensive care unit (ICU) doctor we spoke with in Texas told us that during a 12-hour shift, she could spend 16 hours on documentation, bureaucracy, and compliance activities. Never mind doing any clinical work. Surgeons, too, have complained of compliance expectations leading to 'checklist fatigue' and have flagged a lack of buy-in. They have remarked that if any more checklists would be instituted, they 'would need a checklist for all the checklists' (Stock & Sundt, 2015, p. 841).

Then take anesthesiologists (those of you who have read *The Safety Anarchist* will remember the example). The American Society of Anesthesiologists alone has 91 standards, guidelines, practice guidelines, practice advisories, statements, positions, and definitions. Documents containing them tend to run over 20 pages each. In total, there are over 4 million references to 'Operating Room standards of practice' (Johnstone, 2017). These come from a variety of accreditors, regulators, institutions, bodies, reformers, or educators; some are in response to conflicting guidelines and standards issued by other professional bodies (such as the Association of Perioperative Nurses); many are the accompaniment of new equipment, technologies, techniques, and drugs that get introduced to the OR. The result is such a plethora of practice guidance—for which an anesthetist may be held accountable—that a zealous practitioner (studying 40 hours a week) would have to spend about two thousand years to read it all.

Rules under the radar

It is an enormous paradox. Neoliberalism, the mode of governance and political economy which has become dominant in many countries over the past decades, promised deliverance from excessive regulation, from government overreach, and from the shackles of rules and constraints. And yet, those regulations, that overreach, the shackles of rules and constraints, they have all actually—demonstrably—gotten worse. Not so much because of the strong presence of government, but more because of its absence. Markets have filled the gap. The logic would seem pretty straightforward. If you create a market for everything, then everything needs or gets a price. If everything gets a price, then everything needs to be accounted for. If everything needs to be accounted for, then there must be processes and procedures, and documents and records, to do such accounting with. And it has led to more, even nefarious features of work. If everything needs to be accounted for, then everything needs to go on *somebody's* account. If things go right, that's great, even though it may be great only for some. If things go wrong, it's certainly not great for some. Blame travels easy in a market where you can hunt down the one who's got to pick up the bill. Granted, they might just pass it back to you, claiming that it's not theirs to pay (since they no longer own the rail track, for instance).

The paradox, then, is as follows: free markets have led to unfree, overregulated workers. The number of (internal) rules, the amount of compliance, and the number of the so-called 'compliance workers' have all risen over the past two decades. Internal organizational compliance and business-to-business compliance together now account for some 60% of all compliance demands (Saines et al., 2014). Governments typically impose only the other 40%. And that is an average figure. Finance, legal, and human resources (HR) all sit well above 60% internally imposed compliance. In certain cases, like complying with information technology (IT) requirements, the proportion of self-imposed rules is even higher: it reaches up to 80%. Healthcare also hovers around 80% self-imposed rules (Carayon & Cassel, 2019). Four out of every five rules in a clinic or hospital, in other words, are made by the organization that runs it—they are not imposed, asked for, or expected by governments, by regulators, or by inspectors.

To be sure, it's not necessarily the case that we would have fewer rules if we'd stopped the clock in 1980 and never got into market-favoring, neoliberal policymaking. We would probably still have more rules today, without privatization or deregulation. Take two of the chief market-oriented leaders and policy innovators in the Anglo world: Reagan and Thatcher. Despite the privatization and deregulation under their watch, neither actually succeeded at rolling in their own governments' 'red tape.' On the contrary, by 1993, three years after the end of Thatcher's rule in the United Kingdom (UK), and four years after that of Reagan in the United States, there was *more* government red tape in each country than before they began (Bozeman, 1993). By the 2010s, US businesses had to comply with some 165,000 pages of federal regulations alone (Hale, Borys, & Adams, 2013). Yet for *most* of the rise of compliance pressure over the past two decades, and particularly the way it gets experienced at the front line, on the work floor, we actually have ourselves to thank. To understand where all the additional compliance comes from, we need to look at what free markets have done to our industries, our organizations, our contractor relations, our insurers, our boards, our public relations, our human resources, and to a whole range of other stakeholders.

Governments—because of how they have measured the effects of their own deregulation and privatization—have pretty much missed this growth of internal compliance bureaucracy. The proliferation of rules has literally happened under their radar. As you'll see in Chapter 6, governments, keen to take credit for the cleansing effect of their deregulatory and privatizing policies, haven't been able to know about all these rules. Because they don't measure them. Regulatory Impact Assessments (RIAs) of various kinds have become the norm as an accompaniment to the consideration of new regulations. Some governments actively calculate and track the cost of compliance, and many have numeric targets for deregulation and decluttering their own books. But that applies to the rules *they* make. It doesn't apply to the rules that industries or organizations or departments make because governments have stopped owning that industry, or stopped regulating it as they did before. This means that they, and we, have systematically missed the major source of overregulation that has been hiding in plain sight: the market itself.

Less ownership, more rules, and less (quality) work

Let's go back to the summer of 1986 and to what happened next. The surveying that was once an in-house activity and responsibility of the national railway system is now done by small-to-medium-sized contracting companies that run a couple of vans in their respective part or corner of the country. The rail infrastructure owner—separated from the train operators—is a major client. And the surveyors are not their only contractors. Almost everything that requires technical expertise and equipment is contracted out. The railway, to be sure, had always relied on some contractors for highly specialized work, or work that required specialized machinery. But now numerous other contractors and subcontractors do the actual construction and maintenance work on rail tracks, ballast beds, and overhead contact lines. The surveying contractor also works for, or rather subcontracts, to these contractors, so technically they have multiple clients (a solution that helps them in meeting tax regulations, as you'll see below). The rapidly multiplying and ever denser webs of contractors, deployed by a rail track owner who has little in-house technical expertise left and who doesn't run the trains itself, have led to perhaps predictable problems. Not all of them have to do with a proliferation of paperwork and new compliance demands. One problem, indeed, is that the entire system can be failing as a result of the market rules by which it now operates.

During the first few winters after privatization, train traffic in the Netherlands regularly ground to a halt. Commuters were huddled on frozen station platforms, waiting for trains that sometimes never came. The media was having a field day. Angry travelers make great interviewees. All a journalist needed to do was get a sample that viewers can identify with, and great material was guaranteed. The Dutch are quite forthcoming when sharing their opinions. The footage of station platforms overflowing with shivering people made great B-roll. It wasn't that there was a new problem.

But the new solution to the problem—the privatized, deregulated, and separated solution—managed to make a complete hash of it.

A MARKET FAVORITE: DON'T HAVE PUBLIC TRANSPORT AT ALL

Of course, one solution to the problems above is to not have public transport at all. That is precisely the favorite option of conservative activists in cities across the United States (Tabuchi, 2018). As Tabuchi reported, Americans for Prosperity, a group financed by the oil billionaire Koch brothers, have in the past years campaigned against public transit projects of any kind. Americans for Prosperity and other Koch-backed groups have opposed more than two dozen other transit-related measures—including many states' bids to raise gas taxes to fund public transit or transportation infrastructure—by organizing phone banks, running advertising campaigns, staging public forums, issuing reports and writing opinion pieces in local publications. Public transit plans, they claim, waste taxpayer money on unpopular, outdated technology like trains and buses just as the world is moving toward (ostensibly) cleaner, driverless vehicles. They argue that ride-hailing services like Uber and Lyft are the future of transportation, not buses and trains. Public transit critics have also long raised fears that rail projects are a conduit for crime like pickpocketing, sexual assault and robbery. Or, public transit is only for the benefit of hipster millennials and thus becomes a conduit for gentrification, forcing hard-working Americans to move further away to find affordable housing.

Public transit, Americans for Prosperity says, goes against the liberties that Americans hold dear. Broadly speaking, Americans for Prosperity campaigns against big government, but many of its initiatives target public transit. Indeed, the Kochs' opposition to transit spending stems from their longstanding free-market, libertarian philosophy. It also dovetails with their financial interests, which benefit from automobiles and highways. One of the mainstay companies of Koch Industries, the Kochs' conglomerate, is a major producer of gasoline and asphalt, and also makes seatbelts, tires and other automotive parts. Even as Americans for Prosperity opposes public investment in transit, it supports spending tax money on highways and roads.

The paucity of federal funding for transit projects means that local ballots are critical in shaping how Americans travel, with decades- long repercussions for the economy and the environment. Highway funding has historically been built into state and federal budgets, but transit funding usually requires a vote to raise taxes, creating what experts call a systemic bias toward cars over trains and buses. The United States transportation sector emits more earth-warming carbon dioxide than any other part of the nation's economy.

Compacted snow

So, what is one of the problems with train traffic in the Netherlands since the market started getting a bigger role in running it? Snow and ice, when it occasionally happens, can compact around the underside of the train. And then it can fall off. This often happens when the train goes over a switch (or point, as some countries call it). This is where the track splits to allow trains to swerve onto a parallel track or head off on a track in a different direction. With ice and snow clumps wedged between the rails, switches can get stuck. In previous winters, before 1995, station masters had the authority to use a broom to brush off any snow, and a gas burner to remove the ice build-ups so that the switch could be freed up. Further afield, train engineers, in contact with traffic control, had the authority to nuzzle up toward the switch. The best method was to drive the train all the way onto the switch. If the switch was set in the right direction, the train could simply continue on its way. If not, then the engineer had a tool in the cab to change it. This delegation of decision authority to the front line, to the point of action, worked because the rail track owner and train operator were the same, semi-government organization. There was no coordination overhead, because the work of making trains run was already coordinated. And managers and directors trusted expertise at the sharp end.

With rail track owner and train operators separated and largely privatized, this changed entirely. The simplest question, which wasn't even a question before the separation, turned out to be unanswerable; which organization has the responsibility to help a train across a frozen switch? The people running the train, or the people who own the switch? Organizational paralysis and finger-pointing resulted. The official explanation was that harsh winters were becoming unusual and that there were a lot of switches that could freeze. But a simple probability calculation showed that this was nonsense. There were not enough switches, and there was not enough compacted snow, to grind the entire country's rail system to a halt. To be sure, train timetables in highly developed, uncertainty-avoiding, and densely populated countries (which, say, the Japanese have elevated to an obsessive art) aren't very forgiving. With trains every 15 minutes on most tracks (and 10 minutes on others), waiting longer than 15 minutes for a switch to open up is not an option. Well, it is not an option without consequences because things start backing up in a hurry.

Two trains waiting longer than 15 minutes to go over a switch can quickly lead to a snarl of 20 trains, which takes hours, and often the rest of the day, to disentangle (Heine, 2018). So, what had the procedure become since separation and privatization? And could that explain wait times longer than 15 minutes in front of a switch? It could, amply. Switches are connected to a central reporting system that belongs to the track owner. As soon as it detects a frozen or otherwise unresponsive switch, a message goes to central traffic control and immediately halts all traffic on that stretch of track. Train operators have no choice but to stop driving. As soon as they come to the next signal, it will tell them that the train cannot continue. The engineer, in turn, no longer has the authority to get out of the train and take a look—let alone fiddle with the switch—because his or her company no longer owns the track. It's not theirs to meddle with. Nowadays, switches in a country like the Netherlands have the ability to heat themselves up electrically, so as to avoid an ice or snow dump from freezing them. They can be programmed to do this automatically. Even the overhead wires can receive extended bursts of 'supercharged' currents when there is no traffic on that sector, in order to melt the rime ice that may have accumulated on them. This does require the technology to work, of course, and for the system to know where problems are.

If the technology doesn't work, the track owner, in a bid to save on personnel costs, no longer has its own technicians to go out and solve the problem—whatever it may be. They rely on the market to supply contractors who employ the technicians. These need to be rustled up and sent to the place where the train is waiting in the cold. The contracted technicians travel there by car. But remember, it is winter, and it is likely snowing. Or there may be ice on the roads. The Netherlands is a small and pretty full country; snow and ice lead to traffic jams as far as the eyes can see. It is in those traffic jams that contracted technicians spend most of their day. In the meantime, trains occasionally keep backing up and station platforms often keep overflowing. These are the results of privatization, of a free market for train operators and contractors, of a removal or restriction of front-line authority to act. The new centralized bureaucracy (not measurably smaller in any way than before) that now has to try to pull it all together is one where few people want or dare to take responsibility. It all leads to gridlock as its predictable side effect. As some might put it, promises of market efficiencies have delivered market lunacies.

More paperwork relationships

And that is only when it's winter. Privatization, deregulation, and contracting all create numerous new accountability relationships. The fragmentation of track ownership, maintenance, and train operations across numerous new organizations and contractors has exponentially multiplied the number of accountability relationships—not only between the client and its circle of contractors, but also between contractors themselves, and between contractors and *their* subcontractors. Privatization and contracting also create new accountability relationships with what is left of government oversight. The fact that the surveying contractor has one major client, for instance, requires the contracting company to submit an application for exemption each year to the tax authorities. In this, it can explain how it is not violating regulations which prohibit shadow constructions for employment. If the surveyors are contracted to only one client, then it needs to be shown that the client is not avoiding hiring these people itself in order to duck payroll taxes and pension obligations.

Most of the new rules and overregulation, however, come from each contractor having to demonstrate how it controls its corporate risks, its financial risks, and its health and safety risks. Early indications of the clutter that this can cause were visible in the Netherlands, in which

> ... only 3% of workers surveyed used the rules often, and almost 50% never; 47% found them to be not always realistic, 29% thought they were used only to point the finger of blame, 95% thought that, if you kept to the rules, the work could never be completed in time, 79% that there were too many rules, 70% that they were too complicated and 77% that they were sometimes contradictory.
>
> (Elling, 1991, p. 5)

Results from studies conducted by DuPont in the UK railway sector were similar (Maidment, 1993). So how does this constitute compliance capitalism? The recipient of the compliance demonstrations is less often the regulator than it is the contracting company's client, and its own board and management. In a market, a contractor is accountable more to them—other market actors and its own officers—than to the government. You only need to take a look at health and safety to see what this means. Given that the contractor has more than five surveyors, it now needs to have a health and safety policy statement which, among other things, specifies the person responsible for the health and safety of employees. This person, in turn, needs to sit through and pass annual training (supplied by a consultant who is contracting to the contractor for this purpose), which needs to be recorded and demonstrated to the client or anybody else the contractor works for or with. The consulting contractor also needs to take out liability and indemnity insurances, which need to be appropriately documented and demonstrated to (and then checked and recorded by) the contracting surveyor company, who in turn have to be able to show this to their client in order to be granted the work. The client also records and stores this information. The amount of paperwork going up and down and back and forth is enormous.

Have your contractors completed their annual fire safety training?

And that is not all. Health and safety is an area where the paradox of a shrinking government regulatory footprint and a steep increase in rules and compliance demands is highly visible. As you recall from the beginning of the book, the United States has gradually been defunding and shrinking its Occupational Health and Safety Authority (OSHA) since the Reagan administration, and there have been calls to abolish it altogether. This is based on the argument that OSHA has had a good run but is not able to push down injury and death rates even further with the same logic that got it thus far. By the 1990s, most work-related deaths in the United States were motor vehicle accidents or murder by coworkers or customers. And most of the deaths occurred to the self-employed. Neither of these were seen as amenable to the inspection/fine approach of a federal workplace regulator (Kniesner & Leeth, 1995). Despite these arguments, OSHA wasn't abolished, even though most employers found it the second 'most frustrating' agency to deal with after the Internal Revenue Service (Kniesner & Leeth, 1995, p. 52). But it was considerably weakened.

Workers in the US are now in greater danger of physical harm than in any other recent time, Berkowitz (2020) shows. Black and Latin workers, including immigrants, work in the most dangerous jobs. This year, the Bureau of Labor Statistics reported that Black workers and Latin workers (the majority of them immigrants) suffered higher fatality rates than other workers. In its latest release, the Bureau found that the number of Black workers killed on the job in 2018 increased 16 percent, from 530 to 615, the highest total since 1999. Overall worker fatality rates also increased in the manufacturing industry; agriculture, forestry and fishing; and oil and gas extraction industries.

OSHA now has the lowest number of on-board inspectors in the last 45 years. According to numbers just released, federal OSHA now has a total of 862 inspectors to cover millions of workplaces. Alarmingly, this number is lower than the number of inspectors released last March, when the agency announced it would be increasing the number of inspectors. At this staffing level, it would take the agency a whopping 165 years to inspect each workplace under its jurisdiction just once.

The decrease in the number of inspectors, which has always fluctuated somewhat, but fallen steadily since the 2010s, is a clear result of administration policies to suspend filling vacancies in FY 2017 and then slow-walk hiring by putting in new procedures over the last few years. Overburdening inspectors reduces OSHA's ability to protect workers and spot and change practices that lead to fatalities and injuries. Reducing the number of OSHA inspectors puts more workers in danger of physical harm on the job.

To make matters worse, OSHA has also failed to fill 42 percent of its top leadership career positions, leaving the agency without requisite expertise and direction to protect workers. Key positions such as the director of enforcement, director of training, director of whistleblower protections, and regional directors have been vacant for years. Currently, these unfilled positions are partially staffed by employees who are also holding another job—doing two jobs at once.

As expected, the decrease in the number of inspectors has directly led to a precipitous drop in the overall number of inspections conducted by federal OSHA, as well as a drop in the number of more complicated inspections. New data reveal that the number of OSHA inspections conducted during 2017-19 is thousands of inspections per year lower than any three-year period under previous administrations. Per year, there are now 5,000 fewer inspections than the average yearly numbers in preceding decades.

As the total number of inspections declines, OSHA has also cut back on the number of more complicated, labor-intensive inspections. A lack of resources has led to a 25 percent drop in heat-related inspections; a 66 percent drop in the number of inspections related to musculoskeletal injuries; a 27 percent drop in the number of inspections where OSHA measures workers' chemical exposures; and a 38 percent drop in the highest penalty 'significant cases.' OSHA is cutting back on these critical inspections even though musculoskeletal disorders are the number one occupational illness faced by workers, and the country has had record heat levels over the last few years.

The only kind of workplace inspection that has, tragically, gone up since the early 2000s is inspections in response to fatalities or workplace catastrophes. In 2009 that number was 836. In 2019, it was 978.

The irony is that the number of rules and size of compliance burden related to health and safety has never gone down. Instead, it has risen dramatically. But with a weakened, more distant regulator, where do they all come from? Not from the government. Examples abound. Just imagine the following. The contracted teams of surveyors who go out to sites for the rail track owner have to go through training on how to recognize exposure to new or increased risks, and document their risk assessments for the purposes of archiving and accountability. Their organization asks for it, because the organization it contracts to asks for it. At each site, surveyors need to fill out local risk assessment forms and checklists, which are all gathered and saved for at least five years. All this needs to be reported not only internally, but to the client who has contracted the surveyors. Because if something were to happen there, the client wants to be able to show that it is not the one who is responsible. After all, it asked the surveyors to be maximally prepared in their identification and mitigation of risk, and it has the paperwork to show it. If the contracted surveyors 'make poor choices,' then the consequences shouldn't go onto the client's account, but on the contractors.

The contracting company can then hold its individual surveyors to account for not following the rules and stipulations that it trained them on and got them to sign paperwork for.

Of course, the anxieties around having private contractors stomping around live train traffic (on a railway owned by another company, with trains running on it that belong to yet another company) can be readily imagined. This is why documentation requirements are fairly intricate. Not only that: the contractor has to supply its own full-time safety officer while their surveyors are working anywhere within 50 meters of a train track, but the rail track-owning company sends its own safety official as well. These two are sometimes complemented by a third safety official, from the train operator (if there's only one exploiting that piece of track) who assists in cases of more complex train schedules. The risk assessment forms used by the contractor (which are different from those used by the rail track owner and the train operator) are not developed in-house, but supplied by yet another consulting contractor.

Gas- and electrical safety checking and certification are also required of the surveyor contractor, and fire safety checking and certification take up a day each per person (including all the surveyors) each year. Surveyors actually don't carry a lot of tools that are prone to catching fire. But the office and depot from which they work might have electricity and gas appliances. In addition, the surveying contractor needs to conduct and annually complete portable appliance and device testing to get them certified; conduct and document display screen equipment risk assessments as well as ergonomic risk assessments and mitigation; complete and document first aid needs risk assessments and provide the requisite training to the level required for the various roles; and provide manual handling assessments and training to all of its surveyors for how to lift and transport theodolites and other assorted materials by hand from van to site and back. All of this of course needs to be documented, recorded, and kept up to date. When the railway organization itself still owned the track and employed its surveyors, these things were either non-existent or largely invisible. Managing the various compliance demands for all of its surveyors back in the 1980s—which were less onerous and less voluminous to begin with—could be done at scale, with all the efficiencies this entailed. Now each contractor has to do *all* of these things. And that is just what is needed once they already *have* a contract. The amount and variety of documentation needed to pass through the various stages of bidding and vetting for a contract (for which yet another class of consultancies has brought itself to life) is about three times what is needed to discharge the obligations under that contract—if one were to get it.

Then there is one more example of where the desire for control through bureaucracy and audits can take an organization. After discovering, through audits, that it never succeeded in getting things completed in time or on budget, the rail track owner instituted a process to avoid overruns of its major projects. This of course included the surveying works. It introduced significant new controls, systems, and processes with about 200 auditable control steps. Each of these steps perhaps looked sensible in isolation, but taking the steps (not even considering auditing them) turned out to take some 270 days in total, due to misalignments, delays between handoffs and various forms of bureaucratic lag. Forced to reconsider its approval-for-approval processes, the rail track operator had to conclude that the employee time it invested in all its steps, checks, auditable controls, and self-imposed compliance demands far outstripped the project overrun costs they had sought to reign in.

Soccer ball redux

Yet sometimes deregulation and privatization change nothing. Not long ago, on my walk to the university, I was passed by a pickup truck owned by the private contractor which looks after landscaping on the campus. Two men were in the front, staring at nothing in particular. The back of the pickup was full of what you would expect of a landscaper: a mower, rakes, brooms, and an assortment of other tools of their trade. As they passed, I could see yet another object. Happily bouncing around among all the implements was—you guessed it—a soccer ball. It looked well-used.

2

FREE MARKETS IN THEORY; INTENSIVE MANAGERIAL CONTROL IN PRACTICE

I have a PhD student who works for the Directorate-General for Public Works and Water Management in the Netherlands. The mission of that Directorate today is 'to work for dry feet, sufficient clean water and a smooth flow of road traffic.' These are all considerable challenges in the Netherlands. It is a small country on the flats of the delta of the large European rivers. It is among the most densely populated countries in the world, with 60 dogs, 90 cows, 150 cars, 420 people, and 630 bicycles on each square kilometer. More than half of the Netherlands is below sea level. You can imagine what it takes to ensure all those feet keep dry; the water stays clean and traffic flows smoothly. Does that sound like a task for government?

Rijkswaterstaat, the Dutch name for the Directorate-General, was actually founded by the French in 1798. Yes, they believed this was a task for government. Ruling the Netherlands as a vassal state from 1795 to 1813, the French had long been stronger believers than the Dutch in the virtues of central government. They sorted out a whole bunch of things that only a central government can. It gave the occupied provinces of the Netherlands their first constitution, a federal civil judicial code, a common measurement system (the metric one), street numbers, last names and a centralized population registration, a single land registry, and military conscription. As parting gift, Napoleon took 14,000 Dutch conscripts to join his *Grande Armée* to conquer Russia in 1813. Most of them never made it back.

The French also tackled water management—not a trivial task in a low-lying river delta. The Dutch had long kept the water under control with a patchwork of local water boards that managed water barriers, waterways, levels, and quality in their respective regions. These had been the oldest form of government in the Low Countries, stemming from the 13th century. Water doesn't typically stay in just one region, though. What happens in one, or *doesn't* happen in one, can drastically affect the next one downstream (or even upstream, e.g., through spring tide floods pushing inland from the sea). The French didn't think that mutual coordination between boards was effective or sufficient, so they centralized it into *Rijkswaterstaat*. They only partially succeeded. Even today, there are still 22 local water boards responsible for water levels, quality, and sanitation.

From French to Anglo innovation

It took two centuries before the next major innovation in public works and water management. This time it wasn't a French innovation.[1] It would be an Anglo one. Over a coffee, my PhD student told me that since he has worked there, *Rijkswaterstaat* has the motto 'The market, unless…' In 2003, *Rijkswaterstaat* commissioned an exploratory study into the possibilities of introducing more competition and market forces to the management of water and road infrastructure in the Netherlands (Sterk, 2003). The study identified a number of areas ripe for outsourcing. Dredging, water storage, water level management, and other activities were recommended for submission to the forces of competition. Throughout, however, the study noted that:

> market forces are a means, not an end. Markets must be considered an instrument to serve the common good. Before we do anything else, we shouldn't

elevate market forces to be our goal. They are there to serve the public interest: our health, environment, safety and economy.

(p. 4)

Ten years later, *Rijkswaterstaat* had shed 6,000 jobs. Construction companies trying to compete in a newly created market for what was previously government work offered their bids consistently more than 30% below the expected market price. Within the next three years, some 4,000 construction companies would go bankrupt in their attempts to compete in this new market, leaving only a few big players to dominate it (Koenen, 2015). It became the crescendo of a development that had started in the 1970s. Instead of builder, *Rijkswaterstaat* became administrator. Instead of maker, it became manager. 'Less government, more market' had become the adage. Today, *Rijkswaterstaat* has held onto the governance of public works and infrastructure projects, but it is the market (or what is left of it) that actually does the work.

Mom cooked his dinner

The Anglo-inspired intervention in the Dutch Directorate-General for Public Works and Water Management has roots that predate the French one. They can be traced to the ideas written down by Adam Smith, who was born in Scotland in 1723. But his ideas, interestingly, can be traced back to the French! The best-known of Smith's two books, *The Wealth of Nations* for short, appeared in 1776, in the same year as the American Declaration of Independence. In it (and in several papers that had appeared earlier), he elaborated on an idea that wasn't his, but a French economist's, named Richard Cantillon. In 1755, Cantillon had written his *Essai sur la Nature du Commerce en Général* (translated as *An Essay on Economic Theory*) in which he described an isolated country estate that was divided into competing leased farms. Independent entrepreneurs were invited to run each farm. Their purpose was to maximize the production and returns of the farms they leased. The farmers who were successful were the ones who had found ways to innovate, to introduce better equipment and techniques. And they were selective about what they brought to market, ensuring that it was only the produce and goods that people were willing to pay good (or at least adequate) money for. Cantillon showed that total returns were far higher when an estate was divided into leases that were driven by competing self-interests. The lord-of-the-manor's 'command economy' had no way of competing with the aggregate of self-interested farmers.

Even though his demonstration fits the tenets of Enlightenment like a hand in a glove, Cantillon scrupulously avoided taking a political position. Rather, he wanted to shed light on the mechanics of economic life in the 18th century, and offer different models for how to deal with very real problems of food and other economic insecurities. But the parallel is of course obvious: voluntary private markets are more productive, more efficient, and more profitable than government-run economies. They simply make more sense. Adam Smith thought as much. His 'invisible hand' is a metaphor for the unseen forces that move a free market economy. Like Cantillon's leased farms, individual self-interest and freedom of production as well as consumption end up serving the best interest of society as a whole. As long as players in the market are independent and autonomous, and they enter any trade on that market entirely voluntarily, it works, Smith said. Because then the constant interplay of individual pressures on market supply and demand causes the natural movement of prices and the flow of trade. In his words:

> Every individual necessarily labors to render the annual revenue of the society as great as he can ... He intends only his own gain, and he is in this, as in many other cases, led by an *invisible hand* to promote an end which was no part of his intention ... By pursuing his own interests, he frequently promotes that of the society more effectually than when he really intends to promote it. I have never known much good done by those who affected to trade for the public good.
>
> (Smith, 1776/2009, p. 128)

To encourage a free market, the role of government (or Cantillon's Lord of the Manor) is *laissez-faire*—literally 'let them do.' The market, under those conditions, will find its own equilibrium and fairness. Voluntary, free trade self-organizes competing consumers, producers, distributors, and other intermediaries, each pursuing their individual gains. Each free exchange creates signals about which goods and services are valuable and what it takes to get them to market. Together, all these countless exchanges produce unintentional and widespread benefits for everyone. The best collective results come from letting people serve their individual self-interest. Smith found this realization, in his own words, 'astounding.' He saw how benefits flow not just to individuals, but to an entire society, and that this came from the *absence* of a mastermind, from the lack of anyone dictating or forcibly directing these countless actions. 'No trace of such a person can be found,' he wrote. 'Instead, we find the *Invisible Hand* at work. This is the mystery to which I earlier referred.' He concluded with his famous observation that 'It is not from the benevolence of the butcher, the brewer, or the baker that we expect our dinner, but from their regard to their own interest' (Ibid).

And then his dinner was served. His mother had cooked it for him, because he was living at home when he wrote *The Wealth of Nations*. His father had died shortly before he was born, and, in the words of one of his students, Smith owed his life to 'all the tender solicitude of his surviving parent ... treating him with an unlimited indulgence' (Otteson, 2018, p. 33). Indulgence is of course cognate with kindness, compassion, sympathy, and mercy. It is related to altruism, to the notion of giving something while expecting nothing in return. In other words, it is the very cancellation of self-interest. That was what his mom did for him. To paraphrase his own words, it was from the benevolence of his mother that he could expect his dinner. Between him and his mom, there was no *invisible hand*, no unseen market force. There was only the strong, self-sacrificing arm of a pampering parent. And it doesn't even have to be a parent. A study of the curious blend of private and public practices in post-socialist Czechia (or Czech Republic) in the 1990s showed how the canteen of a former agricultural socialist cooperative continued to function under market conditions, but its:

> economic success in the Czech setting is based on or supported by emotional needs and care. ... food is prepared, distributed, and received in a familiar and affectionate atmosphere. [T]hese practices relate to reconfigurations of the private-public boundaries in wider Czech society and to discourses on 'marketization,' [where] the emotional work performed in the canteen cannot simply be seen as a response to new 'market forces.' The privateness generated through social relations in the canteen is more appropriately interpreted in the light of socialist ideals that stress the centrality and

> importance of the workplace in the community than as the commodification of … labor for profit.
>
> (Thelen & Read, 2007, p. 11)

To be sure, this doesn't invalidate Smith's observation of the self-organizing complexity and the beauty of free markets. But it shows that self-interest is not the only motivation driving people to do things. And it reminds us how the *invisible hand* can work only under the ideal conditions of *voluntary* exchanges by *independent* and *autonomous* actors. As you'll see throughout this book, many of the counterproductive side-effects of market-oriented policies come from the violation of these ideals—violations that stem not from some new Lord of the Manor entering onto the market, but from the very workings of the free market itself.

Governments can actually run things well—or can they?

Let's first take a look at some services which governments had been running successfully for—literally—centuries. In fact, governments often chose to take over the running of a particular service *because* markets were making a hash of it. I will take you back to the country we have already visited—the Netherlands—because it offers nicely contained case observations of the gradual adoption of market-oriented policies. Railways in the Netherlands had long been running outside government control. The first rail line was opened by a private operator in 1839, between Amsterdam and Haarlem. In the next few years, no fewer than six separate companies built and exploited various bits and pieces of railway. In many cases it wasn't possible to have trains from one company ride on the rails of another because of different railway gauges. And all companies had different stations in different parts of the city they travelled to. Making a trip involved many train (and station) and ticket changes, and could mean traveling with foreign companies, since those were the ones who had been constructing and exploiting railways in the country's border regions from the 1850s. The economic consequences of this free market for railways were immense. German, British, and Belgian railways were government-owned and run. Because of this, and due to ample access to coal, these countries' economic performance was rapidly outpacing that of the Netherlands.

It would take a war, the Great War of 1914–1918, to get the Dutch government to intervene. Not that the Dutch were in that war—they were neutral. The country, however, did mobilize its military during the war years. It was the military's top brass who discovered that 75 years of competition had left them with an utterly useless, unreliable, ill-coordinated system that was incapable of supporting any meaningful troop movement. The state of maintenance was deplorable because of the companies' small margins (which themselves had been a result of competition in the market). So, the state nationalized the railways, all of them. And after the Great War, it wouldn't let go. The usefulness and necessity of a nationally coordinated and run system had been proven. It would remain that way until 1995.

The Netherlands postal service was nationalized considerably earlier, in 1799, by the French occupiers. The French figured that the need for reliable and regular postal service was not equally distributed across the country. They rightly anticipated that a competitive postal delivery market would leave out some parts of the country, large parts even. Private operators could be enticed into running stagecoaches along the profitable trunk routes between cities, but that was about it. Nationally collecting, sorting, transporting, and delivering mail required considerable investment, which could only be recouped on a country-wide scale by having it lift the economic performance of the entire occupied territory, not the profit margins of a few market actors. Their new national postal service ensured that every little town was connected to the service, for the same price, and that every address was known. It helped that the French pushed the Dutch to formally introduce street names (and numbers) and last names—without which mail delivery gets a bit tricky. The French left in 1813, but the national postal service stayed. It was quick to embrace innovation and new technologies, such as the telegraph in 1845 and a national telephone network toward the end of the 19th century. The insight the French had come to 100 years before was still valid: if the Dutch had left a landline telephone service to a competitive market, then a national network would never have been built.

The end of Keynes

It was a kind of governance of services and industries that remained popular for a long time during the 20th century. Between the great depression of the 1930s and the 1970s, governments and economists believed that markets could only work with strong intervention and state regulation and ownership. Political-economic arrangements during the first decades after World War II were aimed at sharing the gains of economic expansion and at spreading, preventing, and compensating risk (e.g., workplace injuries and job loss). Governments chose emancipatory, reformist, and redistributive strategies. This made good sense at the time. An important aim was to tame the 'political passions' that had helped ignite communism and fascism (Braedley & Luxton, 2010). And there was no reason to suspect that there was anything wrong with the model. Growth immediately after World War II was spectacular.

British economist John Maynard Keynes' ideas had guided governments through the crisis of the 1930s and now did the same: government spending was encouraged. This would ensure employment, keep up demand, and provide the basis for continued economic growth, even if accompanied by some inflation. Demand can increase only if people can afford to buy things, and in order to afford that, they need to have paid work. Inflation in the Keynesian model meant that the economy was growing; that demand was strong. It was a proven and compelling position. Natural forces and market incentives, Keynes believed, had not been enough to pull the world out of the Great Depression (in fact, they helped the world tumble into it), and they wouldn't lead to equitable, sustainable, and peace-promoting post-war reconstruction and economic growth either. Big governments, substantial government spending, and government ownership of key services and industries were all part of the Keynesian package.

But growth in post-World War II welfare states, driven by Keynesian monetary stability and carefully managed markets, stagnated in the 1970s. The model seemed to have stopped working. Unemployment and inflation were supposed to be inversely related. If one goes down, the other goes up. To promote economic growth, governments could increase their spending and the country's money supply. Inflation would go up, and employment would too, leading to economic recovery. The 1970s, however, was a period of slow economic growth and high inflation (sometimes known as stagflation, a combination of stagnation and inflation). This wasn't supposed to happen in the Keynesian model. An oil supply shortage shock, triggered by Arab countries banning oil exports to countries supporting Israel in the

1973 Yom Kippur War, was widely seen as upsetting the Keynesian model. It was, its proponents explained, an external cost-push inflation, unrelated to the known variables of the model, but with dire consequences for them. A second, similar shock came in 1979 when the Iranian Revolution severely dented global oil production. Governments tried to offset stagflation with more spending, but this time it only increased inflation.

From Mont Pèlerin to the Anglo world

It gave an opportunity for a 'neo' version of Smith's classical liberal economic thought, which had been dominant before the Great Depression of the 1930s. Two colloquia that bookended World War II formed the origin of 'neoliberalism' and cemented its key ideas. The first of these academic meetings was the *Colloque Walter Lippmann*, organized in Paris in 1938. It was held against the backdrop of Stalinist state terror in the east and the rise of fascism in Italy and Germany—all of which relied on strongmen leaders and a totalizing role of the state in the economy and affairs of citizens. The meeting in Paris aimed to construct a new liberalism in support of free markets, free trade, limited government and individual rights. One of the 26 attendees was Alexander Rüstow, a German sociologist and economist who had fled to Switzerland in 1933. He coined the term 'neoliberalism' at the meeting. His vision, though, had little in common with how we understand 'neoliberalism' today. For one, Rüstow had been with the Ministry of Economic Affairs in interbellum Germany, where he worked on the nationalization of the coal industry. And after the war, he promoted Germany's social market economy which affords a strong role to the state in managing markets, the economy, and people's security and welfare.

The *Colloque Walter Lippmann* participants were divided into two ideological camps. Rüstow and others endorsed a kind of social liberalism, which relies on a government-regulated market economy and the expansion of civil, political, and social rights. Poverty, healthcare, welfare, education, and the environment are problems that all deserve strong government intervention, and there is much in social liberalism that cannot be left to (unregulated) markets even as the rights and autonomy of the individual are assured. This type of liberalism would now be known as centrist, or progressive. It tends to be socially liberal and economically conservative. Germany wasn't the only country to embrace this kind of liberalism after the war. There is strong ideological kinship between its social liberalism and, for example, the Scandinavian model; the Rhineland version of capitalism, the Spanish organization of cooperatives, the French *économie du bien commun* or the Italian *economia civile*. These all present capitalism with a human face: a strong, efficient state presence with generous healthcare, education, and environmental and social welfare provisions.

But the other camp at *Walter Lippmann*, led by Friedrich Hayek, an Austria-born economist, did not go that way. It instead adhered to a strict interpretation of the so-called Manchester liberalism. Manchester had been the hub of 19th century textile manufacturing, whose interests led to the birth of that city's kind of liberalism. Factory workers employed in textile mills suffered from England's corn laws, which were the result of a mercantilist policy that imposed steep import tariffs on corn in order to protect the country's land-owning aristocracy. Newly enriched and empowered factory owners, however, had no use for such tariffs and laws. In fact, these disadvantaged them because their workers had to pay more for their food, and had less to eat unless factory owners increased their wages. Free trade was a key point for Manchester liberalism, and even though it would serve the narrow interests of mill owners, its ideals of peace and goodwill among people were as sweeping as those of social liberalism. That said, many of the participants believed that there could be no accommodation between socialism and capitalism. It's either-or. Those participants feared that if you create a national healthcare system today, you will have full-blown communist-style bureaucratic totalitarianism tomorrow. Nowadays this sort of belief would be known as right-leaning, or conservative. It indeed tends to be socially conservative and economically liberal. As Lilla (2014) puts it, countries like the United States and China have embraced this kind of 'neoliberalism' which is organized around a permissive economy with a restrictive culture (a combination he considers unsustainable in the long run).

The second of the colloquia occurred in 1947, a year after Keynes' death. The meeting was organized by Hayek in the Swiss town of Mont Pèlerin, not far from Lausanne. It included Milton Friedman and Karl Popper, among others. Friedman, of course, was inspired by Hayek, whose later position at Friedman's institution was pointedly not paid for by the University of Chicago itself, but by an outside foundation. Wanting to push back on the 'state ascendency of Marxist or Keynesian planning that was sweeping the globe,' the Mont Pèlerin participants saw themselves as a revolutionary corps of capitalist resistance fighters against socialist supremacy (Bregman, 2019). Its participants ended up forming the Mont Pèlerin Society, a forum for neoliberals which promotes free markets and seeks to develop ways in which free enterprise can replace many of the functions that social liberalism would like to reserve for the state. A young Milton Friedman considered himself a naïve, provincial American, yet as equally beleaguered as the others in their own countries (Mirowski & Plehwe, 2009). Reconstruction efforts in Europe at the time were steeped in Keynesian ideals, which curbed free markets and regulated banks. In this environment, the Mont Pèlerin Society was a collection of revolutionaries on the fringe. Yet, in a testimony of how the world's political-economic tastes would change, eight of the society's members went on to win Nobel memorial prizes for economics. In the 1970s, Hayek handed the presidency of the society to Friedman, whose energy and dedication surpassed even that of its founder and his predecessor. Under Friedman, the society radicalized. The free market was soon seen as pretty much the *only* solution to any economic policy problem.

To Chicago and back

Inspired by the Chicago School of Economics under Milton Friedman, governments were encouraged to dismantle capital controls, pull back regulations, implement tax cuts, privatize state industries, and open economies up for the unfettered workings of the free market. Of course, large-scale government spending leads to inflation, Friedman argued. It is literally printing money. With more of it around, it loses value. Thatcher in the United Kingdom (UK) was an early adopter of the ideas, and helped convert them into an electoral platform and policy agenda. As leader of the British Conservative Party, Thatcher had already firmly promoted Hayek's *The Constitution of Liberty*—a book that argues how civilization grows and becomes wealthy because it embraces the fundamental principles of (economic) liberty, and not the other way around. After her election in 1979, she appointed Milton Friedman as one of her economic advisors. The British economy, Thatcher believed, was seen as in dire need of a dose of Friedman.

Friedman advised Thatcher to get rid of aging, loss-making industries and services, submit them to the forces of competition, and let the market sort them out. Competition would lead to more consumer choice, more efficiency, lower prices, and better services. Powerful unions needed to be dealt with too. Anything that had smacked of job losses had previously been successfully blocked, to the point that electrical trains in the UK (and a diesel locomotive between Melbourne and Wodonga on which I rode in 1990, to remind you) still had a stoker in the cab. The task of a stoker once upon a time was to feed a locomotive's steam engine with coal. With new forms of moving a train, the stoker's task had of course disappeared. But unions made sure the job stayed. An employed but completely unoccupied stoker was an icon of ossified, bloated, and expensive stagnation. The British government not only owned the national railway, and the postal service, and public utilities, but the coal mines as well. They were loss-making. Only taxpayer money kept them going. And so:

> During successive Conservative governments between 1979 and 1997 more than two thirds of Britain's state-owned industry was sold to the private sector, transferring about a million jobs and raising £65bn for the Treasury. Mrs. Thatcher wanted to 'roll back the frontiers of the state'; a wider spread of shareholders would create 'popular capitalism', and by exposing state industries to market forces they would become more efficient and offer cheaper goods or a better service to the consumer. The cash raised meant that the government could avoid the more electorally dangerous alternatives of raising taxes or cutting public expenditure. Harold Macmillan, a former and patrician Conservative prime minister, called it 'selling the family silver.' The results were uneven. Several public utilities—the gas, water and telecommunications industries—were sold off *en-bloc* to become private monopolies, no more responsive to the market or the consumer than when they were owned by the state. There was public disenchantment. Advocates of privatization blamed lack of competition, which in their view was the key element in raising efficiency. When the turn came for the electricity industry to be privatized, the government broke it down into more than a dozen generating and distribution companies. This seemed to work; competition between them produced efficiency—lower costs. The promotion of competition became a key element in future privatization schemes, and the electricity industry a model for the railways.
>
> (Jack, 2001, p. 81)

Policies in the UK, and not much later in the United States after the election of Reagan in 1980, encouraged free markets with minimal government intervention, expected unfettered global flow of capital, and prioritized shareholder returns:

> Reagan and his team praised the entrepreneur and heaped scorn on the federal government for its wastefulness and, above all, its appetite for taxes. Taxation was the scourge of initiative, the rack upon which America's vitality was being broken. Reagan's America would come back to its senses and once again be the land of opportunity, of dreams come true, but on one condition: the sacrosanct laws of free enterprise must be allowed free reign. The wealth accumulated by a few individuals would ultimately be of benefit to all, according to Adam Smith and the founding fathers of economic liberalism, whose notion of the 'invisible hand' is more familiar to us as the 'trickle-down' effect. Get rich, Reagan told Americans. And let the rich get richer. Let the poor get to work and stop depending on government handouts and welfare schemes, which are merely an alibi for laziness. The truly needy, the really hopeless cases, will be seen to by charity, not by the state: a simple message, enthusiastically received.
>
> (Albert, 1993, pp. 29–30)

Reagan and Thatcher reduced and re-tasked the role of the state by promoting the privatization of state enterprises. Their successors continued where they left off: in the UK it was actually John Major who started the privatization of the UK railways in 1995. Privatization, to be sure, didn't just entail government withdrawal from a particular service or the selling off of state enterprises and properties to private businesses or individuals. It could also mean the introduction of market principles of exchange (with the state remaining present in that particular sector), the decentralization of previously centrally administered frameworks for service delivery or the re-emphasizing of kinship or community-based networks of services (such as the provision of informal care by family members, churches, or charities). These all invoke notions of 'privateness' and the intimacy of personal responsibility. Seeing these forms of marketization only through the lens of the presence or absence of the state doesn't capture the nuanced ways in which public and private worlds intermesh, or get reformulated or experienced (Thelen & Read, 2007). In addition to the multi-facetted forms of privatization, Reagan and Thatcher drastically reduced top- and corporate tax rates, deregulated industries, dismantled social safety nets, and emphasized individual responsibility for performance, health, and welfare. In Reagan's eight years, the top tax rate was cut from 70% to 28%. During Thatcher's 11-year reign, the top tax rate was reduced from 83% to 40%. In the same period, unemployment in the UK doubled.

Neoliberalism comes to Continental Europe

Market-favoring or neoliberal policymaking has spread far beyond Anglo-Saxon countries (Albert, 1993), in part because of the export of its philosophy, policies, and economics through the International Monetary Fund (IMF), World Bank, and US-based consultancy companies (Kotz, 2002; Kuttner, 2018). It is now:

> a mode of governance that is 'everywhere:' omnipresent and unavoidable… [It] refer[s] to the new political, economic, and social arrangements within society that emphasize market relations, re-tasking the role of the state, and individual responsibility. Most scholars tend to agree that neoliberalism is broadly defined as the extension of competitive markets into all areas of life, including the economy, politics, and society. Key to this process is an attempt to instill a series of values and social practices in subjects.
>
> (Springer, Birch, & MacLeavy, 2016, p. 2)

In France, for example, François Mitterand was elected as president in 1981 on hopes of a socialist transformation of the country. But his pursuit of left-leaning policies lasted fewer than two years. His 'turn to rigor' came in March 1983, and he became the most avid privatizer in French history. Luxembourg, the smallest of co-founders of the original European Union, had a similar about-face. It went from a welfare state supported by its steel-making economy in the years after the war to a sanctuary for money market funds from around the world. Its position between Belgium, France, and Germany made it a reliable provider of various leaders in the ongoing project of European integration. As more countries joined the union, it enabled the gradual spread of 'market-conforming democracies,' with an emphasis on smaller governments and fiscal discipline and financial solvency (e.g., budget deficits of no more than 3% of gross domestic product [GDP]) which Keynes might well have disliked. Economic growth has become the common aim of governments around Europe, and the world. And it has been pursued with unreflective faith in the cost-free benefits of free trade, deregulation, and foreign investment (Lilla, 2014). The development and expansion of state-organized social security nets were once seen as the basis of modern society. Now they were increasingly interpreted as hindering the economic growth (Thelen & Read, 2007).

In the Netherlands, a national makeover with an eye on increasing global competition started with Christian-Democrat prime minister Ruud Lubbers (1982 – 1994). His objective was to run the government like a business, and attain the best possible position for a country always reliant on international trade and export. And of course, there was the anticipated windfall of billions that would flow into government coffers from the selling of state-owned enterprises. First to go were the postal services, and a majority stake in the airline KLM (part of which was recently bought back by the Dutch government because of concern about French co-ownership of the holding that ended up containing both KLM and Air France). But that is where the first small wave ended. Railways and healthcare were not on the privatization radar yet. Looking across the North Sea, the Dutch saw cautionary examples of privatizing coal mines and railways under Thatcher's government. In 1984, angry mine workers battled some 5,000 police near Orgreave in an attempt to keep state owned enterprises open, while privatized railways shed thousands of jobs, increased ticket prices, and let service and safety deteriorate. Market-friendly policies in the UK were not capable of creating enough work to compensate for the many jobs lost in Thatcher's privatization drives. For an ominous tale of capitalist healthcare, the Dutch looked across the Atlantic: the costs of care under Reagan climbed steeply, while cutting off access to millions of citizens. And due to Reaganomic tax cuts, inequality in the United States was on the rise again, for the first time since World War II. Most Dutch said, 'no thanks.'

The opportunity to embrace market fundamentalism—as summed up by *Rijkswaterstaat* in the Netherlands in the motto 'The market, unless…'—came in 1989 with the fall of the Berlin Wall. Fukuyama declared victory for the Anglo model, and essentially called it an end to history itself. In 'winning' the Cold War, it was obvious to him and many others that the Anglo model embodied the final, perfected form of human government.

Imperialism and fascism had been slayed previously. Now communism fell. The prestige of the free market was never higher.

It is easy to overstate the differences, however. Though it was always convenient to characterize (or caricature) Soviet communism as an implicit or imminent attack on the West and its values, it was in reality an attempt to realize the modern western ideal of progress. Soviet communism was conceived in what was a western-style or western-inspired civilization, and would not have been possible without sharing (or wishing to copy or import) fundamental Enlightenment principles. The most important one was the belief in progress—that history is a linear trajectory of improvement whose last act is salvation (like Fukuyama's capitalist victory). This notion reflects a deeply Judeo-Christian commitment, which, interestingly, Karl Marx held to as much as the founders of the United States of America did. Marxism, too, is an enlightenment philosophy, and is a prototypically western doctrine. Ever since Czar Peter the Great (1672–1725), many in his empire believed that nothing would come of Russia if it wouldn't modernize according to western values and examples (J. Gray, 1998, 2003). Some two centuries after Peter's death, communism was one of many failed attempts to westernize Russia:

> From the start the Bolsheviks aimed to copy what they took to be the most advanced features of [Western] life. Rapid industrialisation was imperative. Peasant life had to be eradicated and farming reorganised on a factory model. Mass production—organised on the basis of the American engineer F. W. Taylor's studies of time and motion in the workplace, which Lenin greatly admired—was the only route to prosperity. Following Marx, the Bolsheviks believed that human emancipation required industrialisation.
>
> (Gray, 2003, p. 8)

The differences, then, were perhaps only ever skin-deep. Market fundamentalism tends to embrace aspects of Marx's thought. Like Marxism, it believes in historical materialism. This is the argument that history is largely determined by economic conditions, and not the other way around. Like Lenin in the 1920s, the United States in 1989 believed that it alone had discovered the secret of uninterrupted economic prosperity. Both the Soviets in the 1920s and the Americans in the 1990s believed that their political-economic system could uniquely guarantee a permanent increase in productivity and prosperity. Both believed that economic cycles were a thing of the past. Lenin had supposedly banned them with five-year economic plans. The United States supposedly banned them with unregulated financial markets, free trade, and new technology. And both believed that their political-economic arrangements would do away with bureaucracy. The desire to do so, by the way, wasn't new to either of them. In 19th-century France, Marx observed how the bureaucratic machinery of the French state had survived revolutions of both 1830 and 1848, and that these shuffled around only some surface features of the capitalism the state bureaucracy helped prop up. There had to be a better way, Marx thought.

The short-lived Paris Commune of 1871 became his leading example. For two months in the spring of that year, upon the French defeat by Von Bismarck's Prussian army, a loosely coordinated group of French, without mayor or commander-in-chief, ran Paris. They tried to separate church and state, abolish child labor and night work in bakeries, granted pensions to unmarried companions of national guardsmen killed in action against the Prussians, postponed all commercial debt obligations, abolished interest on the debts, prohibited fines on workmen imposed by employers, and affirmed the right of employees to take over and run an enterprise if its owner had absconded. This was the sort of new society that would make the state apparatus a servant of the people instead of the other way around. The Commune filled all relevant posts by election in the administrative, judicial, and educational apparatus of Paris. Incumbents were paid the same as laborers and could be pulled out of their posts at any time by the people. By 1917, Lenin saw this example as a realistic way forward for the new Soviet state. It would, he believed, gradually eliminate bureaucracy, rules, and create a society free of state compulsion.

Except, of course, it didn't.

Free in rhetoric, heavily controlled in practice

And neither did free markets. The strange thing is that free market rhetoric is seldom matched by liberal management practices. Free markets don't guarantee a life free from the compulsion of rules or the presence of bureaucratic control. The opposite, in fact, appears to be true: free markets have consistently generated intensive managerial control practices and more bureaucracy (Lorenz, 2012). In its starkest reading, workers can now find themselves enmeshed in a centrally controlled and micromanaged bureaucracy, no longer trusted to govern themselves as professionals under a cooperative ethic. The era of choice and freedom that was promised has become a daily reality of conformity and silence for many workers (Braedley & Luxton, 2010).

It is intriguing to consider how members of the Mont Pèlerin Society firmly held the opposite to be true. Workers who were employed by enterprises in state ownership would be reduced to cogs in a vast bureaucratic machine with no space for initiative or free will. In contrast, in an unhampered capitalist system, they would be free people, whose liberty would be guaranteed by an economic democracy where everything could be had, traded, sold, or bought for a price that the market itself determined. It hasn't turned out that way. As you see elsewhere in this book, workers in non-state enterprises are now routinely subjected to a panoptic regime of surveillance, management, quantification, measurement, monitoring, assessment, and control. Amazon, for instance, has patented a wristband that can track its workers' movements, measure productivity, and detect the slightest deviation from protocol—like an unscheduled bathroom break. The specific forms in which the contradictions of market freedoms have manifested themselves would have been hard to predict or expect. But the freedom we were promised, as George Monbiot sums up, turns out to be freedom for capital, gained at the expense of human liberty. As Lorenz explains, the very basis for this lies in the application of the principles of free market thinking to deregulated and privatized industries:

- The first principle, very much in line with Adam Smith, is that free markets mean competition, which means best value for money and optimized efficiency for individuals—whether they are the consumers or the shareholders (co-owners, really) of the private property that produces the good or service. It is in their direct interest, in either role, that the market functions freely. The task of the state is not only to get out of the way, but also to ensure that markets remain free (e.g., by preventing monopolies). In fact, the legitimacy of (and tolerance for) a state stands and falls with its ability to guarantee free markets.
- Free markets shift governance of a society from 'rights' to 'risks.' Fundamental rights previously connected to citizenship—like the

rights to schooling or healthcare—become privileges that you can risk losing, for example, when you lose your job. Flexibilization of jobs offers everyone the right to make money, but precarious employment introduces more risks than it can be worth.

- All former state activities—from education, social security, healthcare, and even some military and security work, can be privatized and commodified so that they would become tradable on a market, which will ensure that they are produced and delivered with maximum efficiency. Collective goods and services, in *neoliberalism*, ideally don't exist. (Classical liberal economic thought still had a place for them, for example, public libraries, national banks, railways, roads, harbors, canals, communications, and postal services).
- Well-organized private companies are key to maximally efficient free markets. Their management equals efficiency, which is demonstrated through calculation and quantification. Companies, and their managers, are literally held 'accountable' for the numbers they demonstrate in everything from productivity, quarterly profit margins, and of course share price (or shareholder value). This 'transparency' is key: consumers and shareholders must have free, informed choices so that they can maximize their own efficiency in the market.

All notions of efficiency in these four principles can be boiled down to a mechanical, numerical efficiency—literally the ratio between a system's work input and its work output. A lot of work, however, cannot naturally be meaningfully measured and held accountable this way.

Just think about a Forest Ranger who patrols a huge mountainous area for fish and game violations, but who fails to find a single violator during an entire day. Consider how the Ranger is there to protect the common good, of course, but could also be seen to have the best interests of individual fishermen and hunters and nature-lovers at heart, making sure that there is enough for everyone and that nobody gets more than the share they are due (or when they are due that share, e.g., hunting season). So, if a day of patrolling yields nothing, was that inefficient, a waste of everyone's time and money? Should fishermen and hunters go to the market and purchase a different Ranger? Or was the work of this Ranger on that day actually super-efficient (i.e., the threat of her or his presence was enough: and it saved the bureaucratic follow-up of fines and sanctions). (I'll talk more about this in Chapter 3 when I discuss the work of Kaufman.)

For free-market policies to derive some sense of the efficiency of a Forest Ranger's work, that work has to be transformed into calculable units. But that takes a bit of effort. In fact, it can take a big effort. Suppose you want to know the efficiency of Forest Ranger's work, then what must you do in order to be able to compare work input and output? You have to ask the Ranger, for instance, to start keeping track of how and where exactly her or his time on the job was spent every x minutes. This of course creates paperwork that needs preparing, quality-checking, processing and auditing, as well as the occasional inspection by someone else, and then managerial corrective or compliance follow-ups). This may seem like a bizarre proposal, but as you'll see below, it is exactly what has been happening in healthcare and homecare.

Government efficiency, of course, is very different from market efficiency. The paradoxical result, then, is that, in order to assure their efficient functioning, free markets are:

> forced to create bureaucratic machinery and formulas to steer and manage [through] a regime of bureaucrats, inspectors, commissioners, regulators and experts … These elementary observations make the claim to be antibureaucratic suspect from the outset.
>
> (Lorenz, 2012, p. 604)

It isn't that markets can't operate efficiently, or that they can't introduce new efficiencies in areas that were previously not exposed to market forces, but, as foreshadowed by Adam Smith, they work efficiently only under certain circumstances or conditions. Where those don't apply, markets can easily produce the opposite of efficiency. Where those conditions don't apply, there's an opening for the ten factors of the next chapters—the factors that lead to additional rules, extra bureaucracy, and more compliance pressure. But before we go there, what are those conditions, and what are some examples of the services that fail to meet them?

Some conditions for free markets to 'work'

Smith explained that the functioning of free markets assumes the presence of well-informed consumers who have sufficient purchasing power and can make rational and voluntary choices to buy goods and services based on their individual preferences and possibilities. His model presents quite a few conditions that need to be met for free markets to actually 'work.' Most importantly for Smith, a free market does not necessarily refer to a market free from government interference. Rather, a free market is free from *all* forms of economic privilege, monopolies, and artificial scarcities, including those that markets themselves can create (for which government intervention may well be necessary). Heijne (2018), in tracing how the Netherlands adopted privatization, deregulation, and free market policies, shows how such conditions often weren't met or quickly subverted. He collated Smith's assumptions into the following corollaries:

- Entrepreneurial interests have to align with public interests.
- The consumer has to choose voluntarily and possess sufficient purchasing power.
- Both providers and consumers need to have freedom of choice.

In the course of his empirical work, he found how these three were regularly violated. Whenever these conditions weren't met, he found the predictable ills or side effects of markets. Bureaucratization and additional compliance burdens constituted one of these side effects.

Entrepreneurial interests have to align with public interests

Initially, entrepreneurial and public interests may seem to overlap. The privatization of a particular service yields some immediate advantages for both the investor and the public. In the long run, though, what gets sacrificed?

Domino's Pizza is repairing roads, stamping a filled pothole with its logo

The pizza chain has announced a campaign to repair potholes. The company is already working with local governments in Bartonville, Texas; Milford, Delaware; Athens, Georgia; and Burbank,

California, to repair roads, filling potholes and stamping the repairs with a Domino's logo. 'We don't want to lose any great-tasting pizza to a pothole, ruining a wonderful meal,' Russell Weiner, president of Domino's USA, said in a statement. 'Domino's cares too much about its customers and pizza to let that happen.' Domino's is allowing people to nominate their own towns for road repair, and many customers are excited for the chance to get potholes filled. Domino's Facebook page has already been flooded with requests. But for some the project raises questions about why a pizza chain is taking initiative to fill potholes. The fact that a pizza chain is stepping up in areas where the government is falling short seems, for some, to be a dystopian solution (K. Taylor, 2018).

In most cases, perverse or counterproductive effects start showing up as a result of the complexities of the privatized arrangement. Some of these could have been foreseen, but for the lack of political will to do so. The railways in the Netherlands are again a good example. They were quite reluctant at first, when the government— newly enamored by free-market thinking—tried to persuade them to split their business into an operational and infrastructure-owning arm. It was modeled after what the UK had accomplished:

> Horizontal separation—the railways as regional monopolies—kept trains, stations, track, signaling and general infrastructure under one ownership, the way they had always been. Vertical separation was a more radical solution. It would separate trains from rails. The owner of the rails would charge the owners of the trains for access to them, on the same principle as a toll road. Different train owners could compete for passengers and freight on the same stretch of track.
>
> (Jack, 2001, p. 82)

When the board realized that a vertical split was inevitable, they proposed to the government that it wouldn't only operate the trains, but also the stations with their shops and highly attractive city-center real estate and potential construction sites. All the areas that only *cost* money (tracks, maintenance, including cleaning and maintenance of station platforms) were left for the newly formed rail track owner. The government agreed. They may have been thinking that when time came to privatize the railways altogether, these profitable business areas could land them a better deal. The railways were never privatized (at least, not yet), but it was already a good deal—for them. People waiting for trains, research showed, are willing to pay up to three times as much for a snack than in a regular shop. The railways retained or took ownership not only of the little kiosks on station platforms, but also of franchises of popular chains that started to show up at stations all over the country, including Starbucks. Within a few years it had become the third largest fast-food operator of the country, just behind McDonald's. Delays now didn't cost money, they *made* money. This is where entrepreneurial interests diverged sharply from public interests: in trains running on time and having access to reasonably priced food. The arrangement seems replete with Smith's anathema: monopolies, artificial scarcities, and economic privileges. And more bureaucracy, much more bureaucracy. Going back to the UK, the 1994 Railways Act that allowed the selling off of British Rail's assets, contained, as Jack called it, a 'flurry of acronyms' that bode well for newly burgeoning bureaucracies:

> The passenger trains were to be run by about twenty Train Operating Companies (TOCS) on franchises which ran from between seven and fifteen years. The trains would be owned by three Rolling Stock Companies (ROSCOS) which would lease them to the TOCS. The railway signaling, the permanent way, bridges, tunnels and some of the larger stations would be owned by one large infrastructure company, Railtrack. Railtrack would contract out the maintenance and renewal of the infrastructure by competitive tender to civil engineering companies (which had bought British Rail's engineering assets). They in turn might put out the work to subcontractors. A new independent body, the Office of the Rail Regulator (ORR), would set the amount that Railtrack was allowed to charge the TOCS—the track access charges—and in general promote competition, efficiency and safety inside Railtrack, to the eventual benefit of passengers. Another new body, the Office of Passenger Rail Franchising (OPRAF) would decide which TOC got which franchise, adjudicate the level of public subsidy required by the TOC (this was a privatization that actually increased public subsidy rather than ending or shrinking it), and reward or penalize train operating performance through a system of bonuses and penalties. Later, under the Labour Government, OPRAF became the Strategic Rail Authority, the SRA. … The Labour party's new leader, Tony Blair, described the privatization plan as 'absurd.' 'The Conservatives,' he said 'want to replace a comprehensive, coordinated national railway network with a hotchpotch of private companies linked together by a gigantic bureaucratic paperchase of contracts—overseen

> of course by a clutch of quangos' [quasi-autonomous non-governmental organizations, then a favourite opposition target].
>
> (Jack, 2001, p. 83)

The divergence of public and entrepreneurial interests is also visible in the privatization of utilities. A global review of the privatization of water utilities declares it, on the evidence, to be a failure. Araral (2009) found that utilities didn't become more efficient. Consistent with the need for additional bureaucracy, accounting processes and administrative overheads required to run a company on the open market, more money went to back office jobs and less to the expertise required to run the actual asset. The review finds no evidence that a change of ownership from public to private is a cure for an under-performing organization. Private ownership of utilities delivered middling performance on the following six indicators:

- Unit production costs
- Percentage of expenses covered by revenue
- Cost to consumers
- 24-hour supply of the service
- Tariff level
- Connection fee.

But privatized companies were better (read: more efficient) at some things. These were:

- Revenue collection
- Minimizing the number of staff per 1,000 connections.

Governments also didn't derive fiscal advantages from selling off their utility assets. New utility owners were not better at raising finances or justifying the cost required to expand or assure service provision. Utilities are considered 'dull,' and suspected of generating only low dynamic gains. Sinking money into them was not considered the smart thing to do. In lease-and-management contracts, there was basically no investment at all, and concessions were frequently terminated. All of this usually means asset-underinvestment and decline. Most private utilities required significant public finance or guarantees from government or government-owned development banks to deliver actual investments. It turned out that the funding sources that private utility companies relied on would also have been available to governments in any case—donors, commercial and development banks, bonds, and operating surplus. Private equity was rarely used by private investors. And of course, when all is said and done, the possibility of foreign ownership of critical infrastructures and assets raises its own problematic policy and sovereignty issues.

The consumer has to choose voluntarily and possess sufficient purchasing power

In the course of 25 years, Dutch medical specialists went from spending 6% to 25–30% of their time on paperwork and fulfilling administrative requirements (Heijne, 2018). The key change, and driver behind it, was marketization. The Netherlands fully embraced market forces for the provision of healthcare in 2006, more than six decades after the first national health insurance (or public healthcare fund) had been introduced by Nazi occupiers during World War II. Capped at a certain income, the public healthcare fund was meant for people who could not afford private health insurance. Over time, this division between public and private healthcare led to inequalities in access and quality. Doctors and other healthcare providers received less payment for taking care of public patients, so they started diverting their time to privately insured patients, who received quicker and better care. Waiting lists for publicly insured patients kept growing, while an aging population crippled the system financially. Something had to be done. A small number of private insurers were chosen to take over the financing of healthcare. Everybody was required to have basic private insurance, and insurers couldn't refuse them on the basis of age, pre-existing conditions, or anything else. Whoever wanted to do so was free to extend their insurance to a menu of broader coverage.

The market-friendly idea was that insurers were going to compete with each other on price. Both healthcare and its patients would benefit: low insurance premiums for the consumer, low cost of healthcare for the country. But things didn't get cheaper. Like in most other countries, healthcare only got more expensive. Premiums and deductibles (or excess) all went up while the basic private insurance package became ever more austere. There are many reasons for this, of course. One is, again, an aging population. Treatment in the last year of life can be up to 15 times the cost of treatment during the person's entire lifetime before that. Other explanations are technological innovations, new drugs, and treatments that weren't available before and all typically increase costs. But marketization added its significant bit. Under the new arrangement, hospitals and clinicians are incentivized to provide as much care (i.e., as many treatments) as possible because that is how they get funded by the patients' insurance company. Markets work well if there is a saturation point at which the consumer either has enough of the thing he or she wanted to buy, or is out of money and simply can't buy anymore.

None of those apply to healthcare. For hospitals and clinicians, there is *always* a next patient. For patients, there is always a next intervention to ask for. There is no natural ceiling that caps demand for healthcare. And so, insurance providers responded with increasingly detailed administrative requirements on clinicians and hospitals to account for the care given. Every single aspirin, band aid, and indeed minute (or block of five or six minutes) needed to be accounted for. Ceilings were introduced to artificially cap the time that could be spent with patients—which of course needed to be accounted for as well. Bureaucracy swelled up on one end of the system to do all the accounting, while the number of frontline people available to meet patient demand shrunk. By the 2010s, popular protest grew against mindless checklists, against caregivers getting sucked into computer screens and tablets instead of paying attention to their patients, against the counting and tabulating of minutes spent per patient, against insurance companies wielding too much power over treatment decisions, against bureaucratization and increased workload. Governments started commissioning inquiries into the conditions.

A report into the lived experience of delivering eldercare flagged how shrinking teams of frontline practitioners needed to deliver the same amount of care in less time. 90% of them share this experience. Their accounting of that time was tightly controlled, top-down, by people who had a distant view of the work as actually done. As one caregiver commented:

> Those people behind their desks have no idea about the work actually going on at the frontline. They call the shots but don't see whether their decisions

are actually possible or not. The bosses only care about money, not about the work actually done.

(Vegter, Gijsbers & Voorn, 2016, p. 23)

Half the respondents couldn't keep up with growing workloads, and virtually all of them worried about resulting absenteeism. 83% said that there was less time to actually spend with patients. Time for a chat, or washing a patient's hair, or helping them eat, or making a stroll could not be recorded in the time accounting sheets, because insurance providers weren't interested in paying for it. And what should a caregiver do with a patient who suffers anxiety attacks and gets out of bed forty times during a night shift, particularly in a night shift staffed by a single nurse responsible for several wards? The next day, an inspector showed up and noted that paperwork and administrative tasks had fallen behind. 90% of respondents found that administrative burdens had risen unreasonably and interfered with their ability to actually do their job. Standing beside a bed, focused on her computer tablet in vexing attempts to make entries to account for her time spent, a nurse wondered aloud whether this was actually what she once signed up for. She couldn't remember the last time she'd taken a patient outside for a stroll or some fresh air (Vegter, Gijsbers, & Voorn, 2016).

Marketization of healthcare divides up incentives across players in a way that Adam Smith could never have intended. Patients, to begin with, are lousy shoppers because they don't fit Smith's ideal of voluntary consumers. If you need care, you need care. If you're sick, you're sick. Not getting healthcare at that point, as the United States demonstrates, drives up the cost for everyone in the end (and of course causes other kinds of suffering). Insurance companies make lousy price-sensitive consumers because it gets them to push clinicians for accountability with ever-expanding administrative requirements, paperwork, and bureaucracy. This erodes clinician productivity and reduces the entire system's efficiency. Increasing deductibles for patients so as to disincentivize them from seeking care takes us right back to the first point. If you need care, you need care. If you don't seek it then, it gets more expensive for everyone in the end. So, sending consumers into a free market who have no choice but to buy something—which they then do with someone else's money—means we end up with a market that is neither free nor really a market.

Both providers and consumers need to have freedom of choice

Let's take a look at the price of the drug Daraprim. Heijne describes how Daraprim was developed in the 1950s as a medicine against parasitical infectious diseases. Only one manufacturer made it, but the price was around one dollar per dose—until the turn of the 21st century. Increasingly, physicians were prescribing Daraprim as part of the daily cocktail required by HIV patients. And the price started climbing, up to a tenfold increase. This had nothing to do with the cost of manufacturing the drug, but everything with the market: more demand meant a higher price (Or did it? One manufacturer of course meant a monopoly, not really a market). The price increases weren't really noticed, however, until Turing Pharmaceuticals, an American company, bought Daraprim. The price went from $13.75 to $750 per dose. It caused an uproar. Hundreds of thousands of HIV-patients are literally life-dependent on the drug, and had nowhere else to go for it. Turing Pharmaceuticals apologized for the commotion and chopped the price by a (supposedly) whopping 50%. Then again, the new price of $375 per dose was still a 27-fold increase over the price of the drug when Turing first acquired it. Any excuse that this was meant to cover the costs of drug development was empty, since Turing never developed Daraprim to begin with. And even if they had, you don't need to charge 27 times more for a drug just to cover development costs. In an analysis published in *Journal of the American Medical Association* (*JAMA*), Prasad and Mailankody (2017) showed that the median cost of drug development was in the $650 million range, whereas the revenue generated in the first four years after introduction amounted to almost ten times as much: $6 billion. They conclude that:

> High drug prices have negative effects on patients and society, and groups of physicians, patients, and policymakers have voiced their opposition to these prices.
>
> (p. 1570)

Opposition from policymakers is guaranteed to be feeble, however, if the market (including one dominated by a monopoly) is 'free.' Consider the interests of insurance providers, lobbyists, patient pressure groups to get access to the drugs no matter what, and media stories celebrating personal stories of disease and loss, and any attempts to intervene in the market with some kind of policy become even trickier. And so, it remains a free market in which consumers have no choice, and a single provider can do what it wants as long as it is able to rally media attention to its cause and counter political pressure for change. Adam Smith would probably stand by if he'd seen this unfold, shaking his head. This is not what he meant with a free market. The 'market' here is peppered with economic privilege, monopolies, and artificial scarcities. Consumers of Daraprim or any other price-hiked drug do not have sufficient purchasing power. They can't make rational or voluntary choices based on their individual preferences and possibilities. They are patients. They need the drug, or they'll die.

Note

1 By 2003, though, even the French themselves—in France—had privatized about 75% of the provision of drinking water. The French government still owns the water infrastructure in France, but its exploitation is contracted out to the market through temporary concessions to the lowest bidder. In reality, there are only three large companies in that market: Suez, Vivendi, and Bouygues. They form an oligopoly which has stifled competition on price. The UK faces some of the same issues, having completely privatized their water management by 1989.

3

THE MACRO

SELL OUT AND PULL OUT

How is it possible that free markets lead to unfree, overregulated workers? How can our new form of economic liberalism produce compliance capitalism in which people are anything *but* liberated from unreasonable, petty rules and constraints? In this chapter, I will run through the macroeconomic factors that make it so. Macroeconomic factors are those related to the decisions of governments and countries, as well as societal, political, and demographic trends underlying these decisions. The relevant factors are, respectively:

- Privatization and corporate, as opposed to state, governance
- Deregulation and performance-based regulation
- Market concentration
- A decline of participatory equality

Privatization and corporate, as opposed to state, governance

It can be hard to believe, but governments may actually need fewer rules to run things. The realization that deregulation and privatization might lead to *more* rules precedes the actual expansion of deregulation and privatization in Anglo countries and beyond. A 1975 study found, counter to people's assumptions and preconceptions about government red tape, that private sector managers expressed greater adherence and commitment to rules than their public sector counterparts (Buchanan, 1975). Middle managers in private business were more rule-bound and procedure-conscious, and paid significantly more deference to formal structure than their government counterparts. One explanation lies in the contingent nature of private employment and hierarchical control and accountability:

> Business organizations clearly have a greater capacity to exert such control, and by implication to heighten individual sensitivity to the structural instruments of control. Such organizations may coerce compliance, if necessary up to the point of discharging an employee. While seldom used and largely implicit, this is a critical power. A middle manager in an economic organization is accordingly under constant competitive pressure to produce results and to display the norms and values prevailing in his administrative climate. Security, advancement, and ultimate success are conditioned on acceptable performance and behavior throughout the managerial career. There is thus little opportunity for coasting or withdrawal.
>
> (p. 436)

While this competitive pressure, filtered up and down through a business, may drive people to greater efficiencies, the deference to protocols, rules, procedures, and other instruments of 'accountability' may again detract from it and turn it into a zero-sum game. Philosopher Gilles Deleuze explained why:

> Corporations focus on short term results. In order to do so, they need constant control, and this is achieved via continuous monitoring and assessment of markets, workforces, strategies, etc. The corporation is a fundamentally different being than the nation-state, because it does not strive for progress

> of society as a whole; it tries instead to control certain specific parts of—increasingly international—markets.
>
> (in Galic, Timan, & Koops, 2017, p. 19)

In government organizations, in contrast, Buchanan found that such control and accountability happens largely by persuasion rather than by control, surveillance, counting, and coercion. He found that mid-level government managers have abundant resources for resisting any structural constraints on their behavior. Some of the reasons he found were as follows:

- A key to this is the tenure system: it isn't as easy to get rid of government employees as it is private ones. The virtual impossibility of dismissal without significant cause keeps employees out of the wind. And because of this, Buchanan found, they approach their rules, procedures, and protocols with more autonomy and discretion than their counterparts in the private sector.
- This is aided by the wider latitude of acceptable performance as defined in relation to the organization's mission. Within a private enterprise, everything (in principle) needs to be focused on the company's mission. In government agencies, this relationship between individual work and organizational mission is less clear-cut (as you will see below, Kaufman would surely have found such leeway and discretion in how forest rangers interpreted their mandates in the face of local situations).
- Government agencies have a stronger system of appeal that shows a sensitivity to the procedural due process rights of individuals (whether employees or citizens) which makes it easier to flag rules that are unduly inhibiting or constraining autonomy or other rights.

The counterintuitive findings reported by Buchanan predated any significant privatization and deregulation efforts across the West. They indicated that we should not think too quickly that privatized organizations are nimbler and less rule-bound. His study indeed indicated the opposite. Herbert Kaufman, one of the 20th century's keenest observers of the inner workings of government, discovered how a government agency can offer the kind of *freedom-in-a-frame* that many private companies today are searching for. *Freedom-in-a-frame* describes the kind of professional autonomy and trust that allows people to know the boundaries of their roles and authority, yet encourages self-sufficiency, adaptive capacity, interpretive discretion, and local innovation. Kaufman's book *The Forest Ranger* (1960) describes how 792 semi-autonomous forest rangers—each with jurisdiction over vast swaths of federal land—were able to make reasonably consistent decisions about grazing rights, timber harvest, fire protection, and scores of other necessary choices regarding the use of public resources.

Kaufman captures the public culture in which rangers internalized certain professional values. This was aided by what could be called neutral competency of the rangers themselves, a *soft oversight* by their employing agency, and a rotation system that kept the rangers from going entirely *native* or *local* inside their own problem spaces, and which also ensured the sharing and distribution of novel solutions across different jurisdictions over time. The advantages of such rotations were 'rediscovered' by high-reliability organization theorists more than two decades later in a study of sailors employed by the US Navy, another huge government bureaucracy (Rochlin, LaPorte, & Roberts, 1987). There is a fascinating and little-known historical footnote to this, which I will save for another book. But to achieve these results, the US Forest Service had been inspired by *Prussian* methods of administration—traditionally seen as the most rigorous and inflexible of Teutonic governance modes—in this case tending mostly toward instilling agency-inspired values and beliefs in those who joined it (Lynn, 2015).

Self-regulation and responsibilization

But what happens when we privatize formerly government-owned organizations? Do the early indications echo Buchanan's? They seem to. Once you privatize, another in-depth study warned in 1979, you create a lot of ties between state and non-state actors where none existed previously. The newly privatized actors, after all, will somehow still have to be accountable to the government for how they provide the service to society (operating a railway, providing drinking water, running a utility, etc.). This gives rise to new formal procedures to govern those relationships. In addition, assurances of transparency and financial accountability, as well as equal access and opportunity to market actors for tendering—consistent with Weber's ideal image of a bureaucracy—tend to exacerbate rulemaking and compliance demands (Meyer, 1979):

> As with the red tape that flows from intergovernmental relationships, this form of red tape stems from the documentation and other administrative requirements that are attached to [the] funds.
>
> (p. 30)

And even if there are no funds that come from government, business-to-business relationships in a deregulated, privatized environment create pressures for new rules; for new assurances through record-keeping and documentation; for the tracing and fixing of financial accountabilities in a market where somebody needs to end up paying for all things all the time, and people are motivated to adopt systems and processes so at least that somebody won't be *them*. Rolston describes the arc in her study of supervision and management in Wyoming mines:

> Longtime miners remember their first years working at the Powder River Basin mines in the late 1970s and early 1980s as being joyfully free of bureaucracy. 'All of us—managers, operators, everybody—were figuring out how to do this together', explained Roger. 'We didn't have any paperwork or anything because we didn't need it. We made our own systems for handling everything, from training people on equipment to safety'. As the mines became more established and were eventually bought out by different companies, employees found their everyday actions increasingly constrained by official policies that emanated from boardrooms rather than the mine itself.
>
> (Rolston, 2010, p. 336)

Workers' everyday actions were increasingly constrained by official policies that emanated from boardrooms rather than the workplace itself—it is an experience that many might share, across all kinds of industries. Meyer's (1979) red tape, associated with documentation and other administrative requirements, stems from the new kinds of ties that bloom in a financialized market place of businesses. And strung across it all is the anxiety that comes from the possibility of being found liable for losses and accidents, in a world that has showed a greater willingness to seek corporate actors behind what is seen as culpable mismanagement of risk (Bittle & Snider, 2006; Goldman & Lewis, 2009; Green, 1997). Privatization, self-regulation, and the possibility of criminal liability together gets company boards to attempt to demonstrate that they have taken all reasonably practicable measures to protect their workers from harm (Jacobs, 2007). Partly in reaction to these trends, researchers have noted an increasing *responsibilization* of workers or individualization of workplace risk (O'Neill, 2003). Workers are assigned ever more responsibility for their own well-being at work: deregulation has pushed more of the self-regulatory effort onto the work floor. 'The burden of each of these strategies rests with the individual worker who is caught up in a neoliberal system that powerfully reasserts itself' (Davies & Bansel, 2005, p. 57). Instances can be seen in:

- Behavior-based programs that eschew expensive retrofits to working conditions and instead aim to 'modify' the behavior of workers to fit the existing situation (Hopkins, 2006).
- Retributive 'just culture' policies that structurally hold frontline individuals 'accountable' for nonconformances and bad outcomes (Dekker & Breakey, 2016).
- Violation notices issued increasingly to workers, not companies. One study indeed shows that over two-thirds of citations handed out by workplace inspectors are now directed at workers or immediate supervisors rather than employers (G. C. Gray, 2009).
- The changing experience of workers' compensation claims processes and a redistribution of work-related injury costs in favor of corporate interests.

The Government Accounting Office (GAO) in the United States recently expressed concern about these trends (GAO, 2012). Assigning individual responsibility to workers who are 'instructed to become prudent subjects who must practice legal responsibility' (Gray, 2009, p. 327) requires behavior-based enticements for them to pay attention, wear protective equipment, ensure the application of machine guarding, use a lifting device, and so forth. A common way to try to induce behavior change is to put up posters in workplaces, which speak directly to the worker (basically telling the worker to try a little harder). Behavior-based policy pushes compliance expectations down to the work floor, often to the detriment of attention to design issues or irreconcilable goal conflicts at the operational sharp end (Hale, 1990; Woods, Dekker, Cook, Johannesen, & Sarter, 2010):

> A behavior-based approach blames workers themselves for job injuries and illnesses, and drives both injury reporting and hazard reporting underground. If injuries aren't reported, the hazards contributing to those injuries go unidentified and unaddressed. Injured workers may not get the care they need, and medical costs get shifted from workers compensation (paid for by employers) to workers' health insurance (where workers can get saddled with increased costs). In addition, if a worker is trained to observe and identify fellow workers' 'unsafe acts,' he or she will report 'you're not lifting properly' rather than *the job needs to be redesigned.*
>
> (Frederick & Lessin, 2000, p. 5)

Non-compliance, injuries, and incidents are thus traced back to individual worker behaviors, not to what the organization and its management have or haven't done or provided. If safe worker behaviors are necessary for good outcomes, then unsafe behaviors can get easily blamed for bad outcomes, which has recently become increasingly formalized in retributive 'just culture' policies that ask what rule was broken, how bad the breach was, and what the consequences for the responsible individual should be (Dekker, 2016). This keeps managers:

> convinced that simply pursuing a policy of tighter controls and stiffer penalties for front-line workers will provide the ultimate solution to their problems. Meanwhile, evidence continues to accumulate that it is precisely this policy that is generating the crises feared by those same politicians and business leaders.
>
> (Amalberti, 2013, p. vii)

In addition, all these arrangements of course demand a managerial and bureaucratic infrastructure to design posters, provide enticements, and assure and track compliance, apply 'just culture' policies and bureaucratically account for all of it to other stakeholders in the organization, insurance provider or regulator. This links to the auditing and regulating of 'organizational culture' itself (Bieder & Bourrier, 2013). States delegate responsibility to organizations, and organizations in turn delegate it to their workers. It thus involves a transfer of liability for the cost of harm onto workers (Henriqson, Schuler, van Winsen, & Dekker, 2014; Silbey, 2009). It is not surprising that, back in Wyoming, miners got so fed up that they did everything to stay as far away from the new rules and programs as they could:

> Many miners minimized their participation in such programs because their emphasis on discipline and individual responsibility often contradicted their already existing informal mechanisms for mitigating hazards and cultivating crew commitments to safety.
>
> (ibid.)

Stifling rules developed by non-experts and non-professionals, petty bureaucratic overreach, imposition of discipline and individual accountability, and a general constraining of autonomy and discretionary decision power on the frontline—this is how deregulation and privatization manifest themselves in workplaces like these mines. Parrish and Schofield (2005) have shown how this kind of policy-making has affected (and in many cases delegated) the day-to-day management and administration of the claims process. These practices run on a corporate-rationalist administrative logic, as any top-down bureaucratic process would. But they find their way into workplace relations that involve systematic suspicion, disrespect, and humiliation of work-injured claimants by insurance company officials (as well as supervisors, peers, and even colleagues). This links to underreporting of injuries, which is often encouraged and abetted by other policies, such as bonuses for injury-free performance or the declaration of 'zero harm' (Saloniemi & Oksanen, 1998; Sheratt & Dainty, 2017).

The commodification of labor, set in motion by the industrial revolution, is a major contributor. The value of human relations gets expressed chiefly, if not uniquely, in terms of its exchangeability for other value. The value of a relationship is nothing if not the value of a thing that you can cash in at the market. Hence, lost time injury (LTI) is a 'meaningful' measure: loss time injuries mean that the worker is not making good on the potential labor which was contractually agreed. It is purely production focused: humans are an instrument for the creation of value (for themselves, sure, but more likely for other more powerful actors in the market). Back in 1944, Karl Polanyi already questioned the commodification of labor, which reduces human beings to human 'resources,' to a means to achieve someone else's ends (Polanyi, 1944). The end result is a skewing of the perennial contest between business and organized labor over the distribution of work-related injury costs in favor of corporate interests (Schofield, 2005). Market-oriented reforms have been designed primarily to reduce the burden of cost associated with employers' insurance premiums. The delivery of such relief to employers has required restrictions on injured workers' rights to legal action and settlements, and an obligation on injured workers to return to work. The latter has led to inappropriate (if not unethical or illegal) use of modified ('light') duties or return-to-work programs. Various kinds of professionals have been coopted into compromised roles in this (Frederick & Lessin, 2000; GAO, 2012).

Deregulation and performance-based regulation

As you've already seen above, an important driver for the spread of internal rules is the shift to process- or performance-based regulation. Other labels for this shift are 'decentered regulation,' 'regulatory pluralism,' or 'smart regulation' (G. C. Gray & Rooij, 2020). The shift has been typical for market-oriented policies, and an important source of savings on government expenditure. Rather than prescribing or specifying the exact actions that regulated organizations must take, performance-based regulation requires them to attain and demonstrate certain processes or outcomes. Performance or process-based regulation might still specify the kinds of risk identification, assessment, and control processes that must be undertaken, documented, and (usually) audited. But these belong to a class of normative goals, driven by principles that give the regulated actor the faith and ability to exercise good judgment. This sort of regulation is most commonly used in contexts in which there are multiple risk sources and multiple feasible risk controls. The regulator offers flexibility in how an organization can meet those principles, goals, or outcomes, and, as said, it might specify certain processes it expects to see.

This shift in regulatory styles—away from prescription—was necessary to allow market-oriented policies and privatization, and to accommodate budget cuts to government regulators. Regulators have had to find more efficient and cost-effective ways to regulate, while having fewer financial resources and less expertise available. Regulatory reformers and supporters of free-market thinking have vigorously promoted performance-based regulation, even though the advantages have long remained ideological and conjectural (Coglianese, 2017), because in reality, a paradox soon became visible. Performance-based regulation can quickly lead to more rules, rather than fewer. Free markets, after all, have increased the likelihood of organizations being sued for not meeting their obligations. The vaguer the principle regulations are under which those obligations sit, the more seductive it becomes for an organization to overspecify the way it demonstrates meeting those obligations:

> A person who is subject to unpredictable liability is likely to hew to the most conservative interpretation of the principle, especially where that person would be a potential deep pocket in litigation. This creates a paradox: unless protected by a regime enabling one in good faith to exercise judgment without fear of liability, such a person will effectively act as if subject to a rule and, even worse, an unintended rule.
>
> (Schwarcz, 2009, p. 175)

Under these circumstances, 'senior management will err on the side of caution,' Schwarcz correctly predicted (Ibid, p. 179). Others have found the paradox as well, explaining how:

> the anticipated error costs for firms of 'getting it wrong' are higher with respect to Principles than detailed rules (assuming the approach to enforcement is otherwise the same), and firms will structure their behaviour accordingly. There is a potential danger that this will lead to 'over-compliance', with firms adopting overly conservative courses of action, thinking that to do otherwise will be considered by the [regulator] to constitute non-compliance.
>
> (Black, Hopper, & Band, 2007, p. 199)

Experience, however, suggests that specifying more (i.e. writing more rules) actually makes it easier to get sued or prosecuted for not following at least some of what was specified (Tooma, 2017). This doubles the paradox. First, having fewer prescriptive regulations may lead to a conservative response that produces more (internal) rules in order to avoid unpredictable liabilities. Yet the likelihood of such liability actually increases the more an organization has specified for itself.

Coglianese has shown this paradox by explaining how 'performance' in performance-based regulation is actually hard to adequately define, measure, or monitor. Regulation research confirms this: 'Process and performance-based legislation also often suffers from an absence of clearly identified standards as to compliance obligations' (Carroll, Deighton-Smith, Silver, & Walker, 2008, p. 98). Because of that, performance-based regulation may define the regulatory relationship, but it is almost never felt like that in most roles inside the regulated organization. Performance-based regulation between what is left of the government regulator and the regulated organization leads almost universally to a doubling down of prescriptive internal regulation in that organization:

> Interestingly, this high-level regulatory approach is supplemented in practice by extensive procedures manuals, developed by all significant operators on the basis of the internal regulatory controls that were in use in former times of vertically integrated government-owned monopolies. These procedures manuals continue to be largely prescriptive in nature.
>
> (Carroll et al., 2008, p. 89)

And it's not just a retaining or doubling down of prescriptive rules about behaviors, technologies, tools, procedures, and processes internally. It is their *expansion*—aided by new markets for contractors and consultants who can monetize bureaucratic advice, sell internal regulatory apparatuses, and profit from the auditing that swirls around and through it all.

In other ways too, performance-based regulation or self-regulation can work quite poorly and even create its own problems (e.g., Gelles & Kitroeff, 2019). Gray and van Rooij (2020) examined what happens when people are supposed to become co-regulators on the frontline, and how their experiences are shaped by various manifestations of asymmetric power. People, their case studies showed, may lack the sheer capacity—financial, informational, social—to apply any self-regulation effectively. They can be burdened with having to regulate themselves but simultaneously get excluded from decisions that could actually make a difference for how they are exposed to risk in the first place. Dependency on a pay check, or on a contingent contract in case of precarious work, was also a powerful disincentive to engage in robust self-regulation and demand the resources and authority to do it with. This also tended to dampen people's claim to any remaining legal rights they might have had. The very way in which the risks to be self-regulated were framed interacted strongly with these other factors. A mine worker with 40 years' experience underground wrote to me recently, explaining:

> When you are a contractor or casual labour hire, you hear the words 'Don't skip your meal break or cut corners, but we're really down on tonnes tonight' in a completely different way to how the permanent worker will hear it. The casual will hear a number of things, one of which is 'You want to be on the plane coming back next swing?'
>
> (Carson, 2020, p. 2)

Let's take a brief look at a different setting for some of the empirical material (Storkersen, Thorvaldsen, Kongsvik, & Dekker, 2020). These studies were carried out by Norwegian colleagues in recent times—in a part of the world known for its generally pragmatic, trusting, and consultative approach to regulation (Peters & Weggeman, 2017). The objective of the research was, through the gathering of qualitative data, to get a sense of the experience of compliance pressure under a performance-based regulatory regime. The results confirm what this chapter has shown so far: a retreating, shrinking government footprint since the 1990s has actually *increased* the compliance pressure felt by people in industry.

One of the industries studied is aquaculture, the other coastal shipping. Aquaculture has recently become one of Norway's largest industries. Of these, salmon farming is the most common and profitable, with companies growing and merging in the last few decades. Most of them have a hundred employees or more, with groups of employees performing inspections and other tasks using boats and cranes, guided by procedures for personnel safety as well as for fish welfare, safe keeping, and quality (Thorvaldsen, Holmen, & Kongsvik, 2017). The other industry is coastal cargo shipping. With a long North Sea coast and innumerable inlets and fjords, coastal shipping has a long tradition in Norway. Vessels transport sand, asphalt, scrap metal, salt, live salmon, salmon fodder, oil, gas, furniture, general cargo in containers, and more. And now they also transport lots of paperwork, paperwork which is not a payload. It consists of management systems, procedures, checklists, and process documentation. As one chief officer of a bulk vessel remarked:[1]

> The system is big. You have [...] ISM companies, you have audits, you have the Devil and his dam. ... We lost control when we had to throw away our simple sheets, and got 23 binders on board.

His captain added, in an echo of research that once showed that spending a lot of time on accountability requirements takes attention away from the actual tasks one is accountable for (Lerner & Tetlock, 1999):

> The paperwork you have to sign out all the time, right. It consumes time that I should've spent to, eh, perhaps be a good sailor. And it brings more tasks for you to do, right. You sit writing reports and checklists.

The workings of a newfound market for the provision of management systems, for allaying liability anxieties, for conducting private certifications, and for supplying insurance and auditing services, are the most important drivers behind the production of most additional bureaucracy and paperwork. All are directly linked to the new deregulatory regime. In an acknowledgment of the interrelated workings of all of these, managerial personnel in fish farms emphasize that they are closely watched by shareholders and media (not necessarily the regulator!), and that bad attention can harm them and their business prospects:

> If we don't have things in order or have the procedures, questions will be raised regarding why we didn't have the right procedures or did this instead of that. ... We need to have a procedure for every work task. If something went wrong during work and we didn't have a procedure for that task, one gets hung.

The many requirements to satisfy the stakeholders that now surround, and make up, the industry, get pushed down into operational areas where they are impossible to reconcile, and impossible to satisfy and still get work done:

> On a vessel, much is pushed from company management to ship management. And it's up to the ships to keep ... make it work in practice. You get lots of procedures and instructions and all this, and you're to plan your day so everything's complied with. Which is close to impossible, in many cases. And if you do something that isn't compliant, you put your head on the chopping block. If it blows – it's your responsibility.

The market for off-the-shelf management systems has grown spectacularly, leading to operators buying procedures that are way over the top for their own purposes:

> The company might not have taken a closer look at it. They buy a system, but it was made for a large offshore vessel, and we get their procedures. That's the tendency, that we get their procedures, but we don't have the corresponding operations and training. ... It's common to buy a system and just start using it. It makes it frustrating and an 'act' instead of reality. It makes people lose motivation. ... We run trainings adapted to our vessel, but it might deviate from what's described, for a larger vessel. When we get the system on board, it's often written for another vessel, that includes the procedures. Then we have the job to make the procedures correspond to what we really do.

These kinds of observations would seem to debunk what is known as 'public choice theory'—the basis of any economic liberalism (and so, indeed, neoliberalism). It is based on the idea of a sovereign consumer who is active, assertive, knowledgeable, critical, prepared to shop around, and who will ultimately achieve the best deal through an exhaustive, fully informed process of option comparison, elimination, and selection. That, of course, is patent nonsense. Or it is at least highly doubtful that this is the kind of process and background through which a fodder vessel would end up with the safety management system of a cruise liner company. The so-called 'ideal customer' of public choice theory is actually not picky, fastidious and fully informed consumer. The ideal customer in a free market, judging from these examples, is an ignorant, anxious consumer – a consumer who can be scared and bamboozled into buying much more than they need. Indeed, 'public choice theory ignores the potential for choices to be manipulated, conditioned or determined by an individual's social location' in the market relation between seller and buyer (Germov, 1995, p. 56). And so, consistent with Saines' (2014) findings, much of the paperwork in a putatively deregulated world is inflicted by the market and self-imposed, self-policed, self-regulated. It is offered, adopted, and enforced by operators and their market stakeholders themselves, without a government regulator specifically asking for any of it:

> A lot of the paperwork seafarers talk about is self-induced. I've thrown away many loose-leaf documents, for example, simply because the company had a rule that all HSE meeting memos had to be put in a binder on a shelf.

Comparing the situation with how the industry used to be governed, an operational manager of a fish farm said how a fear of worst-case scenarios drove this:

> Our internal rules are stricter [than government's], the way we do it. It is. Our basic equipment and such, it's much stricter than the governmental requirements were [...]. It's for the best for the people. All the time you think about what could happen, worst case, and what can prevent it, how to solve it.

Note that there is a great expectation of the usefulness in any practical, operational sense (which we'll revisit in the next chapter). In fact, a sense of resignation among safety managers and other office staff is palpable. The (apparent) need for, yet simultaneous irrelevance of, all the new rules to people who actually do the operational work is well known:

> Not many have read the procedures, but I didn't have great expectations about that either. To expect that procedures are actively used, that's probably ... I don't think one can expect it. One has instructions and such, washing instructions, so one does not necessarily have to read the procedures to understand the washing instructions.

As found by Power (1999), the self-referential game of auditing (by commercial auditors) creates a knowledge loop that is relevant only to itself:

> It's easy for the ship owner to get zero nonconformities and comply with what's to be complied with. And so, it won't be adjusted [to our activity]. They just buy the product and are through with it. [...] You bring apples to school to please your teacher, but you're not getting full yourself. You don't help yourself. ... We answer what we know our parents want to hear. That's very smart to answer, it keeps us out of trouble.

Deregulation (and the shift to performance-based regulation) in these industries was pursued to ease demands on state resources. It pushed responsibility to regulated companies themselves instead. These were to develop management systems and procedures appropriate to their business. As we have seen before, and consistent with Coglianese's warning, the vagueness of knowing how to demonstrate compliance and adequate risk control in a complex, uncertain world makes companies receptive to any help they can get. Here, too, the market came in to meet the need, and met it with compliance capitalism. The Norwegian studies illustrate how deregulation creates insecurity and leads both industry actors and regulators to depend on purchasing services and systems from consultants with over-specified, oversized management systems. The lived experience has led to swelling critiques of internal bureaucratic overreach, stifling cultures of compliance, unfair distribution of risk and accountability, and blindness to actual risk (Anon, 2012; Dekker, 2018; Zimmerman, 1991). Heather and Kearns (2018, p. 4) summarize the lived experience of this type of market-driven management on the work floor:

- Rules and regulations that have become overly obstructive
- Management systems that encourage a dumbing down of individuals and a dilution of personal responsibility
- Higher stress levels due to a sense of loss of control
- Considerable wasted effort
- Systems that have become far too complicated
- Common sense and initiative that have been discouraged
- Cynicism about slogans, stated priorities, and the motivation behind rules
- Safety and other staff that is often detached from the front line either by their inappropriate experience or because of their physical location being remote from the workplace (cf. Woods, 2006).

What this leads to across the spectrum from regulator to work floor is a 'dysfunctional combination of performance and prescriptive standards' (Carroll et al., 2008, p. 97). In performance-based regulation, the onus of proof is on an organization to demonstrate that it has done everything necessary, proportional or 'practicable' to control the risks they themselves identified. As Carroll and colleagues have documented, the field is then left wide open for a volume of behavioral, technical or procedural standards, and rules that can be many times larger than the previous body of prescriptive regulation. A factor that contributes to this is auditing, which tends to construct the very environment it needs to function—one that has things to measure, items to tick off on a list, and legible standards against which to audit. This is quite in contrast to the stated hopes for performance-based regulation. Audits and inspections belong to a world of prescriptive regulation. Performance-based regulation was to build more on an assessment of the resilience of an organization—to what extent it possesses the capacities that allow it to recognize, absorb, and adapt to harms that cannot be prescriptively known or specified in advance. It was to be built on insights, on relationships of trust, and on the realization that risks in the real world are multiple and random, and therefore not easily measurable or auditable. This realization hasn't always reached auditors yet, as we will see in Chapter 5.

Market concentration

There is a counterintuitive macro-economic twist to privatization and deregulation which has recently become obvious, particularly in the United States. Privatization was meant to get the market to enter into activities or industries which were previously reserved for government. From the 1980s onward, they did. There is by now a preponderance of evidence, however, that these private actors are no longer really working in what could be called a 'free market.' They themselves have undermined both the freedom *and* the market. Instead, areas that were privatized and opened up to the market (e.g., telecommunications, railways, garbage collection, and public buses) are increasingly dominated by monopolies, duopolies or, at best, oligopolies (a small group of organizations that have control and the size and means to maintain that control over a particular activity). Competition, as a result, has suffered. Prices typically have gone up and

Table 3.1 Market concentration in the United States, 1993–2001 (Hamel & Zanini, 2020)

	Proportion of US private sector employees' organizations with more than 500 individuals on the payroll	*Proportion of US organizations with more than 5,000 employees*
1993	47.0%	29.4%
2001	51.6%	33.4%

quality has gone down. And, of course, size tends to bring more bureaucracy and compliance.

Market concentration, as shown for the US in Table 3.1, is not a new phenomenon. Karl Marx saw 'market concentration' happen in the 19th century. In *Das Kapital*, he described how ever bigger corporations dominated particular sectors because of economies of scale in industrial production. This, Marx predicted, could only lead to trouble. Today's version of this is highly visible in the United States where utilities and tech giants, for example, have coagulated into oligopolies—to a much greater extent than in Asia or Europe (Philipon, 2019). Today, more Americans are working in large, bureaucratic organizations than ever before. In 1993, 47% of US private sector employees worked in organizations with more than 500 individuals on the payroll. By the early 2000s, that number had grown to 51.6%, and has grown further since then. Large organizations with more than 5,000 employees swelled their employment share the most—from 29.4% to 33.4% (Hamel & Zanini, 2020). This isn't just 'natural' growth or survival of the fittest companies with the best products or earnings ratios. Deliberate economic policy-making lies behind it:

> Deregulation has generally turned out to be a blessing for corporate titans, not for an efficient or equitable economy... Beginning under Reagan, antitrust regulation was all but eliminated. Combined with the demise of antitrust, in industry after industry deregulation has led not to the efficient competition based on price and quality promised by free-market theory, but to concentration, price gouging, anticompetitive predation, deteriorated consumer service, and downward pressure on wages.
>
> (Kuttner, 2018, p. 300)

A free market that strangled free markets

This coagulation of the market into a few big companies—the strangulation of the market by the market—is a most ironic force through which a free market creates unfree workers. The mechanism by which this happens is pretty intuitive: market concentration means bigger companies. Bigger companies mean more bureaucracy because size and bureaucratization tend to go hand in hand. With growth comes a more bureaucratic business structure, due in large part to the need to divide business areas and separate them from staff functions (e.g., human resource [HR], finance, or legal). This also entails more layers of authority such as presidents, vice presidents, directors, managers, supervisors, and foremen (Mintzberg, 1979). Sociologist Max Weber (1864–1920) described how bureaucratization increases people's decision authority and span of control the closer they are to the administrative apex. Specialization and division of labor lead to various chasms between operational, managerial, and staff- or compliance workers. Formalized rules, a chief mechanism by which bureaucracies function, refer to standardized responses to known problems and fixed procedures that govern the collection, analysis, and dissemination of information as well as the processes by which decisions are arrived at, and how both authority and responsibility for decisions are distributed, upheld, and accounted for (Eisenstadt, 1959). In considering what would happen when an activity is deregulated, privatized, and allowed to grow into a bureaucracy, Meyer foresaw much of this in 1979:

> Bureaucratization in the private sector occurs, additionally, as individuals initially engaged in transactions with one another are organized into simple hierarchies, hierarchies are extended through vertical integration, vertically integrated firms reorganize into multi-unit structures, and the conglomerate firm displaces other types. In each of these instances, market failure is said to have occurred, that is, exchanges once conducted across markets are incorporated into organizations and subjected to hierarchical control.
>
> (Meyer, 1979, p. 30)

Big companies now dominate the US economy. Recall from above that more than one-third of the US labor force works for organizations that employ more than 5,000 people. Frontline workers are, on average, buried under eight levels of management and their compliance workforce (Hamel & Zanini, 2020). As you'll see under the 'growth of a compliance workforce,' the 1980s saw the start of a doubling, tripling, quadrupling, and even quintupling of compliance workers in the bureaucratic class—project managers, financial operations auditors, safety officers, HR business managers, and more. It has consequences beyond bureaucratization. Monocultures create fragile systems, and expensive ones at that. Airline tickets, Internet service, cellphone plans—they are today all more expensive in the United States than in Europe and Asia, Philipon (2019) observed. And customer service and product quality in all of those industries in the United States have sunk to new lows. Broadband Internet connections in the United States are on par with Madagascar, Honduras. and Swaziland. Philipon explains that:

> in industry after industry in the United States—the country that invented antitrust laws—incumbent companies have increased their market power by acquiring nascent competitors, heavily lobbying regulators, and lavishly spending on campaign contributions. Free markets are supposed to punish private companies that take their customers for granted, but today many American companies have grown so dominant that they can get away with offering bad service, charging high prices, and collecting, exploiting, and inadequately guarding their customers' private data.
>
> (p. 23)

Anti-trust enforcement has withered in the United States, and not only as a result of the political lobbying power of the corporations which now dominate these markets. A central argument of the *laissez-faire* approach to economics of the Chicago school (more will be discussed about that in the next chapter) was as follows: a monopoly that charges high prices and offers crappy service will actually attract competition, precisely because there's so much to win and it would seem so easy. Offer a service that is just a bit better, or offer it at a slightly lower price, and you're competing effectively. This might work in theory, but in the United States, it has stopped working in practice. New firms don't enter the market. For one, when they do, they get bought up almost immediately. The war chests of the largest corporate players are so well-filled that this is a cost-effective way to snuff out any competitor before it ever gets off the ground. Then there is also a residue of the deregulatory paradox Meyer described in 1979: the rules and requirements that a privatized industry needs market actors to follow can act as a disincentive to smaller, new entrants (Philipon, 2019).

Privatization, in Philipon's analysis, has eventually given rise to new conglomeration, bureaucratization, and ossification—with all their attending compliance demands, accountability processes, and innumerable inefficiencies. The market, in a sense, has ceased to function, or even exist. And this time, there's little or no government around to force anybody's hand to start changing things. Without a strong government, a market cannot work freely; monopolies and plutocrats will emerge and eventually dominate.

To paraphrase Stiglitz, the invisible hand of the market has always been dependent on the strong arm of the government. And, whether by design or happenstance, there is more government in at least some activities in the United States—though probably not in the way that anybody would want. In the United States of the 1990s, it took about four days to open a business. By comparison, doing the same thing in France took 53 days. Now, more than two decades later, it takes four days in France, and six in the United States. In other words, the process of opening a business in France became more than 13 times faster. In the United States, the process became 50% slower.

The decline of participatory equality

Bigger companies also mean more corporate bargaining power, to the detriment of participatory equality. A powerful societal trend of the last four decades, related to privatization, deregulation, and market concentration, is the gradual loss of participatory equality. Participatory equality refers to the actual, meaningful involvement that workers have in decisions about the design, preconditions, implementation, execution, circumstances, monitoring, and remuneration of their work. In the United States, union membership now stands at roughly 10% of the workforce. This is a reduction from 20% in the 1980s (Dinlersoz & Greenwood, 2016). Workers in the United Kingdom halved their membership in the same period (about 60% in 1980 to less than 30% today). You can see this in Table 3.2. And the decline has continued. In the European Union (EU), between 2000 and 2008, union membership:

> dropped from 46 to 43 million. Waged employment (excluding employers, the self-employed and family workers) increased from 120 to 140 million employees during the same nine years, so that density decreased from 27.8 to 23.4 percent. Over a longer period of three decades, while the EU expanded from nine to 27 member-states, union membership stagnated, whereas non-membership more than doubled, causing the average EU union density rate to halve. …after 2000 union density rates fell in all 27 EU member states.
>
> (Bryson, Ebbinghaus, & Visser, 2011, p. 98)

Union 'density' and collective bargaining power are commonly adopted as proxies for participatory equality. Its decline has accompanied the decay of social solidarity and collectivism in civil society. Globalization, deindustrialization and a shrinking manufacturing base in Western countries, and changing labor markets (e.g., flexible employment contracts and part-time work) have all contributed. Financialization (which refers to the growing size and influence of financial institutions and organizations in the economy and politics) has brought about more aggressive management strategies that focused on downsizing the workforce (particularly the bottom half through offshoring, outsourcing, and automation) and distributing (newly freed-up capital) to shareholders (Kollmeyer, 2018). New methods to contract, reward, and control labor, which are less dependent on the intermediation of trade unions, play a role as well, as does the political shift to the right—with a concomitant decline of unions as a political resource or talent incubator. Research has identified endogenous reasons for the decline (i.e., those related to union or other labor representation), too, including union inaction and inadequate services. Unionization, after all, is a costly process. This can show up in a lack of connection with new generations and new social movements, and instead a reliance on traditional organizing methods that hail from manufacturing industries connected to a particular place, and which are tailored for large or public sector organizations (Bryson et al., 2011).

In the United States, participatory inequality and income inequality both followed a U-shape during the course of the 20th century (Dinlersoz & Greenwood, 2016). In an attempt to go beyond correlation, Kollmeyer (2018) used a number of time-series regression models and national-level US data to show how the various processes of neoliberalization create more profound distributional effects (e.g., inequalities in income and participation) than they would have done in isolation. In other words, neoliberal

Table 3.2 Declining participatory equality in the United States and the United Kingdom (Dinlersoz & Greenwood, 2016)

Union membership (proportion of workforce)	US	UK
1980	20%	60%
2020	10%	30%

changes did not just occur contemporaneously with the rise of participatory and income inequality, but interacted in ways that magnified the effects on them. Measurable results can be seen in reduced bargaining power and an erosion of worker rights (Lafferty, 2010), less employment protection and greater restrictions on social insurance, changes in wage structure, and indeed a growth of income inequality (Watson, 2015).

This has consequences for worker health and engagement. McIntyre (2005) has traced how participatory inequality, expressed through management control over the labor process (including division of productive tasks, timetables, tools use, breaks, overtime arrangements, and supervisory styles), contributes significantly to the creation of occupational illness. The expansion of organizational-psychological occupational stress and burnout surveys since the 1980s has made certain kinds of these illnesses more legible (and perhaps in part more prevalent), yet all seem to point to losses of control, security and autonomy, and a rise in bureaucratic accountability and performance demands as central to the problem (Ayers, Culvenor, Sillitoe, & Else, 2013). This is, of course, synonymous with *disabling* workers. Today, unions have a paradoxical role in this. Expansive bureaucratization has handed them a power lever (slowing or stopping work, increasing manning requirements, and restricting site access), such that they are seldom against the imposition or enforcement of rules that otherwise rob members of autonomy.

Note

1 All quotes are from Storkersen, Thorvaldsen, Kongsvik, and Dekker (2020).

4

THE MESO

MISTRUST AND MONITOR

Meso-economic factors are related to the structures and inter-organizational or industry arrangements under which the micro- and macroeconomic forces play out. The ones that we look at in this chapter are the following:

- Deprofessionalization
- The growth of compliance workforces
- Surveillance capitalism.

Together, and in the ways in which they relate to the macroeconomic factors in the previous chapter as well as the micro-economic ones in the next, these factors contribute to the explanation of how free markets lead to unfree workers.

Deprofessionalization

Talk to anyone in a professional role—for example, a doctor, a judge, and an engineer—and you will likely hear how they feel that their professional expertise no longer counts for as much as it might have done 20 years ago, or perhaps when their parents would have possessed such expertise. In the United Kingdom (UK), not long after the deadly rail accident at Hatfield in 2000, deprofessionalization was seen as a contributor to the crash. There was:

> ...a dearth of engineers...a basic lack of engineering competence which is a problem across the board in the industry...not enough people who understand how the infrastructure works or behaves.
>
> (Jack, 2001, p. 84)

Alvin Gouldner spoke of a 'new class,' a bureaucratic officialdom of 'line officials' set above professionals, with board- or political appointees yet above them. These people, Gouldner (1979) observed, are not appointed for their technical competence:

> ...but because they represent money capital or politically reliable 'commissars.' The fundamental structure within which most technical intelligentsia work, then, systematically generates tensions between them, on the one side, and the bureaucratic officials and managers on the other.
>
> (p. 326)

What exactly is it that professionals feel that they have lost in what Gouldner called 'muffled confrontations,' when there is this lack of competence, of competent people even, of people who understand how the thing in question actually works. Professionalism is typically known for the following six factors (Roberts & Donahue, 2000):

- *Mastery of specialized theory*: professionals have to master a body of nuanced theory and knowledge in order to perform the tasks associated with their profession. This is true even if what they do is manual work (e.g., from orthopedic surgery to carpentry). Professionals develop specialized competencies through extensive experience and training. The knowledge base, furthermore, is always incomplete and changing, and therefore professionals need to keep up with developments in their field.

- *Autonomy and control of one's work* and how that work is performed: this is the most important attribute of the professions. It refers to the freedom and power of professionals to regulate and control their own work behavior and conditions, including the order and pace in which it is done. Autonomy also means resistance against supervision by people from outside the profession. Having the authority, and trust, to make choices within accepted practice of the profession, in pursuit of appropriate goals, is critical to professionalism.
- *Motivation focusing on intrinsic rewards* and on the interests of clients: this is commonly seen as the second-most important aspect of professionalism. The recipient of the service provided by the professional (e.g., the buyer of a woodworked piece of furniture, the student receiving a lecture, and the patient being operated upon) typically takes precedence over the professional's self-interests (whether they are expressed in money, or in hours of sleep, or in life–work balance). Professionalism means enjoying intrinsic satisfaction in the vocation. Professionals tend not to think of their work as being closely tied to the number of hours spent on task. A professional simply does the work until it is completed to their (or, more importantly, their client's) satisfaction.
- *Commitment to the profession as a career* and to the service objectives of the organization for which one works: membership in a profession is expected to be taken very seriously. Commitment to the work is long term and may be life-long. This is possible because work and those who reap the benefits of it are seen as the ends with intrinsic rewards. They are not a means to an end. Professionals often continue to do their work even after retirement because of the meaning they gain from the activity. Professionals are loyal to their careers and profession to the point that they invest much of their identity in their vocation. Loyalty to their employing organization exists, but it comes in second place, and mostly as a by-product of their commitment to the profession.
- *Sense of community and collegiality* with others in the profession, and acceptance (or even seeking) of accountability to those colleagues: associations, groups, levels, standards, and other markers can get developed internally to the profession for purposes of entry control, socialization of new members, and enforcement of rules of conduct.

Some professions (like ministry or medicine) in effect sequester their newcomers to enable intensive and intensely focused socialization and bonding with the new reference group—independent of who ends up being the employer of the professional.

- *Self-monitoring and regulation* by the profession of ethical and professional standards: some professions have elaborate written codes, while others rely on unwritten mores and expectations of conduct. Professions typically have procedures for peer review in cases of violation of standards of behavior. This has long been able to assure trust from colleagues, clients, and wider society. For this reason, there is resistance to external forms of control, which automatically mean deprofessionalization.

The *control* or *self-control* created by a group of professionals relies on a kind of horizontal disciplinary force of shared values, commitments, and beliefs that gets produced and reproduced through the reciprocal scrutiny of peers, or of their work products (Orlikowski, 1991). Bureaucratic control, on the other hand, works through direct (or technologically mediated) supervision of workers' performance by reliance on impersonal and universally applicable (i.e., neutral and equitable) rules, procedures, policies, and schemes. These all define or assume certain standards or requirements that are applicable to everyone. These two kinds of 'control' are almost impossible to combine. Bureaucratization, to be sure, does not pursue deprofessionalization as an aim in itself. But as Gouldner already flagged, deprofessionalization is an almost inevitable institutional consequence of it. As Roberts and Donahue (2000) explain:

> Bureaucratization and professionalism always seem to have an inherent conflict, for they operate on contrasting principles of objectives, authority, and loyalty. First, bureaucracy expects its members to promote and represent the interests of the organization; the professional expects the interests of the client to be supreme. Second, bureaucracy sees authority residing in legal contracts that are backed by formal sanctions. As utilitarian and goal-driven formal organizations, bureaucracies focus on contractual arrangements and formal structures. By contrast, professionals tend to think of authority being rooted in expertise of the person holding the position rather than in the power of the status itself. Along these same lines, bureaucracies expect

> their members to comply with directives of the organization; professionals, by contrast, expect to be guided by the ethical standards of their field as spelled out by professional associations. Because professionals develop a reference system focusing on professional colleagues, they are typically more concerned with maintaining a reputation with peers in their field than they are with pleasing organizational superiors. Finally, when disagreement over procedure or policy occurs, bureaucracy expects the organizational management to address or solve the disagreement and to make decisions; the professional looks to professional colleagues for guidance. In each of these ways, the formal rationalization of bureaucracies runs counter to the tendencies of professionals.
>
> (pp. 368–369)

The rise of cultures of administration and bureaucratic accountability makes it so more bureaucratic rationale encroaches on how work is managed, supervised, and executed. The effort to realize fulfillment of job obligations, responsible use of resources, efficiency, and cost-effectiveness is of course as relevant to professional work as it is to any occupation. But the rationalized means by which administrative bureaucracies normally pursue those aims misses the point of professionalism. Predictability, efficiency, and quality control in a profession come not from tight supervision and top-down regulation, but from the motivation and dedication intrinsic to the profession itself. In fact, there is substantial evidence that a long-term result of administrative cultures of bureaucratic accountability is a decline in productivity and expertise (CAIB, 2003; Mintzberg, 2004; Peters & Pouw, 2004; Peters & Weggeman, 2017; Roberts & Donahue, 2000). Flatter, horizontally coordinated organizations enhance creativity and are often more productive than tightly regulated, hierarchical ones, as some corporations are belatedly discovering (e.g., McCord, 2017). Notwithstanding, deprofessionalization has continued apace, with consequences such as the following:

- The professional loses his or her monopoly over knowledge and insight.
- Other people, very much including the newly emerging 'consumers' of the professionals' services, no longer have as much faith or trust in the service or professional ethic.

- The basis for autonomy and decision authority on the part of the professional is gradually being whittled away.
- A new class of 'professionals,' like managers, administrators, HR, or safety people, have more to say about how work is planned and executed.

In this way, professional and technical accountability get supplanted by bureaucratic accountability, overseen and governed by an increasingly non-technical staff. With the appointment of Sean O'Keefe (Deputy Director of the White House Office of Management and Budget) to lead National Aeronautics and Space Administration (NASA) in the early 2000s, for example, the Bush administration signaled that the organization's focus should be on management and finances so as to better control a vast and growing web of contractors and subcontractors (CAIB, 2003). Hierarchical reporting relationships and quantitative measures gradually replaced direct coordination and expert judgment—even when it came to acute safety-critical design and operational issues. Prior to the Space Shuttle Challenger launch decision in 1986, for example, 'bureaucratic accountability undermined the professional accountability of the original technical culture, creating missing signals' (Vaughan, 1996, p. 363).

Market relationships favor the bureaucratic kind of control, though. They have shown to prefer *confidence*—as furnished by audits, pre-tender and supplier assessments, and quantifiable measures—above *trust* (C. Smith, 2001). This means that professionals, and those who rely on them, can use trust only in the margins, where it is out of view, relegated to barely legitimate *work as actually done* between parties. It has no place in *work as it is imagined* by a market that patrols and governs the relationship between the parties. That market relationship, after all, is assured through audited accreditations, driven by contractual obligations and, in the last resort, resolved in judicial arbitration or intervention. Trust, says Carole Smith, has become largely invisible under the cloak of bureaucratic governance and contractual relations. The way this has worked itself into relationships with professionals is now known as the 'proletarianization' of the profession. Here is an example from medicine:

> Our findings can be seen as representing an example of a shift of social preference from trust in the professional and expert judgement of individual

> professionals to confidence in systems of auditable rules and procedures, and that ideas about consistency and standardisation in clinical practice are on their way to becoming 'naturalised' in medical discourse, that is accepted as common sense. ...[T]he increased routinisation of the medical labour process which is implied by our findings can be seen as a manifestation of professional 'proletarianisation.'
>
> (Harrison & Dowswell, 2002, p. 222)

Proletarianization

Even before market-favoring policy-making got underway, Oppenheimer noted how autonomous professional workers were gradually being replaced by, or turned into, a 'white collar proletarian type of worker' (1972, p. 213). It has, explains Giddens (1991), its basis in the very nature of modernity. With the decline of localized practices and the first-hand knowledge that its practitioners had, trust became the stand-in. Trust was a leap to commitment, an irreducible quality of faith in what the other will do. We have no need for trust if the person who does the work for us is in constant view, whose activities we can continually monitor, and when we understand what he or she is doing. That doesn't work with specialized, distant professional work characteristic of a modern, industrialized society. *High-trust* posts are those carried out largely outside the presence of management or supervisory staff, and outside the view of those who consume the products or services rendered by the professional.

Professionals, as Oppenheimer saw them, once had the authority and freedom (and indeed trust) to do their artisan or craftsman-type work—whether planning and executing a surgical procedure, making a diagnosis, writing a book, plotting a ship's journey, floating an idea, designing and building a bridge, etc.—under conditions that they were mainly able to set and regulate for themselves. But market-driven bureaucratic organizations no longer give professionals such high trust and autonomy because the market generally doesn't want to pay for it. Privatization of healthcare has led to proletarianization of medical professionals largely because of this (and because everybody can go online and find out about their own maladies, of course). Professional self-determination has become increasingly difficult to uphold in market-based economies in which professional expertise has become easier to commodify and control—for it to be made more efficient, cheapened, bought, sold, contracted, outsourced, offshored, uploaded, downloaded, or imported. And, as you'll see later on, it has now become easier to supervise and control even specialized, distant work. Professionals can no longer set themselves so easily apart by doing things that nobody else can see or understand. Supervision and control come with the aid of surveillance capitalism, which has eroded professional privilege through technological invasion and observation.

The seeds of proletarianization, paradoxically, lie within professionalism itself—at least in how we have been organizing work in the modern industrial era. Professionals have had no choice but to surrender to the extensive division of labor that first came with the Industrial Revolution. This of course allows them to highlight and celebrate their expertise as a unique possession unavailable anywhere else in the workforce or even society. But it also means that professionals do less broad and diverse work, leaving the planning, billing, marketing, and other activities that help regulate and provide their work to others. As Giddens points out, the specialization that gives professionals their status and professionalism also makes them vulnerable, because it makes them laypersons at almost everything else. This invites or legitimates surveillance and control of all their activities that are not directly related to the application of their professional expertise (e.g., planning or departmental-level organization of work, procurement of resources and equipment, and hiring and use of human resources [HRs]). Most true professionals would rather not bother with billing, or marketing, or recruitment, so being part of a standardized, bureaucratic corporate entity has fairly obvious advantages. But the upsides of this kind of modernization do not outweigh the downsides. Here another example is presented from research into healthcare:

> Corporate employment can provide various advantages to physicians, such as freedom from the business demands of operating a practice, negotiating leverage with health insurers over payment rates, and, potentially, more control over their work schedules. At the same time, the managerial hierarchy in healthcare corporations can have control over many domains that affect clinicians, including the application of clinical algorithms, practice guidelines, standardization of procedures, cost-control measures that affect

> care directly (such as choice of orthopedic prostheses and implantable cardiac devices), quality improvement programs, and supply of clinical information required by insurers. Care delivery strategies such as standardization, cost controls, and productivity targets can create schisms between individual clinicians' values and expectations and those of the organization as well as declines in the clinicians' sense of control, flexibility, and autonomy and a potential erosion of professional values.
>
> (Carayon & Cassel, 2019, pp. 169–170)

A proletarianized professional has less authority and autonomy to determine things like the place and pace of work, the characteristics of the workplace and other people in it, or the uses to which the work is put. These things are governed instead by a growing internal or external (private or public) bureaucratic authority. It isn't as if professionals don't find ways to rebel or at least complain against the encroaching bureaucratization of everything at which they can be considered laypersons. The bureaucratization of professional work that necessarily accompanies its proletarianization produces a new consciousness—of class, of 'us' against 'them'; 'them' typically being 'the bureaucrats': HR, staff personnel, managers, safety people (Gouldner, 1979; Jacobsen, 2017)). The proletarianization of professional work also means that remuneration (typically a wage or salary from some corporate [public or private] entity) becomes more subject to renegotiation, downward pressure, or to market conditions, economic processes and trends outside the organization, and of course bureaucratic control.

Not only is professionalism increasingly circumscribed by the encroaching bureaucratic control of all the activities that surround it. Sometimes standardization, bureaucratization, and compliance enter into the core activities that constituted the one remaining holdout of professionalism. This happens when it can be argued that the profession's outcome data doesn't speak in favor of retaining the kind of autonomous craftsmanship that once defined professionalism. René Amalberti and colleagues flagged how a transition away from craftsmanship, and into the regularity, bureaucratic accountability, and quantifiable quality control of equivalent (and thus interchangeable) actors, might in some cases lead to better (in this case safer) outcomes:

> We believe that to achieve the next increase in safety levels, health care professionals must face a very difficult transition: abandoning their status and self-image as craftsmen and instead adopting a position that values equivalence among their ranks. For example, a commercial airline passenger usually neither knows nor cares who the pilot or the copilot flying their plane is; a last-minute change of captain is not a concern to passengers, as people have grown accustomed to the notion that all pilots are, to an excellent approximation, equivalent to one another in their skills. Patients have a similar attitude toward anesthesiologists when they face surgery. In both cases, the practice is highly standardized, and the professionals involved have, in essence, renounced their individuality in the service of a reliable standard of excellent care. They sell a service instead of an individual identity. As a consequence, the risk for catastrophic death in healthy patients (American Society of Anesthesiologists risk category 1 or 2) undergoing anesthesia is very low—close to one in a million per anesthetic episode.
>
> (Amalberti, Auroy, Berwick, & Barach, 2005, p. 759)

With less individuality—and greater regularity and interchangeability of professional work and workers—you might indeed get more predictable, reliable outcomes. But to get there you need more regulation, more standardization, and more control and bureaucratization. Ritzer (1993) has seen this happen in lots of business sectors. He called it 'the McDonaldization of society.' 'McDonaldization,' a more contemporary form of Taylor's (1911) scientific management of work, has a number of components. These can be recognized in findings about deprofessionalization and proletarianization as well:

- The first is efficiency, which is defined as the optimal method for accomplishing a task. Efficiency in McDonaldization means that every aspect of the organization and its management and administration is geared toward the minimization of time—at least time as measured by the administrative apparatus of the bureaucratic organization. This results in:

> ...professionals having to perform many professional tasks outside of regular work hours by remotely accessing the electronic health records to complete professional work in personal time. Although such work is compensated for

> hourly employees, it is typically not compensated for physicians, advance practice providers, and other clinicians. This can often lead administrators to erroneously conclude that they have 'increased productivity' without increasing costs when, in reality, they have simply extended the work week of health care professionals and stolen time from their families and personal activities. Based on EHR time-stamp data, the average family physician now spends approximately 28 hours per month completing clinical documentation on nights and weekends when he or she is not on duty.
>
> (Carayon & Cassel, 2019, p. 93)

- The second is quantification: the organization's objectives and means to achieve them should all be calculable (e.g., cost of the procedure) rather than subjective (e.g., patient experience). McDonaldization has naturalized the notion that quantity equals quality, and that a large amount delivered by the organization (in a short amount of officially measured time, see above) is the same as a high-quality product. Workers in these organizations are judged by how fast they are instead of the quality of work they do or the quality of the product they deliver.
- The third is uniformity, standardization, and predictability of products, services, and workers. This is another aspect of McDonaldization, as it was in Taylor's scientifically managed system of work. Tasks, guided or even designed by others, are increasingly narrow in scope, repetitive, routine, and limited in autonomy. Execution of these tasks typically requires authorization by other people in the organization.

The growth of a compliance workforce

McDonaldization, deprofessionalization, and proletarianization all relate to another trend foreshadowed by Gouldner: the introduction of additional people who now claim to have something to say about how the professionals do their work. The professionals and their work become but one element in their push for overall system performance improvement. As Carole Smith would remind us, the professional can no longer count as much on relationships of trust, but is now entwined in relationships of confidence that are built on the back of quality control, audits, surveillance, inspections, measurements, and reporting requirements. That is where deprofessionalization starts cutting both ways. On the one hand, moving away from the professional-as-craftsperson has quantitatively demonstrable advantages for overall system performance. Yet when you depersonalize and standardize, when you reduce individuality and autonomy, you typically get less professional job satisfaction, less motivation, less commitment, more burnout, and more intent to leave the profession altogether (Pink, 2009). And you can end up, once again, with worse quality outcomes (Carayon & Cassel, 2019; Grant, 2016; Paget, 2004):

> Administrative burden is a barrier to quality care that diminishes patient care experiences and contributes to the risk of clinician burnout. Health care policy makers, regulators, and standards-setting bodies have a responsibility to identify and eliminate policies, rules, and processes that impede a clinician's ability to perform productive work necessary for quality patient care and that negatively affect the clinician–patient relationship. These entities should engage clinicians and patients in the process to identify and eliminate health care laws, regulations, policies, standards, and administrative processes that contribute little or no value to patient care.
>
> (Carayon & Cassel, 2019, p. 14)

We have dubbed the call above 'decluttering': the identification and removal of bureaucracy that gets in the way of doing actual, professional work (Dekker, 2015; Rae, Weber, Provan, & Dekker, 2018):

> In most cases, local organizations could change or eliminate many of the rules identified in this process without violating any legal, regulatory, or statutory requirement. While the impact of this initiative on the work environment has not been evaluated, it does illustrate a relatively simple process by which local organizations can identify and eliminate wasteful and unnecessary rules that are diverting time and resources and may be contributing to clinician burden.
>
> (Carayon & Cassel, 2019, p. 141)

The advantages would seem obvious. But the obstacles to decluttering are severe. While the autonomy and individuality of *professional experts* and *craftsmen* has declined, other roles within bureaucracies have actually seen their professional status and influence grow (Gouldner, 1979). HR, safety people, managers, and administrators all belong to a group of newly professionalized workers. Their professionalization has established norms, exclusive rights to sources of knowledge (e.g., which universities to go to, or which programs to take in order to qualify for the profession), hiring practices, codes of 'professional' conduct, and certification of people, programs, education, and more. Professionalization confers prestige on those who belong to the new 'professional' class, and tends to devalue or delegitimize the expertise of those who are not part of the class. And in one way or another, their role involves compliance and control of previously autonomous professional experts.

As Carayon and Cassel showed, the supposed productivity gains of a standardized, administrative system typically come from the private budget of its deprofessionalized workers. Yet real productivity gains have lagged considerably behind what technological and organizational advances alone would have predicted. They haven't at all made true on the promises of market-favoring, newly bureaucratized work. Any productivity dividends, in fact, are more or less exactly offset by the risen costs of compliance (Saines et al., 2014) and managerialism, the belief in or reliance on the use of professional managers in planning or administering an activity (Klikauer, 2015). It would seem obvious that it isn't such a smart arrangement; that managerialism costs more than it provides. But such is the influence of marketized economies that internal control and compliance becomes the preoccupation of those in charge. Because it gives them the idea that they can:

- Plan amid complexity and uncertainty
- Pursue consistency across dispersed teams and offices
- Avoid health and safety liabilities
- Reduce risks of malfeasance
- Treat employees and clients (or patients) fairly and equitably
- Reduce legal exposure
- Reduce risks to systems and processes
- Collect business data
- Monitor employee activities and expenses
- ...And do lots more.

And there is something self-justifying and self-sustaining in managerialism, too. Managerial bureaucracies can develop a remarkable entrepreneurism. Bureaucracies can be innovative and 'acquisitive' in their own ways. From the outside, it can sometimes look as if a bureaucracy deliberately sets out to colonize previously unpatrolled areas of practice—such as those seven-page travel risk assessments that need to be approved three levels up (with each level having to add a signature) where a few years back all you had to do was book the trip. In this way, bureaucracies can sustain demand for themselves, creating more work that is to be met with more bureaucratic means. This has indeed been referred to as 'bureaucratic entrepreneurism' (Goyal, 1983; Smith et al., 1978). Members and leaders in a bureaucracy might defend their responsibilities and influence, or may seek to expand them (Mintzberg, 1979). Indeed, those working inside bureaucracies can claim that it is legitimate to expand because of some newly discovered risk or moral imperative (e.g., to protect vulnerable workers, or to counter liability concerns).

There is often no natural brake on bureaucratic entrepreneurism. You would think that operating in a market demands efficiency and that having a large managerial bureaucracy exposes the organization to competitive pressure. But markets not only prize efficiency but also trade in fear and anxiety because markets in their very nature create concerns about cost, about loss, and about paying prices. This can include the fear of being found in non-compliance during an industry inspection or audit, or the anxiety of liability exposure for everything ranging from mental health problems to harassment, discrimination, occupational safety risks, and more. Creating additional documentation and processes (and positions in a hierarchy) to demonstrate the awareness, management, and mitigation of such risks are natural responses to these market pressures. A large healthcare system I recently visited had just proudly announced the appointment of a 'Chief Wellbeing Officer,' whose first initiative—if not sheer existence—was universally derided by every professional I spoke with. For a bureaucracy, this kind of acquisitiveness is easy. The same organization, after all, is often involved in cultivating the rules (or positions) it then gets to implement and administer. The monopolistic explanation is that bureaucracies internal to an organization do not need to be super-efficient with their resources, nor show clear results, because *they* face no competition. A perceived moral obligation, legal fear, or particular interpretation of a regulatory demand can justify even inefficient and ineffective bureaucratic means that an organization and its leadership dedicate to it (Donaldson, 2013). Bureaucracies inside a company in the private sector (e.g., HR department, finance arm, or safety group) can blossom as a result. Here is an example:

> In one case a company became concerned about slips, lapses and mistakes of their staff carrying out routine office operations. The ideal solution in such a situation would be to hire more people or allow sufficient time for people to carry out their jobs but neither of these two options was considered cost-effective. Rather, a solution was found in establishing detailed monitoring of safety and quality indicators. But here is the dilemma. With tighter controls and increased surveillance, the staff felt stressed and uneasy. The next thing for the company was to monitor the stress levels of workers, replace old office furniture with ergonomic equipment and offer free counselling on health and wellbeing to their staff. Being conscious of their brand reputation, the management also felt the need to monitor the activities of their employees on social media. Indicators were set up to ensure the workers were using their holiday allowances and that no amount of annual leave was accrued at the end of every year. A dedicated department was set up and kept extremely busy in balancing the competing goals of business and safety. Soon more people were recruited in this department but elsewhere in the organisation the sentiments were down. A happy workplace soon turned ugly. Productivity dropped further and the organisation was crippled under its own competing goals and metrics. The example is a one-off but the underlying message is not. In many organisations meaningless metrics and indicators have become the elephant in the room—a flawed approach to management and an obvious waste of resources.
>
> (Anand, 2016, pp. 21–22)

In a 1988 issue of the *Harvard Business Review*, Peter Drucker predicted that by 2008 the average organization would have slashed its administrative layers by half and shrunk its managerial ranks by two-thirds. Such were the hopes of a new public management, of market-oriented policies and deregulation. And Drucker's prognostication was actually conservative:

> In the year 1930, John Maynard Keynes predicted that technology would have advanced sufficiently by century's end that countries like Great

> Britain or the United States would achieve a 15-hour work week. There's every reason to believe he was right. In technological terms, we are quite capable of this. And yet it didn't happen. Instead, technology has been marshaled, if anything, to figure out ways to make us all work more. In order to achieve this, jobs have had to be created that are, effectively, pointless. Huge swathes of people, in Europe and North America in particular, spend their entire working lives performing tasks they secretly believe do not really need to be performed. The moral and spiritual damage that comes from this situation is profound. It is a scar across our collective soul. Yet virtually no one talks about it … These are what I propose to call 'bullshit jobs.'
>
> (Graeber, 2013, p. 10)

It wasn't to be. In fact, the opposite happened. Together with the professionalization of new types of workers (managers, administrators, and HR), the proportion of 'compliance workers' employed by organizations to ensure the meeting of all these demands has gone up accordingly. In mature economies, one in ten employees can now be put into the category of compliance workers—inspectors, regulatory officers, contract administrators, office managers, project managers, public relations professionals, information officers, practice managers, policy analysts, health and safety professionals, program administrators, and many more. Instead of Peter Drucker's or John Keynes' hoped-for efficiencies, Greaber's more dystopian conclusion appears to be the right one. Between 1983 and 2014, the number of managers, supervisors, and support staff in the US workforce grew by more than 100%, while the number of people in other occupations increased by only 44% (Hamel & Zanini, 2020). Other figures show that since the late 1990s:

- The number of inspectors, regulatory officers, office managers, and public relations professionals has doubled.
- The number of information and organization professionals, practice managers, and intelligence and policy analysts has tripled.
- The number of occupational health, safety, and environment professionals has quadrupled.
- The number of contract, program, and project administrators has quintupled (Saines et al., 2014).

You could argue that these new roles have made up for the loss of, say, switchboard operators, office clerks, or secretaries to whom letters were once dictated. But that wouldn't explain why compliance roles have grown by 100% and other roles by less than half of that. It is probably one explanation for the fact that getting rid of switchboard operators and typists hasn't demonstrably led to productivity gains either. One problem with that, to be sure, is that labor productivity—the hourly output of a country's economy, specifically the amount of gross domestic product generated by an hour of labor—is determined by so many other factors, that trying to sort out the negative effects of compliance (or any other single variable) on productivity becomes almost impossible (Cauadrado-Ballesteros & Peña-Miguel, 2018).

Nonetheless, there is something to go on. When you look at studies of the effects of privatization on productivity—for which the past three decades have offered plenty of empirical evidence—the results are mixed at best (Brown, Earle, & Telegdy, 2016). In their study of 70,000 privatized firms across East European countries, Brown and colleagues found rises in profitability and productivity, as well as company growth. These effects, however, varied substantially, in part with the company's institutional environment. That can point to issues of governance and the costs of compliance, but of course indirectly so. If you look at data from countries other than those that emerged from communism in the late 1980s and early 1990s, the picture is less strident altogether. Productivity growth during the last 75 years the United States, for instance, was at its most spectacular in 1950, in the middle of an era known for its big governments who controlled markets and chose emancipatory, reformist, and redistributive strategies. This was an era of rapidly expanding government regulation, social welfare systems, and sizable union participation (Braedley & Luxton, 2010), and it yielded the greatest productivity increases (which, of course, were also due to a host of interrelated factors).

In contrast, productivity growth in the United States has been particularly tepid in the last few decades, when privatization and deregulation accelerated (Lafferty, 2010; Ogus, 2004). This is mirrored in data from other Western countries which embraced privatization and deregulation, with some of the productivity dampers over the past two decades directly linked to the growth of compliance cultures (Saines et al., 2014). In the United States, paragon of deregulation, market-oriented policymaking and privatization, productivity growth has pretty much stalled. From 1948 to 2004, the US labor productivity in organizations (that weren't financial firms) grew by an annual average of 2.5% (and most of that growth occurred in the immediate post-war period in which government oversight and ownership were at their height). Since the full embrace of deregulation, privatization, and free-market thinking, productivity growth has averaged just 1.1% (Hamel & Zanini, 2020). And half of this small amount is fictitious:

> American economic statistics employ a method known as *hedonic* accounting, which allows for changes in the quality of goods. The effect of using this method of accounting is to inflate American productivity. Nearly all of the increase claimed ... may be an artefact of this accounting convention. As a British observer has put it: The effect of *hedonic* accounting is that reported US GDP growth overstates the real growth of US output by half of one percent a year. This accounting difference is equivalent to the main part of the productivity miracle that still enthuses in the new economy.
>
> (J. Gray, 2003, p. 51)

No sector of the economy gets spared, it seems. The rise of compliance since the heydays of deregulation and privatization has affected professional services, finance, information and communication technologies, utilities, wholesale and retail, real estate, healthcare, manufacturing, agriculture, transport, education, mining, construction, infrastructure, and many more. Each business group within these industries (HR, contracting, and finance) tends to have its own processes and forms rather than sharing some common framework. Middle managers and senior executives spend some 9 hours per week on compliance activities, with other staff spending an average of 6.5 hours per week. The swell of new internal and business-to-business rules not only robs productivity, but also saps incentive, innovation, and enterprise (Saines et al., 2014).

Surveillance capitalism

Technology has accelerated the growth of *surveillance capitalism*—monetizing the gathering and use of people's data. With increasing computerization, and thereby the 'datafication' of work, it has become possible to monitor much of what people do, and to record it, store it, analyze it, and act on it.

Each task or operation leaves a potentially huge electronic footprint that can be mined for all kinds of things. Reasons that organizations offer for such surveillance include:

- Maintaining productivity
- Monitoring resource use
- Ensuring employee health and safety
- Protecting against defamation, sabotage, data theft, and hacking
- Protecting against legal liabilities.

What is known as 'surveillance capitalism,' in its original sense, refers to a market-driven process where the commodity for sale is people's personal data. In its basic form, this means tracking and recording and repackaging personal data and behavioral information and selling it to advertisers. This is not strictly the case in *surveillance capitalism* as it is meant here. Computer- and Internet-based surveillance, however, creates numerous market opportunities since it shapes—and is shaped by—economic production, circulation, and consumption of data (Fuchs, Boersma, Albrechtslund, & Sandoval, 2012):

> Corporations conduct a systemic gathering of data about applicants, employees, the labour process, private property, consumers, and competitors in order to minimize economic risks, discipline workers, increase productivity, circumvent theft, sabotage and protests ... The overall aim of the employment of multiple surveillance methods and technologies in the capital accumulation process is the maximization of profit and the increased exploitation of surplus value. Surveillance is a method that capital employs for controlling the production and circulation process and for controlling and disciplining the workforce.
>
> (p. 42)

Surveillance necessarily creates additional bureaucracy because of the need to make rules and processes (and hire additional people) for gathering, analysis, storage, and response. Organizations can, and often do, farm out the surveillance work, or parts of it. Surveillance contracting means delegating the harvesting, analysis, and repackaging of data to a third, commercial, market actor through targeted or mass surveillance of people's computer-mediated or -tracked work activities. Zuboff (2015), who introduced the term 'surveillance capitalism,' talks about 'Big Other.' This applies equally to surveillance contracting: somebody who is paid to watch over your shoulder while you are doing your work. This 'Big Other' has the power and authority—however derived—to capture, scrutinize, produce, store, and use the data about how you do your work. Here are some of the data that can get gathered, and scrutinized, often by a contracted, external party:

- Personnel entry and exit to selected areas
- Closed-circuit television (CCTV) cameras in workplaces
- Recording of completed procedures or audit findings
- Psychometric, physiological, and biometric monitoring
- Data-mining for purposes of human resource information systems
- Global positioning system (GPS) observation of personnel or vehicle position (and speed and acceleration/deceleration, such as in intelligent vehicle monitoring systems)
- Electronic tracking of tool use
- Use of camera-equipped drones to monitor compliance on a site (in an example of 'function creep,' drones used for measuring mine deposits were redeployed spontaneously for checking helmet compliance—without employees' knowledge or consent)
- Body cameras that record rule compliance/violations
- Recording of computer usage and surfing behavior
- Review of communications contents
- Use of organization's resources.

Organization and surveillance (or some form of social or other control) go hand in hand, of course, and surveillance itself is nothing new. It happens pretty much wherever work gets done. Today, however, the proliferation and penetration of electronic surveillance in workplaces is enormous. Back in the early 2000s already:

> ...more than a third [of US companies surveyed] with 1000 or more workers employed people to read through other employees' outbound email in search of rule-breaking. Nearly seventy-five percent of US companies monitor worker communications and on-the-job activities.
>
> (Ball, 2010, p. 88)

Surveillance capitalism pulls almost all of the intertwined factors of this chapter together. For one, it creates new markets for additional bureaucracy. Contractors are typically required to install the surveillance technologies, and they, or other organizations, are then contracted to gather, process, scrutinize, and produce the data. Then the organization that has contracted out the work needs its own back office to receive such data and to do something with it. That not only leads to more bureaucratic work, but also to more products of bureaucracy: reports, violation alerts, compliance reminders, HR processes, safety campaigns through posters or memos, the development of new rules, and many more. The possession of such data can be a powerful lever for bureaucratic entrepreneurism. Data can show the existence (and size) of a particular problem that energizes moral concerns (e.g., about speeding or other risk-taking behaviors). This in turn can legitimize and mobilize bureaucratic interventions aimed at stemming the behavior in question. Without the data, that lever would not have been available. Other factors that you have seen in this book are in play here, too. Auditing and financialization rely on surveillance data as a raw commodity that ultimately helps fulfill their needs for compliance monitoring and reporting.

One company that sells and operates vehicle monitoring systems offers an example of the range of functions and data it supplies. It assures positive driver identification, conducts accurate measurement of elevated g-force events (accelerating, braking, cornering), supplies speed zone geo-fencing, identifies high-risk routes, provides in-cab alerts to inform drivers of adverse events, records violations, fuel use, vehicle maintenance status, shows risks ahead, and records forward-facing as well as in-cab facing camera footage. All of this is done during the entire trip. Now imagine that a company that has engaged this contractor has 200 vehicles, and that that each one of them is, on average, in use for 8 hours a day. That alone could mean some 400,000 hours of data recording each year, over a number of input channels (like g-forces or in-cab camera footage). This easily amounts to 4 million hours of data for this one client alone. A lot can be done with such data by automation and artificial intelligence, but it also requires human monitoring or playback (e.g., of in-cab camera footage) to try to make some sense of what might actually have happened. And once the contractor has generated such data and conclusions about them, the client who is paying for it needs to start doing something with it all. It may trigger internal investigations, follow-ups such as carefully monitored individual behavior improvement pathways, human resource performance management processes, sanctions, supervisor conversations about worker productivity and tool use, the creation of peer networks to encourage safe driving and discourage dangerous behavior, new organizational policies, rule development, enhanced compliance and enforcement monitoring—lots of things that can keep an internal bureaucracy busy.

Surveillance also contributes to a sense of deprofessionalization because somebody or something is watching what you are doing. And even if they do not have the skills and knowledge you have, they have the authority to watch and assess your work. This entails a loss of the trust and authority vested in the practitioner. Instead, other people, who sit behind the surveillance technology, get to have a say (whether they actually do or not). Surveillance technologies insinuate rationally driven supervision and bureaucratic oversight into the workplace and workday of a practitioner. Surveillance can happen silently, mostly in the background, without prompts or warnings or visible signs of its presence (unlike some aspects of intelligent vehicle monitoring systems). But it is always there, and it inevitably changes what 'quality' work means. Professional work becomes the aggregate of measurable, calculable units, which are then assessed for their fit within a predetermined bandwidth of what is allowed or desired. And the worker, in the words of Haggerty and Ericson, is not so much an individual worker anymore, but an aggregate of data traces:

> The body is first broken down, abstracted from its physical setting, only to then be re-assembled in different settings through a series of data flows. The result is a decorporealised body, more mobile and measurable than its physical counterpart, re-assembled in the by now well-known 'data double.'
>
> (Galic et al., 2017, p. 22)

A 'data double' is a digital duplicate of our life or work, captured in data and spread across assemblages of information systems. It is the data double that fulfills the duties of bureaucratic accountability, not the worker or his or her actual work. The data double constitutes an additional self, a kind of 'functional hybrid' that is extremely useful and efficient for technologically mediated forms of compliance monitoring and control. Neither the supervisor nor the worker needs to be actually present to make this form of surveillance and disciplining function at all. An electronic footprint of multiple data traces, run through machine logic, pulled apart, re-assembled, and scrutinized against pre-determined criteria, can do the job for both.

Surveillance and the shift in power

Surveillance (literally 'watching from above') is indelibly connected with power. And it implies a moral judgment: who gets to say what is right or wrong in how you do your work? Concern about surveillance goes beyond the workplace, of course, because today the entire society is under surveillance like never before. Research into this is directly relevant to the growth of compliance capitalism. The basis of theorizing surveillance was laid by English philosopher, jurist, and social reformer Jeremy Bentham (1748–1832) and it resonates to this day. Bentham developed architectural *panoptica*, places from which you can see all. They were to be used for watching inmates in prisons, monitoring work done by indigents in pauper houses, and supervising of students in school by an invisible headmaster. His architectural designs used circular structures organized around a central observation post. With these, Bentham was able to remove the need for the physical presence of a supervisor (or *surveillant*), yet still able to impose the sensation of being watched. It vastly amplified the power, reach, and efficiency of the supervisor. Because of Bentham's arrangement, the supervisor is perceived as an invisible omnipresence. This is exactly the quality that sustains perfect discipline in the ones who are being watched. Discipline, Bentham believed, ideally gets internalized, making people behave whether they are actually being watched at that very moment or not. Surveillance applied not only to inmates, pupils, or paupers, but also to jailers, foremen, and headmasters. Bentham's intention was that it should also reduce institutional abuse. In fact, as social reformer, Bentham actually sought to promote self-regulation and self-discipline: this should eventually remove the need for surveillance, panoptica, and prisons altogether.

Foucault (1977) developed Bentham's architectural innovations into the notion of *panopticism*, which still resonates strongly in our ideas about surveillance. *Panopticism*, according to Foucault, refers to (potentially) seeing everything, everyone, all the time. For him, this was one of the distinguishing features of Western societies coming out of the 18th and 19th centuries:

> Western societies can be defined by a new form of power that is capillary and affects 'the grain of individuals, touches their bodies and inserts itself into their actions and attitudes, their discourses, learning processes and everyday lives.'
>
> (p. 39)

Foucault noted how, like the central observer in Bentham's *panopticum*, surveillance ideally remains hidden, in the shadows or background, unnoticed yet palpably present at the same time. A decade earlier, Hannah Arendt (1967) had already observed that it is precisely this mix of features that makes such surveillance so powerful and ubiquitous. As was once Bentham's (charitable) aim, people internalize the discipline imposed by such surveillance. Back in the 1970s, Foucault already foresaw how this mode of governance would become a favorite of technocratic societies. Their disciplining processes rely on what he called 'normation,' the creating and forcing of habits and rituals for how things are done, thereby establishing accepted norms which become central to what people conform to and strive for:

> This can produce 'anticipatory conformity' – where employees behave in a docile and accepting way, and automatically reduce the amount of commitment and motivation they display.
>
> (Ball, 2010, p. 93)

To be 'normal' really means occupying the position of the 'invisible.' The point is to keep one's 'data double' unnoticeable, to stay unmarked by any difference, exceedance, or deviation that shows up in the recorded, surveilled, and analyzed behavior (Galic et al., 2017). A security officer, whose workplace was tightly monitored and surveilled through CCTV and recordings, explained what this does with her, being closely watched and invisible at the same time:

> When I'm working in the checkpoint… I don't know if I necessarily ever want to feel noticed… Sometimes it's hard to be noticed as a good worker. There's people who do their job better than others, and sometimes you don't get noticed for that. [So] most of the time it doesn't really matter about being

> noticed, because sometimes it's just better to float under the radar and not have people know who you are.
>
> (Anteby & Chan, 2018, p. 257)

This obviously is the opposite of creativity, originality, non-conformism, and innovation that we'd like to associate with professionalism and craftsmanship, but this sense of surveillance has even started penetrating workplaces that employ professionals and craftsmen, not just twelve-dollars-an-hour security officers (Grant, 2016; NAPA, 2014). Organizations that deploy hierarchical control and compliance—through technologically enabled surveillance of their members—can undermine the very basis of the professional expertise their core processes may well rely on (Hayes, 2012; Schwenk & Cosier, 1980; Starbuck & Farjoun, 2005). In the example below, you might see how *panoptic* surveillance leads, in the words of its proponents, to a 'culture of trust and safety,' whereas for its detractors it leads to:

> ...a type of power that is applied to individuals in the form of continuous individual supervision, in the form of control, punishment, and compensation, and in the form of correction, that is, the modelling and transforming of individuals in terms of certain norms.
>
> (Foucault & Faubion, 2000, p. 70)

NEW HYDE PARK, NY – Once mainly an instrument to protect your belongings and family, cameras have expanded beyond homes and offices into an area where a mistake can mean the difference between life and death: operating rooms. Long Island Jewish (LIJ) Medical Center has installed cameras in all 24 of its operating rooms (ORs), which performed nearly 20,000 surgeries in 2013.

With the national average of approximately 40 wrong-site surgeries and about a dozen retained surgical objects left in patients every week, the new pilot program at LIJ strengthens patient safety by providing hospitals with real-time feedback in their ORs. LIJ and the North Shore-LIJ Health System's Forest Hill Hospital are the only hospitals in the country using remote video auditing (RVA) in a surgical setting.

RVA ensures that surgical teams take a 'timeout' before they begin a procedure. The team then goes through a patient safety checklist aimed at avoiding mistakes. Each OR is monitored remotely once every two minutes to determine the live status of the procedure, and ensure that surgical teams identify and evaluate key safety measures designed to prevent 'never events,' such as wrong-site surgeries and medical items inadvertently left in patients. The cameras also are used to alert hospital cleaning crews when a surgery is nearing completion, which helps to reduce the time it takes to prepare the OR for the next case. To reduce the risk of infections, the monitoring system also confirms whether ORs have been cleaned thoroughly and properly overnight. In a matter of weeks, patient safety measures at both hospitals improved to nearly perfect scores.

'Within weeks of the cameras' introduction into the ORs, the patient safety measures, sign-ins, time-outs, sign-outs, as well as terminal cleanings all improved to nearly 100 percent,' said Chantal Weinhold, executive director of LIJ. 'A culture of safety and trust is palpable among the surgical team.'

Additionally, all staff can see real-time OR status updates and performance feedback metrics on plasma screens throughout the OR and on smart-phone devices.

The program was designed and implemented by North Shore-LIJ's anesthesiology provider, North American Partners (NAPA) in partnership with Arrowsight, Inc., a developer and third-party provider of RVA services and software.

'At a time when health care reform plays a significant role in all that we do, it is important to engage the full spectrum of stakeholders to improve how safely and efficiently we deliver healthcare to our patients,' said John F. Di Capua, chair of anesthesiology for the North Shore-LIJ Health System and chief executive officer of North American Partners in Anesthesia (NAPA).

The introduction of video monitoring in ORs follows its ongoing, successful use in the medical and surgical intensive care units at North Shore University Hospital. In a 2011 study published in Clinical Infectious Diseases Medical Journal, NSUH demonstrated that the use of Arrowsight's third-party RVA system rapidly improved and sustained hand hygiene rates to nearly 90 percent in less than four weeks. 'The recognition and expansion of Arrowsight's RVA technology is a validater for us, showing firsthand what the RVA system has done to improve patient safety and efficiency at North Shore LIJ Health System, not just in the ICU's but now in the surgical department.'

One of the nation's largest health systems, North Shore-LIJ delivers world-class clinical care throughout the New York metropolitan area, pioneering research at The Feinstein Institute for Medical Research, a visionary approach to medical education highlighted by the Hofstra North Shore-LIJ School of Medicine, and healthcare coverage to individuals, families and businesses through the North Shore-LIJ CareConnect Insurance Co. Inc. North Shore-LIJ cares for people at every stage of life at 17 hospitals and more than 400 outpatient physician practices throughout the region. North Shore-LIJ's owned hospitals and long-term care facilities house more than 6,000 beds, employ more than 10,000 nurses and have affiliations with over 9,400 physicians. With a workforce of about 48,000, North Shore-LIJ is the largest private employer in New York State.

Founded in 1986, NAPA is the leading single specialty anesthesia management company in the United States. NAPA is comprised of the most respected clinical staff, providing thousands of patients with superior and attentive care. The company is known for partnering with hospitals and other healthcare facilities across the nation to provide anesthesia services and perioperative leadership that maximize operating room performance, enhance revenue, and demonstrate consistent patient and surgeon satisfaction ratings. Arrowsight, a Web-based Application Services Provider, is the leading developer of remote video auditing services and software. Arrowsight has helped improve practices, compliance and employee morale in safety-sensitive industries, such as food processing, food services, manufacturing and health care (NAPA, 2014).

That surveillance, particularly with an eye on achieving compliance, changes behavior is probably intuitive. But whether it is the kind of behavior change that was intended is much less clear. A typical assumption of any technological intervention, including one meant for surveillance, is that it represents the tweaking or manipulation of a single variable in somebody's work. First there was no surveillance, now there is. Nothing else has changed, except some measure of output (e.g., efficiency and productivity). This assumption is never correct, however. The introduction of new technology, particularly technology with the potential to watch and (implicitly) make moral judgments about somebody's work, introduces a raft of changes. Many of these changes are qualitative, not just quantitative.

And few of them are actually for the improvement of either qualitative or quantitative measures and indicators of work. Technological surveillance of work is known to negatively affect worker well-being, motivation, work culture, productivity, and creativity. Here are some of the changes documented by the research into this (e.g., Anteby & Chan, 2018; Arendt, 1967; Ball, 2010; Foucault, 1977; Galic et al., 2017; Lerner &Tetlock, 1999; Woods & Dekker, 2001):

- Self-censorship in what is said and done, more inactivity and less initiative to act.
- A sense of resignation and helplessness at being watched all the time—there is nothing, or little, you can do about it, except:
- The development of another type of creativity, aimed at the avoidance of surveillance. This can include finding niches (e.g., camera angles, routes, and encryptions) to avert surveillance. As probably every professional pilot, I quickly learned the exact location of the circuit breaker in a cockpit that disconnects the cockpit voice recorder.
- Less attention to the task, and more attention to how you will be held accountable for that task by the one who could be watching. This is known to lead to the maximization of one goal (a visible, measurable one) at the expense of others.
- Declines in the overall quality of work and increases in stress.
- Behavior changes that lead to more risk. For example, one phenomenon with vehicle monitoring systems has been that people stop driving to the conditions, and only drive to what the system allows. This may be a considerably higher (but still legal) speed than road or weather conditions really allow. The monitoring system is unsensitized to those conditions, and only knows the speed limit. This is the norm around which compliance is organized and thus the norm that drives behavior. As with most technological interventions, there is always a gap between the (mostly) quantitative advantages it promises to deliver, and the qualitative shifts in behavior and outcomes it actually generates.
- Self-fulfilling cycles of coercive surveillance, where surveillance initially leads to attempts to avert it (called 'worker invisibility practices'), which legitimates managerial insistence on more surveillance, and so on.

- The paradox that workers who are constantly seen and observed (remember the 'data doubles') actually feel largely unnoticed as individual human beings by their management.

Given these effects, it is not surprising that:

> ...excessive monitoring can sometimes produce the behaviours it was designed to prevent. If workers perceive surveillance practices as an intensification and extension of control, it is likely that they will try to subvert and manipulate the boundaries of when, where and how they are measured. Studies of call centres demonstrate that intense surveillance increases resistance, sabotage and non-compliance with management. Here, workers are extensively monitored not only in terms of their quantitative outputs, but also in terms of their qualitative manner on the phone, and their overall competence. They work their way around surveillance by manipulating measures by dialing through call lists, leaving lines open after the customer has hung up, pretending to talk on the phone, providing a minimal response to customer queries and misleading customers. Where call-centre managers are also under surveillance, they sometimes collude with workers to produce the desirable results. Incidentally, any resistance that has been observed in call centres so far has involved getting the better of monitoring (sometimes referred to as the application of 'tacit knowledge'), but not actively challenging, breaking, or sabotaging the overall practice.
>
> (Ball, 2010, pp. 93–94)

In a study of Transport Security Administration (TSA) workers, researchers were able to document resistance to what the workers interpreted as coercive surveillance, but which then served as motivation for managers to enact further surveillance, leading to ever-greater workplace surveillance as a self-fulfilling cycle (Anteby & Chan, 2018). Concerns about employee theft of passengers' belongings, as well as efficiency, effectiveness and productivity about the work done at security checkpoints, led to the installation of CCTV. As one officer commented:

> Oh, it's a ton of surveillance cameras. As a matter of fact, within the last three or four months, they have installed so many different cameras. I'm talking in one area you can have six or seven different cameras—all different angles. They want to see what you're doing sitting at this chair, they want to see what you're doing when you get on this computer, they want to see what you're doing when you're operating this machine. . . . You know what? It's weird because, as an employee, you kind of feel like we

should be watching passengers, passenger behavior, passenger activity. But instead, they watch employees.

(Anteby & Chan, 2018, p. 254)

The intention was, initially, to have a record of work so that false passengers' claims about leaving expensive belongings behind could be reviewed. But soon, managers started monitoring video feeds live, and began to correct behaviors, expressions, appearances or attitudes on the spot by remote communication. The only position where a TSA officer could 'speak and not get in trouble' (p. 255) was the one for document checking, which is in direct contact with passengers. Elsewhere, prolonged exchanges with passengers were seen as security problems. As a result of their surveillance, TSA officers routinely get reprimanded or receive letters of guidance and coaching, and so they developed a number of invisibility practices, such as extending scheduled breaks, frequent toilet visits, or disappearing in the hiatuses between body pat downs or manual bag checks and other work. They also sought opportunities to be sent out from their assigned checkpoint, and then wander the airport. The lost-and-found room was a favorite, because it could of course 'take forever' to look for (and maybe not even find) the item in question. As a result of this, the TSA has started collaborating with airport owners and operators to use additional CCTV footage from elsewhere. In turn TSA officers on such breaks or assignments are taking off their blue shirts, or putting something else over their uniform. So, this is to be continued: The conclusion of this cat-and-mouse behavior has not been written yet.

5

THE MICRO

AUDIT AND CASH IN

Microeconomic factors are related to the decisions of individuals and businesses about how prices are set; how money is made, saved, and distributed; and how 'success' is counted. The frame for these microeconomic decisions—the space of possibilities open to decision-makers, of the opportunities and constraints that operate on them—is of course co-determined by meso- and macroeconomic factors. That said, a number of processes and priorities can arise within organizations themselves that all help build and sustain bureaucratic clutter and compliance demands. In this chapter, we'll look at:

- Auditism
- Financialization and short-termism
- The monetization of bureaucracy.

Auditism

Auditing represents a systematic approach to assessing any property of a system for the purposes of, say, regulation or certification. To audit fairly, there is a need for measurable things—things that are standardized, objectified, and preferably quantifiable (Jensen & Winthereik, 2017). Rules standardize tasks; rules make work suitable for documentation and auditing (Hohnen & Hasle, 2011). Rules are a quick and easy basis for checking compliance (Hale & Borys, 2013). When an organization standardizes its tasks, they are documented and can be audited and compared with tasks in other organizations or industries. Standards also allow information to move easily between contexts, since tasks are separated from personnel and organizations from tasks, consistent with Weber's initial take on bureaucracy (Månson, 1996, p. 96). Auditing thus is part of:

> ... the more generalized accountability-based mechanisms of governance that dominate today. An example is the trend towards increased reliance on internal control and self-regulation, where companies are expected to have transparent standardized systems for control. For external auditors and authorities, it is primarily the systems that are subject to control and regulation... If workers perform tasks as the standards prescribe, they are compliant, at least from an accountability perspective, and this compliance is transparent to regulators and others without having to further investigate details of the local setting... [Yet] the rules, which are made to be applicable in several different settings, are more complex, more abstract, and less locally relevant than what is optimal for each setting... Standards are a means of making information mobile across contexts. Decisions and activities enter the systems of accountability by being performed and described according to standards. The bureaucratic methods of accountability depend upon activities and situations of each local context being translated into slots on the accountants' sheets.
>
> (Almklov, Rosness, & Storkersen, 2014, pp. 26–27)

For auditing to work at all, it needs to make work legible on its terms. Auditing relies on the kind of abstraction that offers a synoptic grasp of work and organization. This is a view that sweeps things together, abstracting and collating them and presenting them in one document. It does so by simplifying work, by linearizing the organization in which it happens, and by breaking it down into steps and putting them back together in the rational order of a checklist, an audit sheet, and a procedure. Auditing 'flattens' work and turns it into a monolingual, measurable representation. Auditing contains merely the flat, programmatic language of an organization, which is taught to inspectors, auditors, certifiers, or regulators, who can honestly claim that 'I don't know how to do your work, but my book says you're doing it wrong.' The nuances, messy details, and actual substance of work or organization no longer seem to matter:

> The quality management and auditing industry favour written procedures for these reasons of transparency, and hence create major incentives for companies to write weighty procedure manuals but tend then to be blind to the gap with reality which a paperwork-based system audit does not pick up.
>
> (Hale & Borys, 2013, p. 230)

The audit explosion was happening as I started my research work with the aviation regulator—which you might recall from the Preface. Power (1994, 1999) described how audits were becoming the 'natural solution' to most governance problems, without people ever asking whether other measures might not be better (Hohnen & Hasle, 2011). The audit explosion happened at the same time when deregulation and privatization were ever more tightly embraced:

> During the late 1980s and early 1990s, the word 'audit' began to be used ... with growing frequency in a wide variety of contexts. In addition to the regulation of private company accounting by financial audit, practices of environmental audit, value for money audit, management audit, forensic audit, data audit, intellectual property audit, medical audit, teaching audit, and technology audit emerged and, to varying degrees, acquired a degree of institutional stability and acceptance. Increasing numbers of individuals and organizations found themselves subject to new or more intensive accounting and audit requirements. In short, a growing population of 'auditees' began to experience a wave of formalized and detailed checking up on what they do.
>
> (Power, 1999, p. 12)

More internal rules and more internal bureaucracy often result. To understand how deregulation and privatization both help fuel the audit explosion, consider Power's explanation:

> First, there must be a relation of accountability, i.e., the requirement for one party (the agent) to give an account of his actions to another party (the principal). Second, the relation of accountability must be complex such that principals are distant from the actions of agents and are unable personally to verify them. On this view audit is a form of checking which is demanded when agents expose principals to 'moral hazards', because they may act against the principals' interests, and to 'information asymmetries', because they know more than the principals. Audit is a risk reduction practice which benefits the principal because it inhibits the value reducing actions by agents. Audit will be undertaken by principals up to the point where its marginal benefits equal its marginal cost. Interesting economic models have also been developed which demonstrate that, under certain conditions, agents will rationally demand auditing and will voluntarily contract to be checked.
>
> (1999, p. 15)

Auditing is yet another mechanism that changes relationships once characterized by trust. As privatization, deregulation, and self-control have dramatically increased the number of principals and agents (to use Power's language), the network of accountability relationships has become ever denser. Everybody would likely be, at one point or another, an auditor and an auditee. The transformation of accountability—by taking it to market, in which everything has been given a price—leads to a thirst for control, documentation, traceability, uncertainty reduction, shields from moral hazard, and liability management. Audits have successfully claimed to be able to fulfil these demands. Jensen and Winthereik (2017) confirmed Power's observations about how an audit society enters and spreads and multiplies itself internally in organizations. Audits not only bring with them new rules and compliance demands; they also change the very idea of knowledge—its creation, its acquisition, its use, and its leveraging. Auditing has become a way of thinking about an organization in and of itself, even if disconnected from the supposedly 'actual' organization, its core activities or the work and people in it. It has become an increasingly self-referential process, consistent mostly with itself and independent of the complex, dynamic world to which it purports to speak. Auditing unwittingly writes its own rules for the regulatory, inspection, or certification game, by which all stakeholders, or most of them, then have no choice but to play, independent of their beliefs or skepticism. The so-called audit loops, the researchers found, are:

> ...mutually shaping interactions between auditors and auditees that cross organizational barriers in multiple directions, both 'downstream' and 'upstream.'
>
> (p. 161)

It produces a condition we could call 'auditism.' Under auditism, auditing constructs the very environment it needs to be able to operate at all. The sheer act (or announcement) of auditing tends to make that environment more auditable, more legible—and less authentic to the organization and its actual workings, risks, and people. Practitioners will go to some length just to be auditable. And perhaps to get it over with. This is what it looks like from the perspective of the auditee:

> Most colleagues find audit exercises ludicrous but nevertheless go through the motions of complying with their imperatives lest the wrath of management be incurred. We see straight through the emperor's clothes, so to speak, but feel obliged to stifle our laughter and to hide our sense of ridicule when the emperor's minions approach us 'donkeys' with their managerial sticks and carrots. Repeated viewing of the emperor in his see-through clothing—transparency in the true sense of the word—leads to understandable cynicism towards the system that forces us to carry out the ridiculous chores of audit. A recurrent quip from colleagues is that we're forced, like circus animals, 'to jump through hoops.' The more circus tricks we perform, the more we demean ourselves. After all, the whole idea of forcing someone to carry out a pointless task is to demean that person.
>
> (Lorenz, 2012, p. 620)

And so, playacts are performed, at all levels, to pass the audit and gain corporate legitimacy. Lorenz points out that the effects on people's autonomy and sense of professionalism are corrosive. These literally are performances in the sociological as well as theatrical sense. Making an organization auditable according to, for instance, ISO 14001 has led to vast systems of bureaucratization to feed and support the performance. Together, they produce 'symbolic organizational behavior' that has the chief intentions of achieving a societally acceptable level of corporate legitimacy and passing audits (Vilchez, 2017). Interestingly, any failures of auditing, such as missing something that turns out to be critical in some problem or breakdown down the line, are not attributed to failures of auditing in principle, but as glitches in the efficiency and effectiveness of auditing. Instead, these failures simply call for more or 'better' auditing. Rather than contributing to transparency and democracy, Power (1999) concluded, auditing has become so portable, abstracted, self-referential, and insulated from actual practice that it produces reports full of coded, specialized, cautious expressions that are neither representative nor predictive.

Audit loops are perhaps the perfect achievement of bureaucratic accountability: a system of checks and verifications that has become consistent mostly with itself, and that has less and less to do with the way risk might be building up outside the administrative self-referential knowledge bubble. Turner studied this in the 1970s, ahead of the audit explosion. He referred to the 'incubation period' during which an organization's administratively constructed picture of the world and its hazards slowly drifts away from what actually matters on the frontline. Oversized safety management systems require attention, and as attention is a scarce resource, the systems might function as 'decoys' (Turner, 1978). The fish-farmers and seafarers discussed earlier all describe their safety management in terms of accountability, documentation, and audits—not in terms of practical goals, or difficult work, or risk, or safety. Yet, as has been emphasized in several studies, unpredicted risks may require an opposite approach to following rules, using practical experience and the ability to improvise (Hale et al., 2013).

Rosness (2004) foresaw that coordination of safety-critical tasks would need detailed industry standards on top of the governmental function-based regulations, making deregulation result in increased regulation. Independent of regulatory strategy, it is difficult to find the balance of freedom and control, for regulators and for company managers. The mechanisms found in the Norwegian studies display how deregulation can lead to overregulation when it interacts with other traditions and new market forces that govern how an organization demonstrates accountability. Organizational expectations of market doctrines, of bureaucracy, and of control of work can all turn simple regulations into very detailed, cumbersome procedures inside an organization—ever increasing the distance between how people think work is done, and how it is actually done. It is, as the Norwegians concluded, unlikely that this kind of regime will change without substantial (inter)national initiatives against beliefs in the superiority of market solutions for every societal problem.

Financialization and short-termism

Auditing has risen to such prominence in part because there is so much that organizations need to know and show. Compliance and documentation are thought to meet an auditor's or other stakeholder's expectations. One of the factors driving this need for knowing and showing is financialization. Financialization can explain, to a great extent, an organization's focus on the short term, and its preoccupation with various kinds of indicators, measures, indices, benchmarks, and standards. Financialization, put simply, refers to the increase in size and importance of a country's financial sector (brokers; financial institutions such as banks, investment companies, mortgage lenders, and insurance companies; and money markets and real estate firms) relative to its overall economy. In its wake comes a range of things we associate with rules and compliance. As (newly privatized or deregulated) organizations shift more of their operations, or hitch more of their fate, to financial markets, there is more to track and report than before. This is in large part so because things in a financialized economy can move very quickly. The fortunes of an organization, and those who lead it, can move equally quickly with it. Showing bad numbers is a bad idea. Hinting at a sense that risks are not under control could be a managerial *faux-pas*.

The financialized slice of the overall economy has grown considerably in the last few decades. The revenue for a large slice of the financial sector comes from investments, mortgages, and loans. In the 1950s, the financial sector may have accounted for less than 3% of a western country's economy. Today, financialization represents:

> ...the increasing role of financial motives, financial markets, financial actors and financial institutions in the operation of domestic and operational economies [which] has led to an accumulation of profits in the finance industry and a sharp rise in CEO and top management compensation. Shareholder value ideologies and other doctrines promoting the financial performance of the firm have excluded other stakeholders and

> undermined other productive investment. By 2002, 45 per cent of all profits made in the US economy were derived from the finance industry.
>
> (Styhre, 2014, p. 278)

Financialization is a key parallel to neoliberal governance. Financialization allows corporate entities to trade risk—to sell it for a price to those who are willing (or, in some cases, ignorant enough) to take it on. It also allows corporate actors to make money in its own right. Neoliberalism has helped separate finance from productive activity. Finance had long been expected to work in the service of productive activities in an economy. From the 1980s onward, it became increasingly liberated from onerous regulatory constraints and its societal service expectation. It could become, simply put, a market in itself. This market offered the possibility to pursue unprecedented speculative profits via purely financial operations—disconnected from the rest of the economy. Hyman Minsky, Washington University economist, was an explicit observer of what he called 'money manager capitalism.' Money manager capitalism, he found, was replacing corporate management, the kind of classical economic stewardship that oversees investments in industrial capital and enables actual productive activity. Even companies that had not been active on financial markets diverted their attention to these markets at the expense of their manufacturing base:

> The growing influence of money managers forced business leaders to become increasingly focused on quarterly profits and the stock-market value of their corporations—in other words, on shareholder value. It spurred many nonfinancial corporations to scale back costly and often aging manufacturing operations, engage in mergers and acquisitions at an unprecedented pace, and turn their attention to the sorts of borrowing, investing, and lending traditionally associated with financial firms … The experience of General Electric (GE) is emblematic of the corporate behavior that took root as money management emerged. When Jack Welch became the chief executive at GE in 1981, the firm was a premier US corporation—'as traditional as any large manufacturing firm in the country.' To boost the company's earnings and stock value, Welch sought to transform the company. In the first five years, he closed a dozen plants and sold off 190 subsidiaries, including the entire small-appliances division. He also spent $6.5 billion to acquire RCA (including its broadcasting subsidiary,

> NBC) and $1.7 billion to purchase the Kidder Peabody investment bank and Employers Reinsurance, a financial services firm. The strategy achieved Welch's aims and was widely imitated.
>
> (Whalen, 2017, pp. 3–4)

In financial markets, more means more. And more leads to more. By the early 2000s, fund managers had increasingly outgrown traditional portfolios of stocks and bonds, and helped create and supply an eager market with ever more serpentine financial instruments—securitized mortgages, credit card receivables, collaterized debt obligations, junk bonds, and more. A commitment to the stability and growth of an industrial sector, and by extension a country's economy, was gradually replaced by short-term interests in using funds to make money with money:

> These funds do not buy and hold common stocks for long-term increases in dividend income: the annualized rate of return from catching a short-run swing in interest rates or stock prices can easily dominate interest or dividend income.
>
> (Minsky, 1990 as quoted in: Whalen, 2017, p. 3)

The growth of these markets, and the sophistication of products on them, drove concomitant developments in insurance and program trading. This created additional instruments, which once again established additional markets, which in turn offered more opportunities again for generating financial revenue with financial activity alone. As said, more is more. Like GE, other large companies became little more than highly leveraged hedge funds (J. Gray, 2003). By 2020, the stock market, with an overrepresentation of financial stocks, had little connection to the 'real' economy any longer: what happened on Wall Street had little to do with what was happening on Main Street. Joblessness could go up to unprecedented levels, and productivity could go down in a mass of self-imposed self-regulation rules. Yet stock prices could keep climbing—all at the same time. If financialization has produced an overriding concern beyond making money with money, or making others lose it on your behalf (by selling them your risks), it is the enhancement of 'shareholder value,' a relatively recent term (Hardie, 2008). This prioritizes return on equity and the concomitant rise of:

> ... a different and more carnivorous type of capitalism ... inextricably linked to the willingness, and most importantly the ability, of shareholders to demand that they, as the owners of the company, should see their interests predominate over those of other stakeholders ... it should be recognized that this can cover a wide range of policies [and] demand a reduced influence for the interests of stakeholders such as labour.
>
> (p. 2)

In the words of Albert (1993):

> The golden rule among investors in the new American model of capitalism is that of grabbing the quickest and fattest profit. Taken to its logical extreme, the practice of never refusing a bargain or a higher bid leads to shareholder disloyalty, and this in turn constitutes a major handicap for businesses, who benefit most from a stable, secure capital base. ... Buying a company, for the American capitalist, is ultimately no different from buying a property or a painting. It is therefore perfectly logical for the shareholder-kings to do as they please with the company they have just purchased, breaking it up and selling off the segments which do not interest them. Its employees and managers are treated in the same way as its capital; all are forms of disposable merchandise...If the *Wall street Journal* had a lonely-hearts section for businesses, the messages would read 'Company seeks mature owner' and 'Attractive firm seeks faithful shareholders.' The crowning achievement of contemporary American capitalism is, bizarrely, to have done away with genuine ownership by destroying the logic of shareholder stability.
>
> (pp. 74–76)

Shareholder value is more important than Albert's long-term 'shareholder stability.' The latter, which Albert calls 'genuine ownership,' brings in a whole slew of commitments—to the people who work to earn the firm's money, to the long term, to the community in which the company operates, to the environment around it, to the governance of the country or countries in which it located. The former shrinks decision—and ethical—horizons down to a quarter, or down to a month. With results to be reported quarterly, if not more often, 'money managers certainly felt the pressure of the near term,' Whalen observed (2017, p. 3). A lot of things can impact share price, and thereby shareholder value, but few of them as quickly and decisively as uncontrolled corporate, financial, regulatory, and other risks (Saines et al., 2014). In what Hardie saw as a loss of corporate autonomy, managers and boards became increasingly pressurized to institutionalize risk controls and gather and report the results. Because if they don't, then the possible consequences for shareholder value could be grave. Consider the shrinking tolerance in society for hurting or killing people on the job, and its legal, production disruption and financial consequences for market value. Investors (rather than genuine owners, to speak with Albert) are fickle and their money can flow as quickly as their shifting preferences. The high liquidity of capital markets means that investments can swiftly flow to higher-return or lower-risk organizations. Financialization comes with investments that are tied to short-term company risk and reputation, which can fluctuate per day.

A more subtle illustration of how financial markets are intertwined with self-regulation is the desire for corporate legitimacy, to be demonstrated through displays of accountability (as also explained by Hohnen and Hasle, 2011). This feeds a concern with written documentation and logs—a concern with what auditors will accept or not, even if it is over and above government regulations. Mendeloff (1981, p. 51) already saw how companies accept and follow regulations in order to show 'social responsibility, fear of liability, a desire for competitive advantage.' The desire for such legitimacy doesn't disappear when governments retreat from regulating an industry. It would be more accurate to say that it simply changes hands. In the Norwegian fish farms, for instance, companies relied on a 'good' reputation to stay licensed so that they were allowed (by societal assent as much as government approval) to grow in size (Osmundsen & Olsen, 2017). The need to demonstrate compliance leads, as Power also found in the UK, to audits that are tailored toward an individual auditor or particular stakeholder in the market.

And so, recording and reporting to show risk control and reduction is a key to assuring shareholder value and achieving corporate legitimacy. It leads to more internal compliance demands. Because to do it all, repeatedly and reliably, you need more rules, more control of people's activities, more compliance checking, and more bureaucracy. Tracking, measuring, tracing, analyzing, recording, plotting, archiving, and reporting have expanded into the deepest capillaries of an organization—geared toward gaining and keeping that corporate legitimacy. Efforts at assuring such legitimacy have a 'ratchet effect.' Companies do (or feel they need to do) things like the list below (Provan, Woods, Dekker, & Rae, 2020). Like a ratchet, they take little effort (and almost no evidence for their need) to introduce. But changing or getting rid of them is much harder, because once they're in place, it is almost impossible to convince stakeholders that they are useless (Rae et al., 2018):

- Demonstrate that risks are managed well by means of audits.
- Show programs of work and activity to reflect their commitment to health and safety.
- Respond to incidents and risks in a swift and decisive way.

Every day, every week, every month, or quarter, managers have to ask themselves: how will this look to the markets, the financial markets? What are our profit indices, our performance standards, our market participant receipt amounts, our achievement numbers, our risk profiles, our rule- and procedural- and checklist compliance rates? Financialization has created an entirely new market for accountability – with one indicator at the end of it all: shareholder value. For that is how, and where, they are literally held accountable. Such accountability, of course, needs pathways and vehicles to travel through the innards of an organization. And how is that typically done? How do we know we can trust whether someone is living up to his or her compliance expectations? Interestingly, a popular way to answer this question is to turn to the market itself, which in turn has seen or even created new opportunities for the monetization of compliance and bureaucracy.

The monetization of bureaucracy

In a sense, market-driven policies have delivered spectacularly. Entirely new markets have been set up, opened up, and allowed people to make money. Private actors have the freedom to enter these markets and get in on the trade going on there. The thing is, though, that these new markets trade in bureaucracy. Bureaucratic 'solutions' are the commodity. This is, of course, how capitalism is supposed to work: create a need, or create a fear. Then hawk the product that is designed to fill that need or allay that fear. It constitutes a bureaucratization economy, or, to stay with the title of the book, 'compliance capitalism.' With newly privatized and deregulated industries having to demonstrate to their clients, contractors, and remaining regulators that they have the systems and processes in place to document and adequately manage their risks, backed up by a potentially punitive system of liability claims or legal charges, a lucrative market has opened up for purveyors of all kinds of management systems. And it has kept growing. Just look at the market for safety management systems (Hasle & Zwetsloot, 2011; Townsend, 2013):

- In 2006 there were 26,222 safety companies registered worldwide.
- By 2009, only three years later, there were 56,251.
- In Australia, there were 7,600 registered safety professionals in 1995.
- By 2009 there were 15,000.
- In 2014 that number had doubled again, to 30,400.

By the time a commitment to privatization and deregulation had pervaded most western governments, the so-called *Swiss cheese model* had just been born (Reason, 1990). Safety Management Systems (SMS) were becoming the dominant method of safety assessment, auditing, and regulation. The Swiss cheese model suggests, among other things, that a stronger line-up of defenses and control over the holes showing up in them means better risk management. As with Heinrich's 1931 domino model (Heinrich, Petersen, & Roos, 1980), better barriers mean that accident trajectories are halted before they can cause real trouble. Now these theoretical insights could get translated into a better hierarchical or bureaucratic ordering and documentation of organization and work. In the mid-1990s, this notion could be seen practically in the proliferation of safety management systems, auditing systems, or loss prevention systems across industries. Their stated goal could easily have been to make sure layers of defense line up well, and to patch the holes in them (i.e., at least, what you might read into the function of a safety management system) (Hasle & Zwetsloot, 2011). What it helped legitimate was the creation of additional internal bureaucracy. It was a bureaucracy with a slew of external stakeholders orbiting around it, ready to supply services to feed and grow their stake in an insatiable, market-driven bureaucracy. As Hasle and Zwetsloot concluded:

> ...critics have used harsh words to describe management systems, such as 'scam', 'fraud', 'bureaucracy' and 'paper tigers' and pointed out that workers lose influence. Other issues are their usefulness and cost for small and medium enterprises, and their relevance in the 'changing world of work', where production is increasingly outsourced, and risk can be easily shifted to partners in the supply chain, or to contingency workers. The certification regimes associated with [safety management] systems have also been criticized, e.g., for increasing the cost to businesses and for becoming an aim in themselves.
>
> (2011, p. 961)

Privatization and deregulation created free markets for contractors, consultants, and subcontractors to not only pick up a lot of the work, but also to actually create new markets for even more work. These market places both demand and produce mechanisms of bureaucratic accountability, and have less time or opportunity for trusting professional judgment.

Eat your own tail

Contracting work out is another market-driven and market-enabled trend that has all but become institutionalized over the last few decades in almost all industries and many governments (from local to federal). Contracts specify the relationships that enable and govern the exchange, but also demand bureaucratic accountability through oversight and additional administrative structures. These need measures to compare, reward and decide on, as well as to allow procurement, selection, accounting, and auditing. But the market itself will grow the means to handle all this extra work. Open an activity up for the market, and a whole range of actors may come rushing in, wanting to play in that market. As Kuttner observes in the case of the United States:

> ...the US has become a middleman economy. Private firms make a fortune in excess charges on student loans. Financial engineers extract needless charges on consumer credit and mortgages. Parasitic middlemen attached to the health-industrial complex extract fees for designing systems that

> handle billing, utilization review, pharmacy benefit management, electronic records, and a great deal more—raising costs to patients and making professional practice less fulfilling for doctors.
>
> (2018, p. 301)

As you've seen earlier under the section on deprofessionalization, trust, professional and technical accountability can get supplanted by bureaucratic accountability and a swelling non-technical staff to govern the contracting bureaucracy. Managing, monitoring, and controlling operations across an organizational network of contractors and subcontractors tends to be more complex than doing it all in-house, and therefore bureaucratic accountability becomes the plausible means of trying to do so. The need for bureaucracy then is in the nature of contracting. Contracts between principals and agents in the market are needed to specify how their exchanges get enabled, governed, and enforced. Contracts require drafting, creating, legal certification, follow-up, and bureaucratic accountability through oversight and administrative structures and procedures. Managing, monitoring, and controlling operations across an organizational network of contractors and subcontractors demand a bureaucracy that can institute measures to compare, reward, and decide on contracts, and then set out to monitor and patrol their execution. Bureaucracies create the procedures and processes that allow procurement, selection, accounting, and auditing of contractors. This creates considerable work, perhaps eroding an organization's willingness or ability to participate in tendering or procurement at all. For example:

> ...contracting by government or other larger organizations now requires completed pre-tender/supplier health and safety questionnaires...of varying or increasing complexity and all requiring different information, [and the increased use of a] third party to assess a supplier's suitability to be included on the approved list, [as well as] an assessment fee and annual membership fee.
>
> (Simmons, 2012, p. 20)

A market place has a way of automatically creating more bureaucracy. Because everything has been given a price, or needs to be given a price, everything has to be accounted for. The more parties there are in the free market, the more complicated (and expensive) this accounting can get, as is the experience of the healthcare market in the United States:

> Payment structures can vary...: Each payer has its own set of rules and regulations with different levels of complexity. For example, there is variation in practice requirements (e.g., credentialing); variation in the conditions, tests, and treatments that are covered and the associated coding rules (i.e., Current Procedural Terminology and the International Classification of Diseases, Tenth Revision); variation in the payment-related incentives and penalties employed; and variation in the quality measures required to be reported (Carayon & Cassel, 2019, p. 172)... Payers often require clinicians to obtain prior authorization for medications, other forms of treatment, diagnostic procedures, and referrals. The intent of prior authorization is to deter patients from getting unnecessary medical care and to direct prescribers to less costly treatment options where appropriate (and thus reduce the cost of care); however, these requirements can also create hassles for patients and add to clinicians' burden.
>
> (p. 181)

In a marketplace that only has its own invisible hand, and no strong guiding arm of government, little can be left to trust. Everything needs to be documented and supplied as a basis for the contract between the parties in the market, even if government itself happens to be one of those parties. The strong presence of a market full of newly minted experts, legal advisors, and consultants has been noted (Mintzberg, 2004). As commented by a cargo ship captain in Almklov et al.'s (2014) study:

> Consultant companies have never earned as well... I know many competent people in [this consultant company], but everything is going on paper to be documentable. I have written deviations and commented the formulations on the deviations, and they are sent back and forward. It's silly.
>
> (p. 27)

And it can set up a dilemma for all stakeholders:

> Safety specialists are often agents in relationships characterized by principal-agent dilemmas: The agents hired to help a company with the safety systems do not necessarily have the exact same interests as their principal. We have suggested that at least in some cases, it can be in the interest of the hired

> safety specialists (the agent) to work with more standardized systems and systems that require less local adaptation.
>
> (Almklov's 2014, p. 33)

New public management promised, and has indeed in many countries and industries delivered, free markets. These are 'places' where goods and services could be traded, bought, and sold (like off-the-shelf safety management systems and the advice that goes with them) without much interference from above or outside, where people were free to set up shop, become an entrepreneur, and participate in the market without anybody bothering them in the execution of their free trade. It has, however, created a market whose incentives—for liability fear-mongering, for exclusive claims on knowledge and products that can offer regulatory assurance, for vastly overselling protective equipment, procedures, checklists—have become so perverse that the market itself is now the main engine behind overregulation, bureaucratization, and increased compliance pressure. A larger compliance burden is a good thing, as vast amounts of money can be made off of it. It's neoliberalism chasing, and feeding off, its own tail.

6

HOW COULD GOVERNMENTS HAVE MISSED THIS?

From the 1980s onward, with a considerable acceleration over the last 20 years, governments in many countries have made efforts not only to deregulate, but also to track the success of their efforts at doing so. The growth of cultures of internal compliance is a consequence that runs directly counter to the original intentions of deregulation and privatization. But it is one that privatization- and deregulation-oriented governments have failed to see, mostly because it has happened under their measurement radars. This chapter dives into why and how this is the case. We take a brief step back into history to understand some of the legitimate reasons for bureaucratization, the origins of 'red tape,' and governments' growing desire—in the last few decades—to quantify the compliance burden it imposes. In the process, we learn little to nothing more about how privatization and deregulation lead to more internal rules and compliance demands, because this is not what governments measure. What we do learn is that they probably wouldn't know *how* to measure it either, even if they wanted to. As you'll see, getting any sense of compliance pressure or overregulation is marred by complexity and ambiguity. There is merit in the efforts of governments and researchers, however, because they do give us a starting point for understanding why free markets have led to the experience by many of being so unfree in their employment and work.

The balance of bureaucracy

The expansion of bureaucracy has fascinated researchers and frustrated citizens and entrepreneurs for the longest time. Concern about bureaucracy getting in the way of people despite its benign, rationalizing intentions dates back to the time of post-World War II (WWII). Lots had to be rebuilt, channeled, and managed; people needed houses, jobs, factories, offices, transportation, healthcare, and schools (Dickson, 1968). And governments stepped in. Between the end of the war, up to the 1970s, governments and economists believed that capitalism could only work with strong intervention and state regulation.[1] Political-economic arrangements during the first decades after WWII were aimed at sharing the gains of economic expansion and at spreading, preventing, and compensating risk (e.g., workplace injuries and job loss). Governments chose emancipatory, reformist, redistributive strategies—in part to tame the 'political passions' that had helped ignite communism and fascism. For this, they needed government bureaucracies (Braedley & Luxton, 2010). The contours of two perspectives on this came into view early on (Eisenstadt, 1959):

> The first point of view defines bureaucracy mainly as a tool, or a mechanism created for the successful and efficient implementation of a certain goal or goals. Bureaucracy is seen as an epitome of rationality and of efficient implementation of goals and provision of services. The second point of view sees bureaucracy mainly as an instrument of power, of exercising control over people and over different spheres of life, and of continuous expansion of such power either in the interests of the bureaucracy itself or in the interests of some (often sinister) masters. This point of view tends mainly to stress the process of bureaucratization, i.e., the extension of the power of a bureaucratic organization over many areas beyond its initial purpose, the growing internal formalization within the bureaucracy, the regimentation

> of these areas by the bureaucracy, and in general a strong emphasis by the bureaucracy on the extension of its power.
>
> (p. 303)

The term 'red tape' dates back to the early 16th century, to the Spanish administration of Charles V, King of Spain and Holy Roman Emperor. Ironically, he started to use red ribbons in an effort to modernize the administration of his vast empire and introduce some key efficiencies. The red ribbons were a kind of prequel to today's sticky note or colored folders. Charles' administration started using red ribbons to bind the most important administrative dossiers that required immediate attention and discussion by his Council of State. This way everybody was able to see and separate them from issues that could wait, or which could be treated by ordinary administrative processes. The latter were bound by ordinary string. Other European monarchs heard about it and loved the idea. Its use multiplied throughout the 17th and 18th centuries. By the 19th century, the English were using it so much that Charles Dickens had his David Copperfield character complain about it. By this time the term had flipped its meaning. Instead of separating out the things that actually mattered, red tape now stood for rules, procedures, documents, and processes that got in the way of doing the things that mattered.

In 1977, the Brookings Institution in Washington published a searching yet sympathetic *cri-de-coeur*, with a litany of complaints about government 'red tape.' But it was balanced with a consideration of what such tape was possibly good for (Kaufman, 1977).The question that the author Kaufman wanted to answer was how it could be possible that something persisted and even kept growing throughout society even though it was so universally abhorred. Even though he didn't provide an exact definition for 'red tape' (for reasons of complexity that should soon become clear), he noted that:

> [w]hen people rail against red tape, they mean that they are subjected to too many constraints, that many of the constraints seem pointless, and that agencies seem to take forever to act.
>
> (pp. 4–5)

The bureaucratic procedures imposed on people and industries, he found, were messy; they took too long, lacked local knowledge, were easily out of date, often made insane demands, increased costs, and slowed progress. Red tape, in short, was a burden on people, on industries, and on society. And many times, it delivered no measurable positive outcome. Kaufman was able, however, to mirror the dismal landscape of red tape against its other side. A few years before the election of Reagan (together with the United Kingdom [UK] Prime Minister Thatcher, one of the first post-war leaders to actively and comprehensively promote free markets and deregulation), Kaufman warned his readers not to forget about that other side. Red tape, he argued—however inefficiently it is rolled out and applied—is how government protects us from tainted food, from shoddy products, from disintegrating airplanes, exploding cars or trains running off the tracks, and from unfair, exploitative, dangerous labor practices. It guarantees a social safety net for the elderly, the disabled, children, veterans, and victims of natural disasters. It offers protection against theft and fraud, assures representative democracy and due process of law, keeps government public, and helps uphold honesty and equity. One person's red tape, in other words, is another person's protection. Or, paraphrasing Kaufman, one man's red tape is another's treasured safeguard.

As a result of his balanced views, Kaufman didn't come with the kinds of radical proposals that would become the norm in the United States and the UK only a few years later. In other words, he offered no early comfort to those looking to build arguments for deregulation or privatization. Kaufman thought that broad-scale reduction or devolution of government responsibilities would be unwise or impractical. Smaller government advocates always had strong support, particularly in the United States. But Kaufman told them that red tape doesn't come from malevolent or incompetent bureaucrats. Instead, it arises from two compelling and interrelated reasons:

- To ensure that government processes are representative and accountable.
- To meet the demands, often fragmented, always highly diverse, and sometimes conflicting, of citizens and interest groups.

In other words, there is not really a choice but to accept red tape. For all its ills, it is inevitably connected to and co-produced by the society that both calls for it and despises it. Bozeman, too, reflected on this duality. In 1993, he suggested that the origins of red tape could be described as an administrative 'tragedy of the commons.' Kaufman would probably have agreed. As he put it:

> Every restraint and requirement originate in somebody's demand for it. Of course, each person does not will them all; on the contrary, even the most broadly based interest groups are concerned with only a relatively small band of the full spectrum of government activities… But there are so many of us, and such a diversity of interests among us, that modest individual demands result in great stacks of official paper and bewildering procedural mazes.
>
> (p. 29)

This is why there is so much red tape: the sheer number of specialized demands for government action, intervention, regulation, and protection barely leaves another option. Red tape may be the inevitable by-product of protecting the way things are done and run in a country. Kaufman explains, 'Had we more trust in … our public officers, we would feel less impelled to limit discretion by means of minutely detailed directions and prescriptions' (1977, pp. 58–59). He points out that much red tape could be avoided were we willing to reduce the checks and safeguards that we impose on government employees; we could get less red tape, at least theoretically. But Kaufman didn't believe in this option. If we'd do away with red tape, 'we would be appalled by the resurgence of the evils and follies it currently prevents' (ibid).

Government, he found, basically could not be shrunk or withdrawn from the protective and regulatory functions and powers it was endowed with, without losing the essence of what it was to be a transparent democracy. Indeed, it would be a mistake to see red tape or paperwork as a residual waste product which could be easily separated from what we actually want of government. The messiness and misguidedness that were featured in the horrendous examples and the discontent they generated formed the inevitable by-product of attempts to make government work for everybody in a huge, diverse democracy. So, he put his faith in existing political and administrative processes to continue to peck away at the red tape problem, realistically acknowledging that it could at best be contained, never eliminated.

For some, the red-tape-versus-protection chickens came home to roost in 2017, when a fire broke out in London in the 24-storey Grenfell Tower block of flats in North Kensington. It was started by a malfunctioning fridge-freezer on the fourth floor, quickly spreading to the building's exterior and its other floors. It turned out that the building's cladding, together with its external insulation and the air gap in-between, created a smoke stack effect that kept sucking the fire and fanning its flames. The worst residential fire in the UK since the Second World War, it burned for 60 hours, causing 72 deaths and injuring another 70 people. Kaufman would have been interested to learn that in the years prior, the Conservative-Liberal Democrat government ran a Red Tape challenge that intended to reduce the 21,000 statutory rules and regulations in force at the time. By the end of the 3-year initiative, 2,400 regulations had been scrapped, more than 10% of the total. One change as a result of this initiative was that businesses with good inspection records could get their fire safety inspections reduced from 6 hours to 45 minutes, so that the business' managers could get on with their job and focus on what mattered. This reduction was highlighted following the fire, with some suggesting that the extent of fire spread would have been limited if the reduction hadn't occurred.

The idea that 'red tape' is an objective term, then, isn't sustainable. Kaufman said as much in 1977, and the example of Grenfell 40 years later might suggest he was right. The creation of rule-based bureaucracies and our attempts to reduce uncertainties and control risks remain an indelible part of how we enact our values in our societies. That, however, doesn't mean that people (or governments) are taking it lying down. The trend since the 1970s has been to express concerns about rising bureaucracies and rule-based orders. There has been a growth in the desire and commitment to measure the impact of new and existing rules, to quantify the cost, and ultimately to reduce the compliance burden—most decisively through deregulation. None of these efforts have proved simple.

The cost of compliance

It's nice if we all agree that there *seem* to be more rules than ever before, and that none of us like it very much. But how can we make that case more formally? The problem starts and ends, perhaps tediously, with measurement. At the front end you have to measure the number of rules that are made. Are there more now? How can you answer that question if you can't measure the number of rules made? And there is another problem: how do you decide what is 'a rule'? Indeed, what is actually a measurable rule, so you can say, now we have one additional rule when another one shows up? And that's not all. At the back end, you have to decide how to measure the cost of complying with that rule. If you think the former is tricky, try the latter.

Counting the rules

The problem of knowing whether you actually have got an additional rule (let alone counting the cost of that rule) was flagged by Bozeman (1993). He set out to build a 'theory of red tape.' This is the kind of a first step if you want to start measuring the amount of red tape. If you don't have a definition, you don't know what you're measuring to begin with. Bozeman found that:

> ...one major flaw in most concepts of red tape is that the concept is too encompassing. Some authors make no distinction between formalization and red tape. Some take the view that most red tape is simply extensive rules and regulations. Such a concept of red tape leads us inexorably to unsatisfactory and ultimately ambiguous notions... (p. 279). [An] empirical question then is, Under what circumstances are extensive rules and procedures red tape and under what circumstances are they actually 'white tape,' providing benefits along with the delays and frustrations[?].
>
> (p. 275)

He didn't really answer the question, but suggested that there were at least three kinds of 'red tape':

- Organizational red tape: rules, regulations, and procedures that remain in force and entail a compliance burden for the organization but have no efficacy for the rules' functional object.
- Stakeholders red tape: organizational rules, regulations, and procedures that remain in force and entail a compliance burden, but serve no object valued by a given stakeholder group.
- Multidimensional red tape: rules, regulations, and procedures that remain in force and entail a compliance burden for designated stakeholders but whose contribution to stakeholders' objectives or values is less than the compliance and implementation resources expended on the rule.

But even with a distinction like that, the problem of 'counting rules' isn't easily solved.

Because what is a rule that you can 'measure,' and then say: 'look, we have an additional rule that we need to follow!'? This rule creates 'red tape' for us! Bozeman defined a 'Rule Sum': the total number of written rules, procedures and regulations in force for an organization (1993, p. 280). But this turns out to be far from simple. Take a piece of legislation that requires company directors (that is, the board of a company) to ensure appropriate controls for safety risks are in place. Is that a rule? Of course, that is a rule. But what happens with that 'rule'? The board tells the chief executive officer, or other relevant officers of the company, to start doing something about this new 'rule', because that's their job. So, they do. They delegate this down, probably to general managers. General managers may look to their colleague in human resources, or workforce, or safety, and ask, 'what do we need to do internally so that the board can live up to this legislative requirement?' (They probably wouldn't even ask it that way.) The general manager for safety then likely asks her or his people to (1) check if these things are already in the company's safety management system. (2) If not, then they will have to add something. Is that a new rule? Probably, but does that then nullify you counting the first one, given to the company's board? Because you can't very well count the same rule twice, even if it is written and directed at different audiences. If something is added to the safety management system, it could be something like 'supervisors are required to assure that appropriate risk controls are in place…' If indeed it is already going to be that detailed in that document. But it doesn't stop there. You probably get the picture. Eventually, this thing then winds its way down to the driver of one of the company's commercial vehicles, who has been notified (by means typical for that company) of a new rule that says that vehicle wheels have to be chocked on both sides upon parking. So, what does that new rule do to the other ones? Should we count all of them, because they all leave a strong residue of compliance pressure with the level, group, department, team. And how do you measure the cost that this winding, filtering, percolating rule-making exacts on all of these parts of the organization? Pages of documents produced? Hours of meetings spent? Minutes of workers chocking their truck wheels on both sides even when they are parked on a hill? Nights lost in sleepless anxiety by board members? You might begin to see here that counting may not really be the way to go if you want to learn more about this.

It turns out that even the passing of laws (bills that become acts of congress or parliament) is also a lousy indicator. Laws turn into delegated legislation, which the English call 'statutory instruments.' Delegated legislation confers powers on ministries to turn the law into more detailed orders, rules, or regulations.[2] Versions of this conversion process happen traceably in all democracies. For various reasons, Anglo countries actually don't pass that many laws as compared to, say, Scandinavian or Germanic ones. In the

United States, an important reason is the federated nature of the country; states themselves are responsible for passing the majority of laws. In the UK, a rich tradition of common law and jurisprudence governs a lot of its civil code instead of laws.

What matters here, however, is the ratio between passed laws and delegated legislation. It is the latter, after all, that turns into the kinds of things that filter down into people's lives and companies as experienced overregulation. In 2007, the UK parliament passed fewer than 100 laws, Austria (also a federation) passed about 100, whereas the Netherlands passed more than 300, and Finland passed over 650 laws (De Jong & Zijlstra, 2009). But as the country that produced the fewest laws (a neoliberal dream scenario), the UK actually produced the *largest* volume of delegated legislation. For every law passed, the UK generated between 15 and 40 statutory instruments (which then turned into even far more rules and regulations). The Finns did it with just two for every law passed. Even the Austrians, who didn't pass a lot of laws either, contented themselves with only about four pieces of delegated legislation per law passed.

Don't count the rules, count the cost

Governments, however, were never so much interested in counting the rules that their own rulemaking or legislation led to, but rather what it all *cost* for the national economy. The 1977 report of the US Commission of Federal Paperwork, for instance, came with a figure. The cost of compliance, as embodied by government paperwork, it concluded, was $100 billion annually for the whole of the United States. Yet that was only federal, not state or even lower levels of government. Blaming faulty organization, poor management and unnecessary procedural obstacles, mission creep and the constantly growing of scope and reach of the federal government bureaucracy, the commission offered 770 recommendations. These, it believed, could reduce the paperwork burden by 10%.

The UK has also long been concerned with the cost of compliance. Various commissions have tried to quantify the cost of legislation and the administrative burdens these create for society. According to the 2005 Hampton review, for example, the costs of compliance could be split into two types (p. 11):

- *Policy cost* is the cost inherent in meeting the aims of a regulation. This could be a direct cash cost, such as installing a new waste incinerator prescribed by legislation, or it could come indirectly, for instance, through changes to a factory in order to meet new health and safety regulations.
- *Administrative costs* are those costs that are incurred in gathering information about a business, or checking on a business's compliance. So, for instance, filling in a form is an administrative cost, as is showing an inspector around a site.

The Hampton review was triggered by rising discontent in the complexity, confusion, and density of regulations. It defined (or tried to define) the cost of compliance like this:

> The administrative burden of regulation is the cost in time or money of regulators' inspection and enforcement activities. The review has considered the burden imposed by licensing, form filling, inspections, and enforcement activity including prosecutions. It has also looked at how the structure of the UK's regulatory system affects the ability of regulators to minimise administrative burdens when interacting with, and encouraging compliance from businesses.
>
> (Hampton, 2005, p. 9)

Hampton recommended that the government substantially reduce the number of regulatory bodies with which business had to deal. Consolidation of regulators was thought to be one route forward, also because 'smaller regulators which undertake fewer inspections also appear to have higher inspection costs' (p. 13). A couple of simple sums laid out the case persuasively:

> The review believes that some of the problems identified above are rooted in, or exacerbated by, the complicated structure of regulation in the UK. Regulatory inspection and enforcement are divided between 63 national regulators, 203 trading standards offices and 408 environmental health offices in 468 local authorities. When the Department of Trade and Industry coordinated a Government-wide list of priority areas for trading standards departments, it resulted in a list of 59 issues, all of which were identified as top priorities.
>
> (Hampton, 2005, p. 6)

If its recommendations were to be followed, the Hampton review promised that the need for inspections would be reduced by up to a third (around one million fewer inspections carried out per year across the country), and reduce the number of forms regulators send out by about 25%. It foresaw, unsurprisingly, how its proposals had the potential to significantly reduce the direct cost of regulation to Government as well as regulated industries. The Hampton review never actually spoke of deregulation. Its analysis, however, and its conclusions and recommendations, probably leave little doubt. Deregulation was surely a way to reduce the cost of compliance. But how could governments be sure?

Deregulation and measuring reductions in the cost of compliance

Governments are trying to measure (and, since a few years, celebrating) their success at quantitative rule reductions. The European Union recently embraced the numeric target of 25% deregulation—the measurement and tracking of which of course entails a new heap of bureaucratic processes, administrative procedures, and indeed additional government rules. It has a running competition that offers awards for the 'best idea for red tape reduction,' aiming to identify innovative suggestions for reducing unnecessary bureaucracy stemming from European law. In 2008, the European Commission even held a conference entitled 'Cutting Red Tape for Europe,' which had the goal to reduce red tape and overbearing bureaucracy in order to help business people and entrepreneurs improve their competitiveness. The United States has a government department dedicated to this very task: the Office of Information and Regulatory Affairs, a creation of the Reagan administration. It itself operates by a slew of rules, bureaucratic procedures, and impositions on other parties to get what it needs to do its job. It can tell us that US businesses are known to be supposed to comply with 165,000 pages of regulations covering all kinds of areas, some of them undoubtedly related to the requirements of the Office of Information and Regulatory Affairs.

Pioneers of a numeric deregulation target were the Dutch, who have been shooting for a 25% reduction for years. As the UK Better Regulation Task Force looked on from the other side of the North Sea (Arculus, Graham, & Rowlatt, 2005), it saw their neighbors act on a realization from the early

1990s. The Netherlands, an international economy focused on trade, had recognized that it was critical for its regulatory climate to not get in the way of international competitiveness or undermine the prosperity of its citizens. Wholesale removal of regulation, like what was done in Anglo countries, would have been more controversial politically in the Netherlands. Deregulation was perceived by some parts of the Dutch political spectrum as removing necessary safeguards against various risks. So instead, in the mid-1990s, the Dutch started to focus on reducing the administrative burden in order to improve the quality of government and reducing unnecessary regulatory costs. Their approach took aim at the bureaucracy that had been put in place to implement regulations, with a couple of things in it that were hoped to drive its success:

- Measuring the administrative burden: every government department had to use the same Standard Cost Model (see below) to measure the administrative burden which was imposed on business through its regulatory activities. This measurement included all the administrative obligations imposed by central government departments and regulatory agencies under both national and European legislation.
- Commitment to a target: Dutch ministers agreed that one of the priorities for their term in office was to reduce the administrative burden across the whole of government regulation and they set a reduction target.

The point was not to question the policy objectives of the regulations themselves. Instead, the government wanted to ensure that the way the policies got implemented with a minimum of regulatory bureaucracy swirling around it. At first, between 1994 and 1998, the government of the Netherlands set itself an administrative burden reduction target of 10%. But how would they know whether they were anywhere near target? Without an agreed measurement method and monitoring structures, it was impossible to even try to aim for a target. So, in 2014, the government put out a 'Handbook Measurement Compliance Pressure.' In 99 pages, this handbook explains how the government went about measuring the cost of compliance so that they could take this into account when considering the introduction of a new rule, or changes to an existing one. They called it the 'Standard Cost Model.'

The Standard Cost Model

The Dutch Standard Cost Model works as follows. Each information obligation associated with every regulation has to be separately identified. The regulatory burden imposed by each information obligation in euros per year is then estimated using the formula:

$N \times W \times T$

N = the number of businesses affected by the obligation;
W = the hourly tariff of those involved in meeting the information obligation (formalised into low, medium, or high);
T = the number of hours taken to meet the administrative obligation in a year.

Multiplying the time taken by a business to fulfil the information obligations of a regulation by the appropriate hourly tariff and by the number of businesses affected allows the aggregate cost to business of meeting the information obligations of that regulation to be estimated.

The example offered by the UK Better Regulation Task Force was that of 1,000 farmers (N) spending an average of five hours per year (T) informing the relevant regulator of notifiable diseases under section 88 of the UK Animal Health Act 1981. If the average cost of a farmer's time were £50 per hour (e.g., medium), the estimated Administrative Burden to business of that section of the Animal Health Act would be £250,000 per year. The Standard Cost Model provides a stylised estimate of the Administrative Burden. It does not pretend to measure the true level of the Administrative Burden. Rather, it produces a standardised set of numbers which when aggregated together gives the government an overall picture of regulation, thereby enabling it to identify actions that will reduce the burden.

The first of these is actually quite straightforward: three out of four administrative burdens imposed by new rules are completely independent of company size. It doesn't matter if you're a two-person mom-and-pop shop or a behemoth with 20,000 employees, except that the administrative cost of the rule gets amortized across a whole lot more people in the latter (and that the larger company likely has people on the books who can more easily accommodate extra tasks associated with complying with a particular rule). As a result, the cost of compliance (measured here as a proportion of the company's annual sales tax) can be up to ten times higher in a business with one to nine employees as compared to those with more than 100 employees (Vergeer, 2017).

Despite its strident approach, the initial uptake in the Netherlands was slightly anemic. In 2003, the Dutch set out to re-energize the process and correct a couple of things, such as a lack of ministerial commitment and accountability (Arculus et al., 2005). With this out of the way, the government demanded a 25% (not a 10%) reduction in administrative burden between 2003 and 2006. This target was a *net* target, meaning that the 25% reduction had to be achieved *after* taking into account any new burdens from regulations brought in by the government or the EU during the period of the target. It divides the cost of compliance into:

- Direct financial costs (taxes, fees, charges, premiums, as well as fines and liabilities in case of non-compliance)
- Substantive compliance costs (measured by the constraints imposed on particular activities and the costs involved in making oneself familiar with the existence of those constraints or need for permits)
- Administrative costs (those associated with the internal processes and bureaucracy necessary to confirm and trace compliance).

It was proud to show that government-imposed compliance costs had been slashed by 2.5 billion Euros over five years (MEZ, 2017). Seeing the successes from across the sea, the UK Better Regulation Task Force recommended in 2005 that its Government adopt the Dutch approach to reducing administrative burdens (see also Hampton, 2005). The advantages it recognized in this were as follows:

- An outstanding return on investment for the UK, potentially an estimated £16 billion increase in gross domestic product (GDP) for an investment of some £35 million.
- An opportunity for government to help increase the innovation, productivity, and growth of business.
- A mechanism for increasing the quality and efficiency of government through increasing the effectiveness of regulation.
- A robust method for the government to improve its control over the flow of new regulation and a driver to reduce the burdens imposed by the stock of existing regulation.

The Dutch had established an independent public body (called ACTAL) to act as a watchdog for its debureaucratization efforts. Government departments were obliged to send ACTAL details of all new legislative proposals and their calculation of the administrative burden involved.

ACTAL reviewed the calculations before the proposed legislation would be sent to the Dutch Council of Ministers and to Parliament. It also issued its own opinion. In addition, ACTAL evaluated the administrative burden reduction programs that departments were obliged to present annually to Parliament. And so, the efforts to reduce bureaucracy spawned, as they inevitably do, their own bureaucracy. To track compliance costs and manage their reduction, the Dutch government (in addition to its 99 pages of calculation procedures) created an 'integral trade-off framework,' a 'company effects test' and instituted a new 'compliance pressure assessment board,' supported by a 'compliance pressure advisory board.'

Together with the reporting of its work and the results of these initiatives, all these things have started to form what we might call a 'compliance pressure government-industrial complex.' This is a dense network of political, commercial, academic, legal, legislative, and regulatory interests driven by concerns for (at least the legitimate image of) small government worthy of re-election. Government reports about the success of regulatory reductions (which include the achievement of the targets set) are part of this effort. They have come out regularly in the Netherlands and the UK alike, and other countries have been following suit (Haythornthwaite, 2006). This sort of complex network has proven so resilient that the idea of the cost of regulation has never been off government radars since (Vergeer, 2017). And yet, despite all their efforts, those tasked and preoccupied with counting and measuring rules and cost reductions appear to miss something vital about the lived experience of the cost of compliance. Because the problem was that *few people seemed to notice* the effect of government efforts to reduce the cost and burden of compliance. The way people experience these appears to be driven by many things that fall outside any government's measurement instruments—or perhaps any ability to measure quantitatively. Let's look at that now.

Compliance pressure

Bozeman noted that it is often not the sheer number of rules, regulations, and procedures that cause people to experience problems. The sheer number of rules is not what seems to add up to the 'burden' that people feel. Indeed, red tape, he observed in 1993, usually means:

- Excessive or meaningless paperwork
- A high degree of formalization and constraint
- Unnecessary rules, procedures, and regulations
- Inefficiency and unjustifiable delays
- Frustration and vexation as a result of the above.

All of these are judgments, of course. What is excessive? Or unnecessary, or meaningless, or high degree, or unjustifiable? With all those things, it depends on whom you ask. To help figure this out, Bozeman suggested that we needed to learn more about the resources and energy people were expending to comply with a rule, and came up with the following definitions:

- **Compliance requirement** means the total resources (i.e., time, people, and money) formally required to comply with a rule (regulation and procedure).
- **Compliance burden** means the total resources (i.e., time, people, and money) *actually* expended in complying with a rule.

Bozeman then decided that he needed even more theoretical sophistication to make sense of the experienced compliance burden. For this he coined the phrase 'rule density.' It is not easily operationalized (and thus not easily measured), but he offered the phrase to make analytic distinctions for the conceptualization of (organizational) red tape:

- **Rule density** means the total resources devoted by the organization to complying (i.e., compliance burden) with all its rules, regulations, and procedures (i.e., its rule sum) as a percentage of total resources expended by the organization.
- **Organizational red tape**: rules, regulations, and procedures that remain in force and entail a compliance burden for the organization but have no efficacy for the rules' functional object (i.e., the thing or process they seek to influence, control, improve, and affect).

With this out of the way, though, another important question kept pushing to the fore. Where does the red tape come from? What are the sources?

Rules that are born bad and rules that have gone bad

Bozeman made a distinction between rules that are 'born bad' and rules that have 'gone bad.' It is a useful distinction, because it might suggest different places and times for intervening in the overregulation and bureaucratization of work. Rules that are born bad are ineffective from their inception. They create a compliance burden without addressing the functional object.

Having to chock both sides of a commercial vehicle's wheels when parked on a slope is an example of this. Chocking one side (the downslope side) may make sense and have an effect for the functional object. (This is to stop the vehicle from rolling away. To be sure, there are already other controls and rules for that, like setting the parking brake and leaving the vehicle in gear rather than neutral). But the functional object is not addressed by chocking the upslope side, since the vehicle won't ever spontaneously roll upslope. The idea behind the blanket rule may be that drivers are not qualified to judge what is up or down, or that doing the same procedure the same time every time offers a kind of assurance that ensures 100% compliance and control of the critical risk. All of this breathes a lack of trust and confidence in the capacities and capabilities of the people you employ, of course, but that is a different topic.

How is it possible that some rules are born bad? Bozeman (1993) identifies the following reasons:

- *Inadequate comprehension* of the relationship between the means (the rule) and the ends (e.g., controlling a risk): people designing the rules have insufficient understanding of the problem that (supposedly) needs solving, and don't have a good understanding of how the work is actually done in the first place.
- *Self-aggrandizement and illegitimate functions*: Bozeman sees this happen when employees have the space to demand others to furnish them with something, and to back it up with a rule-to-comply-with, even when it is illegitimate for them to do so. An accounting employee or director may set an additional reporting requirement on travel reimbursement forms for the purpose of expanding organizational influence and power, for instance.
- *Negative sum compromise*: decisions about rules often reflect a kind of compromise. Some parties or levels in the organization may demand

accountability because they themselves are held accountable. A new rule could be the compromise that seeks to do too much and ends up doing not only nothing, but actually making it more difficult for other people to do their job.

- *Overcontrol*: managerial control is usually a legitimate purpose in itself, but it is, as Bozeman points out, also a value that tends to get overemphasized. Rules, after all, cannot cover every contingency or even begin to match the complexity of most actual work. Yet, the most common response to the ambiguity and uncertainty this represents for a manager or staff organization is through additional formalization.
- *Negative sum process*: participation can also become a source of red tape or rules that are born bad. The attempt to have everyone participate offers everyone a contribution or a say, and not wanting or risking to disenfranchise anyone can lead to formal rules and procedures for participation in decision-making and other organizational processes. This detracts from efficiency.

In contrast to rules that are 'born bad,' rules can also go bad over time, despite their initial effectiveness and good intentions. Bozeman (1993) identifies the following reasons why notionally good rules can go bad over time:

- *Rule drift*: this happens when the meaning and spirit of the rule get lost in organizational archeology. Individuals in the organization can also inadvertently but subtly shift the rule or its meaning. Sometimes individuals enforce rules or comply with them without having any idea why they are in place or what function they serve. It could well be that the need for the rule no longer exists. Rules may be observed ritualistically and even may be venerated without anyone knowing what function they serve other than a historical ritual. Rule drift doesn't have to be measured in the length of time that has passed since a rule first came out. Other factors that may be related to rule drift include personnel turnover (in the case of internal rules), changes in client composition (for external rules), or even changes in which inspector comes by to check things on behalf of a regulator.
- *Rule entropy* is a special case of rule drift; rule entropy occurs as rules get passed from one organization to the next and from one person to the next. This happens easily in case of reorganizations or program

changes. The more organizations, organizational levels, and accountabilities are involved in rule creation and application, the more likely the meaning will be lost through entropy.

- *Change in implementation* happens if the rule itself stays essentially the same but individuals begin to implement it in a different manner. For example, a rule may be applied with less discretion than it was in the past or it may be interpreted more stringently than it was in the past.
- *Change in the functional object*: sometimes the functional object of the rule changes in ways that render the rule obsolete or otherwise useless. For example, a rule requiring an annual report of hiring needs is dysfunctional if there is a multi-year hiring freeze.
- *Change in the rule's efficacy*: even if the functional object remains constant, changing circumstances can erode the rule's usefulness or effectiveness. Requiring employees to fill in an ergonomic 'how-to-sit-at-your-desk' checklist, for example, ceases to be effective or useful when the company introduces 'hot-desking' whereby employees no longer have their own desks. The functional object is still the same, but the rule no longer addresses it effectively or meaningfully. Training in how to sit at a desk (if you must...) can be a more effective and useful intervention instead.
- *Rule strain*: organizations with a certain number of rules, even if all are separately effective and useful, can create strain and inefficient use of resources. Rules that are notionally effective and useful can still be so abundant that together they have a net negative effect. The more there is to comply with, the less there will likely be complied with, and other (actual) work may suffer as well.
- *Accretion*: rules tend to build one on top of another. This means not only a historical encrustation of the organization in rules that are no longer effective or useful, but can also lead to inconsistencies or cross purposes (e.g., safety vs. security rules in aviation). The net effect could be damaging (even if a particular rule remains effective with respect to its functional objects). The interesting aspect of accretion is that rules have an impact that is more than the sum of their parts. Weber warned about this a century ago: create a hyperrational organization, add rationality to rationality, and the sum will likely be irrationality.
- *Misapplication*: rules can get misapplied for a whole host of reasons. Sometimes rules may be difficult to interpret or apply because they have

been written poorly and thus quickly evolve into an undue compliance burden. The purpose of a rule (perhaps a legitimate purpose; perhaps for an effective rule) might never have been clearly communicated to the people who need to check and enforce compliance with it.

'Overregulation'

Bozeman's analysis clearly suggests that there are complexities behind the experience of compliance pressure—and complexities behind the production of the rules that help cause it—that a simple characterization of 'red tape' doesn't capture. The same goes for the label 'overregulation.' 'Overregulation' is a tricky term because it contains an implicit standard. *Over*regulated relative to what? Relative to what we believe regulation should give us? More than is necessary to accomplish the goal of the regulation, whatever that goal is? But more *what*? More paperwork, burdensome bureaucracy, inspections, pointless audits, meddling, time, effort, administrative nonsense? Some would say 'all of the above'! Others would pick out some and build their favorite hit list. It depends, and it differs. As Bozeman reminds us, we:

> … need to recognize that organizational administrative rules, regulations, and procedures are not—in either number or content—inherently good or bad, but only good or bad from the perspective of values posited and the extent to which they seem to serve or thwart those values.
>
> (1993, pp. 283–284)

Indeed, it turns out that the experience of 'overregulation' is psychologically quite complex. Most critically, it is only loosely coupled to the rise or fall in the quantity of regulations governing a particular activity. That means that it is wrong to think that 'overregulation' is an objectively measurable thing, something that can get a figure that applies to everyone, something that is a target that can be pursued, reduced, or achieved. Of course, the sheer quantity of rules matters. Without rules, you can't really claim to be overregulated (nor can others claim that you are non-compliant). But it is safer to say that overregulation is a label that denotes an experience—the experience of being overregulated. Many attempts to rein in overregulation have led to an increased experience of overregulation, or they have done very little to lessen it (Fisscher, Stoeten, Németh, & Slingerland, 2019). This insight, and this repeated finding, has been around since the 1970s.

This is why it makes more sense to speak about 'compliance pressure.' Compliance pressure puts cause and effect in one phrase. The cause is the need to comply; the effect is the experience of the need to comply—the pressure of the costs, the administrative work, the distraction, and the uncertainties that compliance activities generate. A recent analysis of compliance pressure builds on the insight that mere quantitative measures related to compliance—as used by most governments—miss important aspects of the lived, daily experience of that compliance. This is why a government's numbers about deregulation and rule-making can widely diverge from what people actually experience. The research shows that three main attributes of a rule co-determine the extent to which it will generate the experience of compliance pressure: its cost, its doability, and its perceived usefulness (Vergeer, 2017). Let's look at those three in more detail now.

Experiencing compliance cost

Governments have tended to measure the direct cost of compliance when deciding to institute a new rule, or removing an existing one. People who need to comply, however, also count, or experience, the indirect costs that make up their compliance pressure. The most important sources of indirect costs noted in the literature, and which are not typically taken into consideration in calculations, are the following:

- The hiring of external advisors and consultants to assist with regulatory interpretation and implementation
- Rule-making officials who lack an understanding of, empathy for, or even interest in the difficulties faced by companies or departments or workers who need to adopt the new compliance requirements
- Extra internal, inter-departmental and inter-agency paperwork, which may often differ from one department to another.
- A lack of coordination between the various agencies or departments who may be involved with the rule, or whose own set of rules interacts with the new one.
- The costs of sanctions, delays, holdups, or fines when compliance is not achieved.

It shows that introducing a new rule is not just a matter of manipulating a single variable in an otherwise stable landscape of business activities and costs. Instead, doing so induces changes—or causes perturbations—in a complex, networked system of interrelationships and interdependencies. As always with complexity, controlling the effects of such a supposedly singular change is impossible: the reverberations and influences stretch into all kinds of corners of the complex system, including areas not thought of beforehand (Capra, 1996). Even when a new rule does little or no good, then you can't automatically conclude that at least it does no harm. Because it might, and you might not even know it. Interestingly, it also suggests that the proposal (as the UK has implemented) to remove one rule for every new one is not going to yield easily predictable or measurable effects. This would be the case if rules can be set in place and excised cleanly, without dragging along the lint and fuzz of a whole additional set of organizational activities and implications. But that is not the case. There is always an experienced cost to rulemaking. Rulemaking doesn't happen in a linear, mechanistic, predictable world where you can take one thing out and stick another thing back in without anything else changing in the process. You could, in fact, argue that it wouldn't even *need* to happen in such a world. In spite of the UK's best intentions, there is no zero-sum rulemaking.

Doability of a new rule

One aspect of the *doability* of adopting a new rule or compliance demand is obvious: can the rule actually be carried out? You might be surprised how often even this rather basic requirement isn't met.

I recall working with an organization that ran a number of offshore drilling platforms in a colder part of the world (which, incidentally, still has months-long warm summers). Drilling platforms at sea are exposed to the elements and corrode rather quickly, which means that there is always sandblasting and painting going on. The grit used to clear the corrosion off the rig has a way of getting into people's eyes, which then requires a wash-out, and the recording of an incident. The latter is particularly problematic, since rig leaders are held accountable for the number of recorded incidents on their rigs. So the fewer incidents, the better the performance appraisal. To prevent the common eye incidents from occurring, the organization decided to invest in a new kind of safety goggle. This new goggle has a foam lining where it sits against the face, like a ski goggle, creating a supposedly perfect seal that won't allow any grit to go through. What it also doesn't allow through, though, is a sufficient amount of circulating air.

And so, during the summer months, workers on the rig were finding that their goggles fogged up in minutes. They had to take them off and wipe them clean, so that they could see where they were going, and see what they were doing. This of course exposed their eyes to the environment, including its grit, at regular intervals. But it didn't stop there. The year before, the company had decided that safety goggles need to be attached to the back of workers' hard hats, where a little leather strap with a pushbutton on it holds the goggle's strap in place against the back of the hard hat. Now every time a worker needed to take off the new safety goggle, she or he also needed to remove the hard hat, otherwise the goggle wouldn't slip up over the bill of the hard hat in the front and couldn't be wiped clean. This left workers without goggles and without hard hats for many occasions on each shift (incidentally 'violating' the organization's own golden safety rules).

Seeing the problems associated with the introduction of its new goggles, the organization decided it had a training problem, not a design or fit-for-purpose problem that challenged the sheer doability of its new requirements. It instituted a new rule that specified that each employee needed to be trained in how to wear the new safety goggles. This new compliance requirement of course dragged along more bureaucracy in its wake, because platforms now needed to start keeping track of who had, and who hadn't yet, been given this training, and when they would be due for a recurrent course. With rotating workforces that only partially overlap, this is not a simple task. Platforms called on the on-shore organization to institute a new role (in the safety training coordination office) to try to keep track of it all. With the organization scrambling to fill one absurd, bureaucratic, self-imposed hole with another, it started to dawn on some that perhaps the original intent, and motivation behind it, should be subject to another look. When we left, the organization was all wrapped around the axle with itself trying to decide whether it should allow the workers the discretion to choose a safety goggle of their liking—from a very limited, company-determined choice of two, of course.

Doability of a new compliance demand, however, is not just limited to its practical doability. What researchers have included under this label too is whether people even understand the rule, and to what extent there has been cooperation and consultation between those making the rule and those having to live by it so that the rule actually fits the situation in which it needs to be applied. These aspects actually have a large influence on people's experienced compliance pressure, and (presumably) on their ability and willingness to comply at all. If the various departments involved (wittingly or not) in the new rule are themselves ill-coordinated (which can lead to rules that clash or are otherwise incompatible), or people in them eschew their responsibilities for creating the new demand, then the experience of compliance pressure would go up. Being kept up to date in a predictable, transparent way about adaptations or changes to a new rule, was also shown to lower people's experienced compliance pressure. And when departments or people were able to adopt a new rule without external advice or expertise, compliance pressure was perceived as less, and the willingness to comply was higher (Vergeer, 2017).

Usefulness of a new rule

In a final twist, Vergeer found that the experience of compliance pressure is driven in part by factors that have little or nothing to do with the actual cost of the new rule. Instead, the psychological experience of pressure to comply varies in relation to:

- The perceived goal of the new rule
- The perceived effectiveness of the new rule in achieving that goal
- The constraints created by the new rule.

Together, Vergeer calls these the 'usefulness' of the new rule, or—perhaps more accurately translated—its perceived utility. When people don't really see or understand what the goal of the new rule is, the experience of compliance pressure goes up. The willingness to accommodate the new rule, let alone the willingness to consistently comply with it, goes down. The key idea here is people's perception of the goal: this is what drives their sense of compliance pressure, and it can be quite separate from the actual goal that whoever made the rule wants to pursue with it. This goes for effectiveness too. What confidence does a person have that the rule can actually help them or their organization achieve the goal it putatively pursues? (Hopkins, 2010).

> Remember the rule to chock a parked truck on both sides of the wheel, even when that truck is parked on a slope, and when it has its handbrake engaged and its shifter in gear. The usefulness of at least the upper chock is anybody's guess. Then there is the rule for linemen in an electrical utility company. Their cherry picker trucks, which are stabilized and immobilized on stilts when the lineman is working at height in the

personnel basket, still need their wheels chocked. The wheels in these cases are themselves mostly off the ground. It is intuitive that rules like those—which neither have a clear perceived goal, nor any effectiveness in achieving that goal—are met with the kinds of sighs and eyerolls that contribute to the experience of intrusive, useless compliance pressure. The rule in fact imposes constraints on the lineman's time, and for no reason. This is time that could be better spent actually doing the job and assessing its real risks, rather than running around the truck with chocks for wheels that have just been elevated off the ground.

Notes

1 Government expansion into areas of social welfare and economic regulation in the modern era in fact stems from the 1930s, when the global depression forced states to step in and act on behalf of those who did not have those means themselves.

2 As explained by the House of Commons Information Office, the scope of these powers varies greatly, from the technical (e.g., to vary the dates on which different provisions of an Act will come into force, to change the levels of fines or penalties for offences or to make consequential and transitional provisions) to much wider powers such as filling out the broad provisions in Acts. Often, Acts only contain a broad framework and statutory instruments are used to provide the necessary detail that would be considered too complex to include in the body of an Act. Secondary legislation can also be used to amend, update, or enforce existing primary legislation. Statutory instruments are just as much a part of the law of the land as an Act of Parliament. The courts can question whether a minister, when issuing an statutory instrument, is using a power he or she has actually been given by the parent Act but cannot question the validity of the statutory instrument for any other reason.

7

A RETREAT INTO RULES

Markets, and the deregulation and privatization that gave them ever greater reign, can explain a good part of why we have more rules. They explain a good part of why we have a greater sense of being overregulated today. In this, we may be discovering that something is not as good as we believed it to be. Free markets haven't led to free people. Free markets have led to unfree people, to overregulated workers. Four decades of market-favoring economic policies, embraced across much of the world after their adoption in the United Kingdom and the United States, have left most of us with more rules and compliance demands in more areas of our lives than ever before. It wasn't supposed to be this way. Deregulation and privatization were supposed to give us freedom. But paradoxically, freeing ourselves from government ownership, control, and oversight has led, in the words of John Gray (2003), to unlimited government. Not unlimited 'government' as embodied by a state, but unlimited government—the unlimited governing—of ourselves.

And this is where we need to pause because it is unlikely that markets can carry the entire explanatory load for our greater compliance burden.

It says something about us too. Because we constitute the markets, we are somehow players, creators in them. The successful removal or retreat of state government from some of our activities has freed up new spaces, arrangements, and revenue models for the imposition of compliance and bureaucracy. The removal or retreat of government may well have removed all constraints on us governing ourselves. There is no ceiling on the amount of compliance we will put on ourselves. Nothing or nobody stops us from piling up self-imposed regulation, rule-making, and compliance demands. For sure, the very workings of the free-market aid and abet this, rendering additional rules and compliance necessary, profitable and seemingly unavoidable. But what about our own role?

Bystanders or accomplices?

Let's ask that question about ourselves. Are we hapless bystanders, looking on as the invisible hand of the free market rolls out more and more rules over us? Or do we, or perhaps some of us, actually *like* more rules? Do we, or they, derive something else from demanding and expecting compliance? And have free markets created the kinds of political, economic, and social conditions that make us more liable to retreating into rules? In this final chapter, we look at three dynamics. These may help explain why we, under certain conditions, are more accepting or even welcoming of more compliance. They are:

- **Safetyism**—our increasing sensitivity and risk aversion. This has led to a search for, and expectation of, protection by second or third parties from any kind of harm, whether physical, emotional, or psychological. In return for this protection, we welcome (or, in many cases, have little choice but to acquiesce in) the shrinking bandwidth around what is considered acceptable behavior.
- **Moral entrepreneurism**—the promotion of more rules, conformity, and obedience, which is driven by the belief that norms are slipping, that 'accountability' is eroding. It is animated by a kind of righteous indignation about a loss or some crisis we face. This, in turn, is linked to an assent of more authority, and to conformity with what it imposes.
- **Escape from freedom**—the notion that escaping from freedom also delivers a freedom from thinking, and alleviation from the burdens of choice

> and responsibility. If someone else makes and enforces the rules for us, it reduces uncertainty and ambiguity. Add to this that people have long been willing to trade their freedoms for economic prosperity, and a compelling link to the promises (if not delivered realities) of neoliberalism becomes visible.

There are many interactions between these three. Together, the three dynamics move us to not only accept, but sometimes even invite, a greater imposition of rules and constraints into our (working) lives.

Safetyism

Brad Wilcox wanted to give a name to the growing overprotective impulse that has crept into society. He was fascinated by the success of that phenomenon. A sociologist at the University of Virginia, he coined the term 'safetyism.' It includes the shaming and banning of acts and expressions that could possibly hurt or offend particular societal groups. Terms and books from the historical literature canon—*Catcher in the Rye, The Great Gatsby, The Grapes of Wrath, To Kill a Mockingbird*, to name just a few—have been banned from some American schools and college campuses, because they would give rise to hurt and offense. The ultimate aim of safetyism is to turn the world into a series of 'safe spaces' where people are shielded not only from any kind of physical harm, but also from psychological and emotional harm—by trying to protect them even from words and ideas that could make them uncomfortable. Radio programs, lectures, and publications need, by social convention if nothing else, to avoid a range of topics and expressions, and issue 'trigger warnings' if something unavoidable could possibly arouse a strong emotional response.

> Conor Friedersdorf, writing in The Atlantic, cites the example of a long-time University of Southern California professor who was recently removed because of a Mandarin word he used correctly, but which sounded like a racial slur in English (Friedersdorf, 2020). During a Zoom class on August 20, the 53-year-old professor told students that in business settings they should avoid filler words such as 'um' or 'er.' Then he gave another example of a filler word that he added to his lecture perhaps five

years ago to be more inclusive of international students. 'Like in China, the common word is that—that, that, that, that,' he explained. 'So, in China it might be nèi ge—nèi ge, nèi ge, nèi ge. So, there's different words that you'll hear in different countries.'

To some students, the Mandarin word, rendered 那个, sounded too much like the n-word for their liking. They sent a letter of complaint to administrators and pressed their grievance in a meeting. The offended students characterized the burden and harms that they purported to suffer. 'Our mental health has been affected,' they wrote. 'We would rather not take his course than to endure the emotional exhaustion of carrying on with an instructor that disregards cultural diversity and sensitivities and by extension creates an unwelcome environment.' His 'careless comment' affected their ability to focus on their studies, they claimed, 'and to expect that we will sit through two more weeks of this class, knowing that the professor lacks the tact, racial awareness and empathy to lead and teach an audience as diverse as ours is unacceptable. We should not be made to feel ignored and belittled.'

Soon after, Patton was removed from the class, investigated, and excoriated in a mass email. The 'professor repeated several times a Chinese word that sounds very similar to a vile racial slur,', the School's dean wrote. 'Understandably, this caused great pain and upset among students, and for that I am deeply sorry. It is simply unacceptable for faculty to use words in class that can marginalize, hurt and harm the psychological safety of our students.'

And what did this do to the rest of the faculty? A member of the school's faculty council described 'an overwhelming sense of vulnerability, worry, insecurity, fear and anxiety' among faculty who worry that they could be 'cancelled' anytime due to a misunderstanding. The faculty feel 'anger, disappointment, betrayal, and outrage' at Patton's treatment. They support 'efforts to bring greater diversity and inclusion into our classrooms,' but 'a large proportion' of faculty members mentioned that 'given the atmosphere of fear and perceived lack of support, they think it is too risky for them to continue discussing certain topics with students. This includes topics related to diversity and inclusion, but it also includes such topics as politics and international relations.'

Safetyism presumes, according to Lukianoff and Haidt (2019), an extraordinary fragility and helplessness of our fellow human beings, whose only display of strength is the assertion of the right not to be offended by anyone else. What they describe is a sense of the decline of mental resilience. This was no longer new by the time safetyism was coined. In 2015, Gray published an article in *Psychology Today* in which he tried to figure out the dwindling coping skills that people have to deal with their own discomfort. A lack of mental resilience has been bred especially into the millennial generation, Petersen (2020) argues. Their fragility stems from an overbearing, overbooked, overcontrolled, helicoptered upbringing, where their childhoods were seen mainly as a means to an end: getting somewhere in life. Space for spontaneity and the formation of independence and confidence were compressed, or eliminated altogether. The one remaining assertion of the right to not be offended comes from millennials having been conceived as mini-adults even when they were children. Behaviors, postures, and skills were cultivated under what sociologist Ara Francis has called 'vigilante parenting', which turns unyielding watchfulness and advocacy for the child into a righteous moral quest. This has included encouraging children to advocate for themselves whenever they felt something was unfair (Francis, 2015).

It would all make fertile ground for safetyism. Safetyism has as its sacred (if not only) value the protection of people who are deemed vulnerable (or deem themselves vulnerable), or not in control of all choices that affect their exposure to risk. Safetyism unquestionably legitimates maximum precautionary measures, and obeisance to them. The conviction, after all, is that there is no goal loftier than protecting people against (involuntary) risk, because they:

> ...have been convinced that they really are too fragile to hear certain ideas, and that they are honestly trying to prevent themselves and others from facing what they see as real emotional pain.
>
> (Shibley, 2016, p. 377)

Enforcing compliance with the demands of safetyism, Altemeyer (1988) found, works when there is a high degree of perceived legitimacy of the authority (whether a state, a person, or a more abstract entity, like a behavioral code or set of rules), and when a general aggressiveness against nonconformants is perceived to be sanctioned by that legitimated authority. It is increasingly possible to effectively police people's compliance with these conventions, particularly in a networked world where people can swiftly set up echo chambers for their own opinions and convictions. Altemeyer's general aggressiveness is recognizable in what Haidt and Lukianoff called 'vindictive protectiveness.' This is the tendency to shield people from perceived injury (including criticism) by attacking the putative aggressor (Shibley, 2016). It is a way of patrolling safe spaces by censuring or sanctioning anyone who interferes with the aim of complete, assured protection from any kind of harm.

Here too you can see the paradox of a retreating state. People attach importance to social conventions endorsed by a legitimated authority, but in this case that isn't an authority embodied in a state or a particular person. It is the authority of majority opinion, or the opinion of a vocal minority:

> You'd think it would lead to a very small state that would leave a lot of freedom for people. In fact, it leads to a big, intrusive state. If you strip away all the communal commitments that help people govern themselves from within, then very soon you find you have to pass all sorts of laws to govern them from without. If you privatize meaning so that people get to follow their unrestrained desires, they immediately start tramping on one another, and public pressure grows for restrictive laws, like hate speech regulation, to keep things from getting out of control.
>
> (Brooks, 2018, p. 11)

Under these conditions, a new kind of authority (which might be as amorphous as a social consensus, a convention) starts making rules and policing them instead. To be sure, the state has done its bit, too, particularly by codifying into legislation or statute the legal requirement to provide a 'safe' workplace, including one free from harassment, emotional hurts, and psychological risks. A problem, of course, is the local, spontaneous nature of the actual definitions of these harms—with vindictive protectiveness arising out of instances of indignation and confrontation, and the relative difficulty of laws and regulations to confidently exclude even vague perceived harms. The response of others to the latest shrinking of behavioral bandwidth is often to think twice before speaking. It is to over-correct so as to not even approach the margins of the freshly re-contoured norms of acceptability (Friedersdorf, 2020).

Moral entrepreneurism

Remember Beck's *Risk Society* from its mention in the Preface: the risks we occasionally and randomly encounter in the society we have created tend to be faceless as well as inevitable. Beck argued how the economic gains from modernity—from the application of science and rationality—are increasingly overshadowed by the unintended production and distribution of the downsides. The risks produced and distributed by modernity are highly complex in their causation, they are latent and unpredictable, they are not limited in time, space, or social class, and they are not detectable by our physical senses, Beck explained. But, most fortuitously, they are ultimately the result of human decisions. Somewhere, somehow, we can trace these risks back to a place and time where some human didn't manage the risk effectively enough (Green, 1997). This is fortuitous because one of the most reliable ways in which society explains and handles misfortune, unanticipated occurrences, and deviance from the norm (Luhmann, 1991) is to designate a perceived source of risk as 'the other' (Foucault, 1976, 1977). Turning risks into something that comes from 'the other' fits with our late-modern quest for order and extinguishing existential anxiety: it gives risk a face and reduces its inevitability. It renders risk knowable, decisionable (or actionable), and potentially controllable. A construction of risk that promises to resolve unpredictability and ambivalence by producing identifiable victims and blamable villains is highly attractive (Hollway & Jefferson, 1997). When we discover that a modern risk wasn't adequately managed, that condition or episode can give rise to what Cohen once called a 'moral panic':

> Societies appear to be subject, every now and then, to periods of moral panic. A condition, episode, person or groups of persons emerges to become defined as a threat to societal values and interests; its nature is presented in a stylized and stereotypical fashion by the mass media; the moral barricades are manned by editors, bishops, politicians and other right-thinking people; socially accredited experts pronounce their diagnoses and solutions; ways

> of coping are evolved (or more often) resorted to; the condition then disappears, submerges or deteriorates and becomes more visible.
>
> (Cohen, 1972, p. 9)

Cohen was writing in relation to social deviance and youth criminality. Unger (2001) took the idea and tested its fit with the conceptual shifts that are necessary when risks are seen to emanate from the economic and technological nature of modernity itself. He did this by evaluating the relevance and application of the five criteria for a moral panic as enumerated by Goode and Ben-Yehuda (1994). The first is that there needs to be heightened concern about the risk. The problem here is that threats posed by a risk society are ubiquitous and long-term, not easily localizable and ephemeral or episodic as they were in Cohen's sense. Risk is always there. A 'risk society is characterized, in other terms, by a stream of emergencies and would-be emergencies' (Unger, 2001, p. 276), but that doesn't mean that risks are easy to identify or deal with:

> Risks...induce systematic and often irreversible harm, generally remain invisible, are based on causal interpretations, and thus initially exist only in terms of the (scientific or anti-scientific) knowledge about them. They can thus be changed, magnified, dramatized or minimized within knowledge, and to that extent they are particularly open to social definition and construction.
>
> (Beck, 1992, pp. 22–23)

And then, to boot, we have to doubt how much faith we can put in even further modernization and technology to control the risks produced by those two in the first place:

> In Beck's assessment, the proliferation of risks in late modernity gives rise to an acute awareness of monumental uncertainties and anxieties, as '... the unknown and unintended consequences [of modern industrial production] come to be a dominant force in history and society'. (op. cit.: 22). Simultaneously, society becomes an issue and problem for itself, precipitating a confrontational reflexivity and a 'globalization of doubt' concerning the degree of faith instilled in science and technology.
>
> (Hier, 2003, p. 6)

So, if modernity cannot seem to solve the unanticipated problems created by modernity itself—if its institutions (organizations, politics, and regulators) aren't trusted or are expected to fall short, then what? It has the consequence of 'instilling fear in people and, in so doing, encouraging them to...adopt a gung-ho "something-must-be-done-about-it" attitude' (McRobbie, 1994, quoted in Ungar, 2001, p. 277). The one who might be able to do something about it is the moral entrepreneur (Becker, 1963). A moral entrepreneur is someone who actively creates awareness of the issues and follows them through to a solution that targets a limited, seemingly manageable foe. A moral entrepreneur not only promotes (new) norms or revives old ones. He or she also offers a clearly identifiable deviant person, group, societal segment, or set of ideas or behaviors that can receive the corrective compliance directed at it by the moral enterprise. Sociological research into this consistently shows that there is a disproportionality in how that person, group, segment, or idea are linked to the perceived risk—to the point that if it weren't for them, the risk would supposedly be negligible or non-existent. '*The 'war on error'* is such a moral enterprise. It instills the fear that McRobbie talks about as follows:

> The initial threat assessment proved stunning in terms of sheer magnitude. Hundreds of thousands of people die unnecessarily each year around the world as a direct result of human error. In healthcare settings alone, it is estimated that well over 100,000 patients die per year due to iatrogenic (doctor/nurse-induced) causes... In business, billions of dollars are lost each year as a direct result of human error, and not just from accidents, injuries, lawsuits, or increased insurance premiums. As evidence mounts about the causes of the global economic meltdown in the first decade of this century, it is becoming readily apparent that human error played a major role. Miscalculations and unchecked egos were principal components of the fiscal collapse of many organizations—add to this the number of senior executives and fast-rising managers who derailed themselves through completely avoidable human error. The list continues with error-induced product defects, inefficiencies, supply chain delays, and poor customer service, and it becomes obvious that human error puts the very engine of our profitability and economy at great risk.
>
> (Kern, 2018, p. 275)

Turning 'human error' into the threat to be dealt with fits with Beck's stereotyping of an enemy into a form of 'bureaucratic stranger.' Institutions (e.g., businesses, banks, and hospitals) harbor unreliable elements—people—who are the source of trouble. The institutions themselves are no longer to be trusted with any meaningful solutions: 'the government, industry and society have failed,' says Kern (Ibid, p. 285), so now we have only ourselves to fall back on to deal with this threat. Human error is the categorically decisive bureaucratic construction of the enemy, which replaces the constant but incomprehensible societal undertone of modern risk (Hier, 2003). This enemy of human error is the antithesis to security and offers an unambiguous distinction between 'self' and 'other.' Those who produce errors and are not committed to reducing them are the enemies of everybody else's in modern society. Order can be achieved by instilling discipline in them, by shrinking the bandwidth of what constitutes acceptable performance. Exaggerating the threat, and uniquely focusing on it through all kinds of claims-making activities is an important tool (Ungar, 2001):

> Human error is the thief of human happiness and the slayer of dreams, careers, potential, and all too frequently life itself. Viewing it as anything less hostile is to willfully expose your throat to the knife. These are harsh words, but they are intentionally so … avoidable errors end lives, poison relationships, squander wealth, feed addictions and ruin careers.
>
> (Kern, 2018, p. 283)

Such exaggeration not only reduces the complexity and intangibility of existential insecurity (collapsing it neatly into the omnipresent threat of 'human error'), Hier (2003) explains. It simultaneously satisfies the desire to belong to a community; to share a communal goal, purpose, or project (the 'war' on that error), contributing to the consolidation of a sense of own-group identity. Sociologists suggest that the desire to be part of something, to identify with a larger goal or community, has grown ever more pressing in modernity (Giddens, 1990). People will not just be drawn to a community offering a sense of belonging and identity, but especially to one that issues declarations and practices that offer the promise of social order and social control in the face of the kind of existential risk that modernity entails (Hollway & Jefferson, 1997). The chances of people submitting to authoritarian control over deviance go up even further when the community considers itself both victimized by the abstract risks and newly and redemptively empowered to do something about it now that the risk has been given a 'face', a clearer identity itself. The '*war on error*' recognizes this:

> Error is a persistent and progressive thief who will continue to steal from you and your potential as a human being on ever-greater scale until you make a conscious decision to stop being a passive victim.
>
> (Ibid, p. 283)

The route to greater social order and social control, according to the war on error, is 'personal accountability' (Ibid, p. 279). It means deviance control as an imposed, or self-imposed discipline, as a self-regulating, compliant way of life. And the suggestion is that this can be promoted and imposed and taught. Tightening the frame available for human intention and action and demanding compliance are not only reasonable but also necessary recipes for restitution of control and order. Submitting to a kind of authoritarian control in a 'war' on deviance, Paxton observed, is not uncommon when people can be persuaded that there is widespread moral decline and degeneration—an erosion of standards, norms, and 'accountability.' This animates the 'war on error' too:

> The world has gone braindead on the issues of personal responsibility and accountability... In many circles, accountability seems to be a four-letter word.
>
> (Kern, 2018, pp. 278 and 285)

The 'obsessive preoccupation with community decline' (Paxton, 1998, p. 1) translates into a sense of some overwhelming and universal crisis which lies beyond the reach of any traditional solutions. It is one of Paxton's 'mobilizing passions' that can get people to rally behind an authoritarian intervention. This intervention typically casts itself as the *only* real way to deal with the problem, just like the 'war on error' does, which repudiates traditional approaches to risk management, shoves aside the 'failed' state, government and institutions, and announces itself as 'the cure for the disease of human error' (Ibid p. 280).

Concern about the disappearance of a single center of authority, about commonly held norms and values, has been noted as a fundamental consequence of modernity. It, after all, has 'disembedded' people from a whole range of familiar and comforting structures and arrangements (Giddens, 1990). Such concerns have become accentuated even further with the spread of neoliberal governance and global capitalism. These have unraveled the post-war social consensus about who ran what, and who could own how much, and how things (power and money) were distributed among everybody. Kuttner (2018) observes that globalization and financialization have played havoc with the livelihoods and previously taken-for-granted stabilities and securities of large groups of people. These become more likely to embrace a moral enterprise which identifies (or, more likely, mis-identifies) a common foe, which promises to preserve security and restore a sense of belonging and order and control.

Free markets have replicated the conditions under which people retreat into rules and compliance. Just think of the consequences of neoliberalism and market domination for workplace relations (Springer et al., 2016). Governments have retreated from labor arbitration, wage protection, social insurance, workplace inspections, and from owning or running anything at all, except a smaller version of themselves. The promotion of privatization, self-regulation, and 'self-reliance' between employers and employees has shifted the power balance and largely eroded people's employment conditions (Watson, 2015) and negatively impacted workplace health (Schofield, 2005). Economic insecurity and flexibilization of labor have gone up, real wages have not (Saull, 2015). And of course, free markets have not improved economic and social conditions for many people. Recall from earlier in the book how inequality has risen sharply, how flexible and precarious (instead of tenured and secure) employment has too, how jobs have been sent offshore, access to healthcare has in many places become more difficult and less affordable, and life expectancy in countries like the United States has actually declined. At the same time, free market policies that endorse self-regulation and responsibilization of the individual have produced social conditions that leave people feeling alone, without the ties that bound them to others before:

> ...ominously, it has increased the slide into what sociologists call 'mass society.' In a mass society, there is a loss of institutions of representation or of political voice that connect people to one another. This atomization, in turn, leaves people alienated and primed to embrace [moral entrepreneurism].
>
> (Kuttner, 2018, p. 17)

For such a moral enterprise to work, though, people need to be not only susceptible, but somewhat gullible (Arendt, 1967; Scott, 1998, 2012). Gullibility means that people are easily persuaded to believe something and abide by it, often because they don't know any better or because it sounds better, in any case, than their current predicament or crisis. In his study of people surrendering to bureaucratic control, Scott (1998) speaks of a 'prostrate populace' as one of the conditions for the success of a moral enterprise that demands compliance. Prostrate means overcome, helpless, in submission. A 'prostrate' populace has to be gullible to some extent, otherwise it won't submit to rules issued by the moral enterprise, even if these rules are emerging and governed by a consensus authority of newly shaped social conventions about what is acceptable and what isn't. In the words of Arendt:

> A mixture of gullibility and cynicism had been an outstanding characteristic... [people] had reached the point where they would, at the same time, believe everything and nothing, think that everything was possible and that nothing was true... [The] audience was ready at all times to believe the worst, no matter how absurd, and did not particularly object to being deceived because it held every statement to be a lie anyhow: they would take refuge in cynicism.
>
> (p. 382)

This type of submission succeeds particularly when resistance is cast as a personal moral failure, as a character defect on the part of individuals who won't get with the program, who don't lift their game like everyone is expected to. It's these individual people who are the problem; they lack, in the words of the 'war on error', 'the individual will to proceed' (Kern, 2018, p. 285). The running fear of moral weakness, of not having the 'individual will to proceed', of individuals making poor choices, of clouded minds and rotten souls, is typical for fundamentalist answers to a plurality of views, rules, standards, and norms (Law, 1997). One solution to the problem of plurality is more 'educational interventions', or that more sinister (if honest) suggestion of 'behavior modification'—all in the name of the eradication of deviance and disorder (Krause, 1997). When applied to workplaces, the premise—going back all the way to Taylor (1911)—is that there is one best way to do the task, figured out by those who actually don't do that work themselves. The one best way is then codified in rules, procedures, checklists, and safe-work method statements for others to follow. Deviance should be declared unacceptable.

Once regimes of compliance and order are established, the social-psychological dynamic that plays out underneath it so that it is maintained turns out to be rather subtle. A prostrate populace, Scott as well as Arendt explain, is one of a dissociated psychological state. People believe that they are better off following the rules they don't believe in. People find that complying, though onerous, is still easier than dealing with the consequences of not complying—unless they can do it undiscovered and thus get away with it. So, people submit, more through a calculated trade-off than out of committed conviction. In her searching investigation of totalitarianism, Hannah Arendt (1967) found an interplay between submission and two other factors:

- *Submission*: we yield to the authority imposed on us; we do as we're told (so we actually do fill out that checklist before executing a simple task). We submit because the alternative (disobedience, non-compliance) only creates more trouble for ourselves.
- *Resignation*: we accept the existence of these rules as undesirable but inevitable. We resign because whatever we try to do about them, we know that it won't have any effect anyway.
- *Cynicism*: we no longer believe (if we ever did) that such rules help anything at all, or that they actually do what they're advertised to do. We might, in fact, recognize that rather than managing our own lives, the rules are in place to make us protect the liability of people higher up in the hierarchy.

Beyond this dynamic, there remains a simple attraction: with rules and compliance, we can 'escape from freedom.'

Escape from freedom

Psychoanalyst Erich Fromm found that instead of thinking for ourselves, we frequently allow society or a subculture to dictate how we should behave or what we should aspire to in life. A member of the Frankfurt School at Goethe University, Fromm was fascinated with the way in which people regressed into rules and compliance—away from everything that Renaissance humanism and the Enlightenment had fought for. Individualism, self-determination, autonomy, and freedom—all these things could get thrown to the wind under certain social and economic conditions, he observed. Fromm called his debut book *Die Furcht vor der Freiheit*, which was translated as *Escape from Freedom* (though it literally means *The Fear of Freedom*) (Fromm, 1941). Pre-empting Beck and Giddens by decades, he found how the freedoms achieved through Renaissance, Enlightenment, through industrialization, urbanization and revolution, could produce feelings of isolation and fear, and the loss of belonging, of self, and of identity. It drove, Fromm figured, a desire for and return to authoritarianism, to conformity.

From community to autonomy to alienation

Consistent with his background as a psychoanalyst (and not a sociologist like Beck or Giddens), Fromm observed that industrialization and the rise of liberalism resulted in what he considered 'the complete emergence of the individual.' Modernity offered many pathways out of being identified by reference to the whole from which you came (the town or region, the trade, guild or profession, the family, and the social class). Psychologists call this individuation. Individuation not only comes from the newfound freedom of modernization; it also creates even more such freedoms. What it also did, however, as we've seen Giddens observe with his reference to 'disembedding,' was break primary ties that had once offered people security and a sense of belonging, of being rooted somewhere. At work, people were part of a 'class', of a union, of an association, or of multiple associations—family, educational, avocational, religious, political, neighborhood, and ethnic, to name but a few. In 1835, prior to large-scale industrialization and urbanization, de Tocqueville was intrigued by what he called 'the spirit of association,' which he saw everywhere on his travels through America at the time. To him, it was a key ingredient for the success of democracy. Democracy happens in a shared community, Brooks (2018) agrees. It reminds people that they're created equal; they share a common enterprise.

Modernization and industrialization changed this dramatically. Giddens observes that the more that tradition loses hold, the more people are forced to make choices among an ever-growing plurality of options and claims to 'truth.' Modernization and industrialization freed people from traditional authorities, conventions, prohibitions, taboos, and compliance demands that had, in a sense, greatly limited them. But these conventions, rules, and linkages also provided people with a sense of security and meaning in life, without them having to necessarily ponder any difficult (life) choices that made it so. The conditions in which they lived pre-existed, were set, and would post-exist beyond the person's lifetime. Becoming an individual, in contrast, makes people stand-alone, facing the world in all its perilous and overpowering aspects. Fromm writes:

> Growing individuation, means growing isolation, insecurity, and thereby growing doubt concerning one's role in the universe, the meaning of one's life, and with all that a growing feeling of one's own powerlessness and insignificance as an individual.
>
> (1941, p. 45)

The escape from freedom is crucially linked to economic, social, and political conditions. Like Karl Marx, Fromm believed that capitalism had turned human beings into cogs in a machine, sapping them of their individuality and creativity, and leaving them alienated and susceptible to authoritarian forces. The way 'capitalism is done in the 21st century' would certainly have accelerated this tendency:

'How capitalism is done in the 21st century'

A prominent engineer and vice president of Amazon's cloud computing arm said that he had quit 'in dismay' over the recent firings of workers who had raised questions about workplace safety during the coronavirus pandemic (Zaveri, 2020). He criticized a number of recent firings by Amazon, including that of an employee in a Staten Island warehouse, Christian Smalls, who led a protest in March calling for the company to provide workers with more protections. Mr. Smalls' firing has drawn the scrutiny of New York State's attorney general. Mr. Bray also criticized the firing of two Amazon employees, Maren Costa and Emily Cunningham, who had circulated a petition on internal email lists that called on Amazon to expand sick leave, hazard pay and child care for warehouse workers. They had also helped organize a virtual event for warehouse employees to speak to tech workers at the company about its workplace conditions and coronavirus response. Mr. Bray, who had worked for the company for more than five years, called the fired workers whistle-blowers, and said that firing them was 'evidence of a vein of toxicity running through the company culture.'

Employees have protested at several Amazon facilities, saying they feel unsafe and fear warehouses have been contaminated with the coronavirus. Other employees are demanding better pay or more sick leave. Not long before, Amazon had set up an 'Amazon relief fund,' which offers grants between $400 and $5,000 to independent delivery companies, gig workers and seasonal employees. Public donations to the fund, though not solicited, are possible because of the way Amazon set it up. Meanwhile the retail giant is worth around $1 trillion, and its online shopping during the Covid-19 pandemic drove sales to $75.5 billion in the quarter, up 26 percent from a year earlier. But the public is asked to make donations so that Amazon can pay its workers a fair wage.

The company had previously said it fired Mr. Smalls because he had violated its policies by leaving quarantine—he had previously been exposed to a sick worker—to attend the protest at the site. Amazon told Ms. Costa and Ms. Cunningham that they had violated a policy that forbids Amazon workers from asking their co-workers to donate to causes or sign petitions.

Senator Sherrod Brown of Ohio and Senators Robert Menendez and Cory Booker, both of New Jersey, have written to Amazon's chief executive, Jeff Bezos, to express concern about warehouse safety. The company has rolled out various safety measures at its warehouses across the country, such as temperature checks and mandatory masks.

Mr. Bray acknowledged that Amazon was prioritizing warehouse safety. But he said he also believed the workers. 'Amazon treats the humans in the warehouses as fungible units of pick-and-pack potential. Only that's not just Amazon, it's how 21st-century capitalism is done'.

This creates the tension that Fromm was concerned about. Human individuation depends on the conditions of modernity. But this increasingly means market-driven, globalized, industrial, and financial capitalism. That means that the conditions of 21st-century capitalism no longer typically offer a basis for the realization of individuality: just think of the example above. At the same time, people have lost those ties which gave them security and a sense of belonging and community. Fromm concludes that this lag, this gap, makes freedom an unbearable burden. When the freedom to individuate has outpaced the economic and social conditions that afford people the resources to do something meaningful, worthwhile, and relational with that freedom, instead leaving them alone and unprotected, powerful tendencies arise to escape from freedom. Fromm warned us that people will seek refuge in a submission to new compliance demands. They become willing to reconcile themselves to an authority (rules and conventions) which offer(s) even a shred of economic security (e.g., employment, even if temporary, precarious or contingent) and promises at least some relief from uncertainty.

The cognitive shortcut

And so comes the submission to more rules. Rules eliminate the need for us to think for ourselves, except about the applicability of the rule to the situation we find ourselves in. We need to take responsibility neither for the rule nor for its inherent (in)justness or its consequences. Rules, and compliance to them, shrink cognitive complexity. They are a shortcut to solutions and action, even if our embrace of them means we are unwilling, or avoiding, to make trade-offs demanded by other practical and moral concerns. Research into fundamentalism—the insistence that one set of claims is foundational, indubitable, and decisive—notes how rules can end confusion, fear, and provide satisfying and sure answers to the uncertainties of life (Law, 1997). What is attractive about it is its oppositional stance toward the disembedding and uprootedness of the modern, industrialized, urbanized world. A more fundamental stance on rules and compliance represents a critical—and, if embraced, a successful—confrontation with the general problem of uncertainty and insecurity.

Free markets have plowed up a terrain that is enormously favorable for compliance-driven approaches to the management of uncertainty and risk. Privatization and deregulation and market concentration have all shaped (and in ways are still shaping) the political-economic conditions of possibility for the growth of compliance. Deprofessionalization, the burgeoning of compliance workforces, and surveillance capitalism have all undermined the foundation of trust. The leap of faith we all had to make when absent in time and space from when and where work was done can be made with procedures, checklists, self-regulation, and risk assessments—and now with optical fiber cable. Faith is no longer necessary to make that leap. We can be (virtually) there, we can watch—even down to a surgeon's moves in a hospital's operating theater. Financialization, short-termism, contracting, and the infatuation with auditing have all both necessitated and abetted more rules and formal processes of bureaucratic accountability inside as well as between organizations. And finally, the market itself has been great for bureaucracy and compliance. Bureaucracy and compliance mechanisms themselves can be monetized, commodified, bought and sold. Just think of the enormous market for safety management systems. When more paperwork and compliance are your revenue model, then free markets are your friend.

And yet, it doesn't carry the whole explanation. For sure, free markets have led to unfree, overregulated workers because of all the mechanisms above, as has been detailed in chapters 3, 4, and 5. But as a collective of political-economic policy directions and consequences, they are more than the sum of their parts. Together, in interaction, they have fostered the societal and psychological conditions for those mechanisms to thrive. The erosion of workers' rights, the liberation of finance, the acceleration of downward mobility and precarious employment—these have all produced a sense of loss and possibly even crisis. A plurality of values and ideas offers only possibilities but nothing consistent to grab hold off, while states and institutions appear less and less equipped to deal with the risks of modernity. These conditions are ripe for welcoming more authoritarian control, where demanding a singular set of rules and compliance with them is—paradoxically—the liberation people might be looking for. It suggests that efforts to declutter the growing bureaucracy of work, efforts to persuade organizations to decentralize their decision-making, efforts to devolve authority as closely to the professional frontline as possible, and calls to find ways to once again cultivate trust could remain cosmetic, temporary, and tenuous. But the mechanisms that have created unfree workers, and the emergence of the conditions that give them fertile ground, were not inevitable. Nor are they irreversible. We can once again harness entrepreneurism and capitalism in a way that serves trust, equality, and participation if we strive to help change the rules of the political-economic game.

REFERENCES

Albert, M. (1993). *Capitalism against capitalism*. London: Whurr Publishers.

Almklov, P. G., Rosness, R., & Storkersen, K. (2014). When safety science meets the practitioners: Does safety science contribute to marginalization of practical knowledge? *Safety Science, 67*, 25–36.

Altemeyer, B. (1988). *Enemies of freedom*. San Francisco, CA: Jossey-Bass.

Amalberti, R. (2001). The paradoxes of almost totally safe transportation systems. *Safety Science, 37*(2–3), 109–126.

Amalberti, R. (2013). *Navigating safety: Necessary compromises and trade-offs—theory and practice*. Heidelberg: Springer.

Amalberti, R., Auroy, Y., Berwick, D., & Barach, P. (2005). Five system barriers to achieving ultrasafe healthcare. *Annals of Internal Medicine, 142*(9), 756–764.

Anand, N. (2016, 15 September). Managers must face up to the risk of creating meaningless safety metrics. *TradeWinds*, 21–22.

Anon. (2012, 5 January). David Cameron: Business have 'culture of fear' about health and safety. *The Daily Telegraph*, p. 8.

Anteby, M., & Chan, C. K. (2018). A self-fulfilling cycle of coercive surveillance: Workers' invisibility practices and managerial justification. *Organization Science, 29*(2), 247–263.

Araral, E. (2009). The failure of water utilities privatization: Synthesis of evidence, analysis and implications. *Policy and Society, 27*(3), 221–228.

Arculus, D., Graham, T., & Rowlatt, P. (2005). *Regulation—Less is more: Reducing burdens, improving outcomes. A BRTF report to the Prime Minister.* London: Better Regulation Task Force.

Arendt, H. (1967). *The origins of totalitarianism* (3rd edn). London: George Allen & Unwin Ltd.

Ayers, F. G., Culvenor, J. F., Sillitoe, J., & Else, D. (2013). Meaningful and effective consultation and the construction industry of Victoria, Australia. *Construction Management and Economics, 31*(6), 542–567.

Ball, K. (2010). Workplace surveillance: An overview. *Labor History, 51*(1), 87–106.

Beck, U. (1992). *Risk society: Towards a new modernity.* London: Sage.

Becker, H. S. (1963). *Outsiders: Studies in the sociology of deviance.* London: Free Press of Glencoe.

Berkowitz, D. (2020). Worker safety in crisis: The cost of a weakened OSHA. *National Employment Law Project, 50*(4), 1–6.

Bieder, C., & Bourrier, M. (Eds.). (2013). *Trapping safety into rules: How desirable or avoidable is proceduralization?* Farnham: Ashgate Publishing Co.

Bittle, S., & Snider, L. (2006). From manslaughter to preventable accident: Shaping corporate criminal liability. *Law & Policy, 28*(4), 470–496.

Black, J., Hopper, M., & Band, C. (2007). Making a success of principles-based regulation. *Law and Financial Markets Review, 1*(3), 191–206.

Bozeman, B. (1993). A theory of government 'red tape'. *Journal of Public Administration Research and Theory, 3*(3), 273–303.

Braedley, S., & Luxton, M. (Eds.). (2010). *Neoliberalism and everyday life.* Quebec: McGill-Queen's University Press.

Bregman, R. (2019). *De meeste mensen deugen: Een nieuwe geschiedenis van de mens.* Amsterdam: De Correspondent.

Brooks, D. (2018). The privatization of meaning. *New York Times*, p. 11.

Brown, D. J., Earle, J. S., & Telegdy, A. (2016). Where does privatization work? Understanding the heterogeneity in estimated firm performance effects. *Journal of Corporate Finance, 41*(12), 329–362.

Bryson, A., Ebbinghaus, B., & Visser, J. (2011). Causes, consequences and cures of union decline. *European Journal of Industrial Relations, 17*(2), 97–105.

Buchanan, B. (1975). Red tape and the service ethic: Some unexpected differences between public and private managers. *Administration & Society*, 6, 423–444.

CAIB. (2003). *Report Volume 1, August 2003*. Retrieved from Washington, DC. www.nasa.gov/columbia/home/CAIB_Vol1.html

Capra, F. (1996). *The web of life: A new scientific understanding of living systems* (1st Anchor Books edn.). New York: Anchor Books.

Carayon, P., & Cassel, C. K. (2019). *Taking action against clinician burnout: A systems approach to professional well-being*. Washington, DC: National Academy of Sciences, Engineering, and Medicine.

Carroll, P., Deighton-Smith, R., Silver, H., & Walker, C. (2008). *Minding the gap: Appraising the promise and performance of regulatory reform in Australia*. Canberra, ACT: ANU Press.

Carson, S. (2020). [An observation from forty years underground, email received by author, October 22, 2020].

Cauadrado-Ballesteros, B., & Peña-Miguel, N. (2018). The socioeconomic consequences of privatization: An empirical analysis for Europe. *Social Indicators Research*, 139(1), 163–183.

Coglianese, C. (2017). The limits of performance-based regulation. *U. Mich J. L. Reform*, 50(3), 525–563.

Cohen, S. (1972). *Folk devils and moral panics: The creation of the Mods and Rockers*. London: Routledge.

Davies, B., & Bansel, P. (2005). The time of their lives? Academic workers in neoliberal time(s). *Health Sociology Review*, 14(1), 47–58.

De Jong, P. O., & Zijlstra, S. E. (2009). *Wikken, wegen en (toch) wetgeven: Een onderzoek naar de hïerarchie en omvang van wetgeving in vijf Europese landen (Onderzoek en Beleid #280)*. Amsterdam: VU University Amsterdam Centre for Law and Governance and Wetenschappelijk Onderzoek- en Documentatiecentrum, Ministerie van Justitie.

De Wannemacker, W. (2020, 13 June). Time to slim down aviation's ever-expanding rule book. *Flight Global*, 12, 13.

Dekker, S. W. A. (2015). *Safety differently: Human factors for a new era*. Boca Raton, FL: CRC Press/Taylor and Francis.

Dekker, S. W. A. (2016). *Just culture: Restoring trust and accountability in your organization*. Boca Raton, FL: CRC Press.

Dekker, S. W. A. (2018). *The safety anarchist: Relying on human expertise and innovation, reducing bureaucracy and compliance*. London: Routledge.

Dekker, S. W. A., & Breakey, H. (2016). 'Just culture:' Improving safety by achieving substantive, procedural and restorative justice. *Safety Science, 85*, 187–193.

Dickson, D. T. (1968). Bureaucracy and morality: An organization perspective on a moral crusade. *Social Problems, 16*(2), 143–156.

Dinlersoz, E., & Greenwood, J. (2016). The rise and fall of unions in the United States. *Journal of Monetary Economics, 83*(10), 129–146.

Donaldson, C. (2013). Zero harm: Infallible or ineffectual. *OHS Professional, March*, 22–27.

Eisenstadt, S. N. (1959). Bureaucracy, bureaucratization, and debureaucratization. *Administrative Science Quarterly, 4*(3), 302–320.

Elling, M. G. M. (1991). *Veiligheidsvoorschriften in de industrie (safety rules in industry)*. PhD thesis, University of Twente, Enschede, the Netherlands. (WMW No. 8)

Fisscher, L. A. D., Stoeten, M. M., Németh, A. A., & Slingerland, W. (2019). *Ervaren regeldruk bij mkb-ondernemers: Een onderzoek naar ervaren knelpunten en mogelijkheden tot vermindering van regeldruk*. Deventer: Saxion Hogeschool, Lectoraat Weerbare Democratie.

Foucault, M. (1976). *Mental illness and psychology* (1st edn.). New York: Harper & Row.

Foucault, M. (1977). *Discipline and punish: The birth of the prison* (1st American edn.). New York: Pantheon Books.

Francis, A. (2015). *Family trouble: Middle-class parents, children's problems, and the disruption of everyday life*. New Brunswick, NJ. Rutgers University Press.

Frederick, J., & Lessin, N. (2000). The rise of behavioural-based safety programmes. *Multinational Monitor, 21*, 11–17.

Friedersdorf, C. (2020). The fight against words that sound like, but are not, slurs. *The Atlantic, 163*(9), 40–44.

Fromm, E. (1941). *Escape from freedom*. New York: Farrar & Rinehart.

Fuchs, C., Boersma, K., Albrechtslund, A., & Sandoval, M. (Eds.). (2012). *Internet and surveillance: The challenges of Web 2.0 and social media*. London: Routledge.

Galic, M., Timan, T., & Koops, B. J. (2017). Bentham, Deleuze and beyond: An overview of surveillance theories from the panopticon to participation. *Philosophy and Technology, 30*(1), 9–37.

GAO. (2012). *Workplace safety and health: Better OSHA guidance needed on safety incentive programs (Report to Congressional Requesters, GAO-12-329)*

(GAO-12-329). Retrieved from Washington, DC: Government Accountability Office: www.gao.gov/assets/gao-12-329.pdf

Gelles, D., & Kitroeff, N. (2019). F.A.A. Leaders face scrutiny over Boeing 737 Max Certification. *New York Times*, p. 7. Retrieved from www.nytimes.com/2019/07/31/business/boeing-max-faa-senate.html

Germov, J. (1995). Medi-fraud, managerialism and the decline of medical autonomy: Deprofessionalisation and proletarianisation reconsidered. *ANZJS, 31*(3), 51–66.

Giddens, A. (1990). *The consequences of modernity*. Stanford, CA: Stanford University Press.

Giddens, A. (1991). *Modernity and self-identity: Self and society in the late modern age*. Stanford, CA.: Stanford University Press.

Goldman, L., & Lewis, J. (2009). Corporate manslaughter legislation. *Occupational Health, 61*(2), 12–14.

Goode, E., & Ben-Yehuda, N. (1994). *Moral panics: The social construction of deviance*. Oxford: Blackwell.

Gouldner, A. W. (1979). *The future of intellectuals and the rise of the new class*. London: Continuum.

Goyal, A. (1983). Coping with bureaucracy, contractors and big industry. *Economic and Political Weekly, 18*(50), 2086–2087.

Graeber, D. (2013, August 17). On the phenomenon of bullshit jobs. *Strike, 8*, 10–11.

Grant, A. (2016). *Originals: How non-conformists change the world*. London: W. H. Allen.

Gray, G. C. (2009). The responsibilization strategy of health and safety. *British Journal of Criminology, 49*, 326–342.

Gray, G. C., & Rooij, B. V. (2020). Regulatory disempowerment: How enabling and controlling forms of power obstruct citizen-based regulation. *Regulation and Governance, 13*(5), 1–22. doi:10.1111/rego.12328

Gray, J. (1998). *False dawn: The delusions of global capitalism*. London: Granta Books.

Gray, J. (2003). *Al Qaeda and what it means to be modern*. London: Faber & Faber.

Green, J. (1997). *Risk and misfortune: The social construction of accidents*. London: Routledge.

Hale, A. R. (1990). Safety rules O.K.? Possibilities and limitations in behavioral safety strategies. *Journal of Occupational Accidents, 12*, 3–20.

Hale, A. R., & Borys, D. (2013). Working to rule, or working safely? Part 1: A state of the art review. *Safety Science, 55*, 207–221.

Hale, A. R., Borys, D., & Adams, M. (2013). Safety regulation: The lessons of workplace safety rule management for managing the regulatory burden. *Safety Science, 71*, 112–122.

Hamel, G., & Zanini, M. (2020). *Humanocracy: Creating organizations as amazing as the people inside them*. Cambridge, MA: Harvard Business Review Press.

Hampton, P. (2005). *Reducing administrative burdens: Effective inspection and enforcement*. London: HM Treasury.

Hardie, I. (2008). *Financialization, loyalty and the rise of short-term shareholder value*. Paper presented at the ESRC Seminar 'Financialization and Competitiveness', Northumbria University, Newcastle.

Harrison, S., & Dowswell, G. (2002). Autonomy and bureaucratic accountability in primary care: What English general practitioners say. *Sociology of Health & Illness, 24*(2), 208–226.

Hasle, P., & Zwetsloot, G. I. J. M. (2011). Editorial: Occupational Health and Safety Management Systems: Issues and challenges. *Safety Science, 49*(7), 961–963.

Hayes, J. (2012). Operator competence and capacity: Lessons from the Montara blowout. *Safety Science, 50*(3), 563–574.

Haythornthwaite, R. (2006). *Risk, responsibility and regulation: Whose risk is it anyway?* Whitehall, London: Better Regulation Commission.

Heather, S., & Kearns, G. (2018). *Poll: Mining OHS rules polarise the industry and risk friction*. Perth, WA: Mining People.

Heijne, S. (2018). *Er zijn nog 17 miljoen wachtenden voor u: Dertig jaar marktwerking in Nederland*. Amsterdam: De Correspondent.

Heine, S. (2018). *Er zijn nog 17 miljoen wachtenden voor u (there are another 17 million people ahead of you): Dertig jaar marktwerking in Nederland*. Amsterdam: De Correspondent.

Heinrich, H. W., Petersen, D., & Roos, N. (1980). *Industrial accident prevention* (5th edn.). New York: McGraw-Hill Book Company.

Hendrich, A., Chow, M. P., Skierczynski, B. A., & Lu, Z. (2008). A 36-hospital time and motion study: How do medical-surgical nurses spend their time? *The Permanente Journal, 12*(3), 25–34.

Henriqson, E., Schuler, B., van Winsen, R. D., & Dekker, S. W. A. (2014). The constitution and effects of safety culture as an object in the discourse of accident prevention: A Foucauldian approach. *Safety Science, 70*, 465–476.

Hier, S. P. (2003). Risk and panic in late modernity: Implications of the converging sites of social anxiety. *British Journal of Sociolgy, 54*(1), 3–20.

Hohnen, P., & Hasle, P. (2011). Making work environment auditable: A 'critical case' study of certified occupational health and safety management systems in Denmark. *Safety Science, 49*(7), 1022–1029.

Hollnagel, E. (2018). *Safety-II in practice: Developing the resilience potentials.* London: Routledge.

Hollway, W., & Jefferson, T. (1997). The risk society in an age of anxiety. *British Journal of Sociolgy, 48*(2), 255–266.

Hopkins, A. (2006). What are we to make of safe behaviour programs? *Safety Science, 44*, 583–597.

Hopkins, A. (2010). Risk-management and rule-compliance: Decision-making in hazardous industries. *Safety Science, 49*(2), 110–120.

Jack, I. (2001). The 12.10 to Leeds. *Granta, 73*(1), 67–105.

Jacobs, D. (2007, November/December). A catalyst for change in workers' compensation. *Professional Case Management, 12*, 357–361.

Jacobsen, M. (Writer) & M. Jacobsen (Director). (2017). *Safety Differently* [Documentary]. In R. Miller (Producer). West End, Queensland, Australia: RideFree Media.

Jacobsen, M. (Writer) & M. Jacobsen (Director). (2019). Doing safety differently [Documentary]. In R. Miller (Producer). West End, Queensland, Australia: RideFree Media.

Jensen, C. B., & Winthereik, B. R. (2017). Audit loops and audit implosion. In A. Lebner (Ed.), *Redescribing relations: Strathernian conversations on ethnography, knowledge and politics* (pp. 155–181). New York: Berghahn.

Johnstone, R. E. (2017). Glut of anesthesia guidelines a disservice, except for lawyers. *Anesthesiology News, 42*(3), 1–6.

Kaufman, H. (1960). *The forest ranger: A study in administrative behavior.* Baltimore, MD: Johns Hopkins University Press.

Kaufman, H. (1977). *Red tape: Its origins, uses and abuses.* Washington, DC: The Brookings Institution.

Kern, T. (2018). The war on error: A new and different approach to human performance. In J. U. Hagen (Ed.), *How could this happen? Managing errors in organizations* (pp. 273–285). Cham: Springer/Palgrave MacMillan.

Klikauer, T. (2015). What is managerialism? *Critical Sociology, 41*(7–8), 1103–1119.

Kniesner, T. J., & Leeth, J. D. (1995). Abolishing OSHA. *Regulation, 18*(4), 46–56.

Koenen, I. (2015). *Prijsvechten: Van bouwfraude tot uitverkoop*. Roelofarendsveen: BIM Media.

Kollmeyer, C. (2018). Trade union decline, deindustrialization, and rising income inequality in the United States, 1947 to 2015. *Research in Social Stratification and Mobility*, *57*(10), 1–10.

Kotz, D. M. (2002). Globalization and neoliberalism. *Rethinking Marxism*, *12*(2), 64–79.

Krause, T. R. (1997). *The behavior-based safety process: Managing involvement for an injury-free culture*. New York: Van Nostrand Reinhold.

Kuttner, R. (2018). *Can democracy survive global capitalism?* New York: Norton.

Lafferty, G. (2010). In the wake of neo-liberalism: Deregulation, unionism and labour rights. *Review of International Political Economy*, *17*(3), 589–608.

Law, J. (1997). *The limits of fundamentalism* (Master of Arts in Humanities Thesis). Dominguez Hills, CA: California State University.

Lerner, J. S., & Tetlock, P. E. (1999). Accounting for the effects of accountability. *Psychological Bulletin*, *125*(2), 255–275.

Lilla, M. (2014). The truth about our libertarian age: Why the dogma of democracy doesn't always make the world better. *New Republic*, *100*(6), 1–10.

Lorenz, C. (2012). If you're so smart, why are you under surveillance? Universities, neoliberalism, and new public management. *Critical Inquiry*, *38*(3), 599–629.

Luhmann, N. (1991). *Risk: A sociological theory*. New York: De Gruyter.

Lukianoff, G., & Haidt, J. (2019). *The coddling of the American mind: How good intentions and bad ideas are setting up a generation for failure*. New York: Penguin Books.

Lynn, L. E. (2015). Herbert Kaufman, The forest ranger: A study in administrative behavior. In M. Lodge, E. C. Page, & S. J. Balla (Eds.), *The Oxford handbook of classics in public policy and administration* (pp. 1–14). Oxford: Oxford University Press.

Maidment, D. (1993). *A changing safety culture on British Rail*. Paper presented at the 11th NeTWork Workshop on 'The use of rules to achieve safety, Bad Homburg.

Månson, P. (1996). Max Weber. In H. Andersen & L. B. Kaspersen (Eds.), *Klassisk og moderne samfundsteori*. Copenhagen: Hans Reitzels Forlag.

Mark, R. (2020). Regulation or inspiration? *Flying*, *147*(7), 40–45.

McCord, P. (2017). *Powerful: Building a culture of freedom and responsibility*. San Francisco, CA: Silicon Guild.

McIntyre, D. (2005). 'My way or the highway': Managerial prerogative, the labour process and workplace health. *Health Sociology Review, 14*(1), 59–68.
Mendeloff, J. (1981). Does overregulation cause underregulation: The case of toxic substances. *Regulation, 5*, 47.
Meyer, M. W. (1979). Debureaucratization? *Social Science Quarterly, 60*(1), 25–34.
MEZ, R. (2017). *Goed geregeld: Een verantwoorde vermindering van regeldruk 2012-2017*. Den Haag: Ministerie van Economische Zaken, Directie Regeldruk en ICT Beleid.
Mintzberg, H. (1979). *The structuring of organizations: A synthesis of the research*. Englewood Cliffs, NJ: Prentice-Hall.
Mintzberg, H. (2004). *Managers not MBAs: A hard look at the soft practice of managing and management development*. San Francisco, CA: Berrett-Koehler.
Mirowski, P., & Plehwe, D. (Eds.). (2009). *The road from Mont Pèlerin: The making of the neoliberal thought collective*. Cambridge, MA: Harvard University Press.
Morgensen, V. (2003). Occupational safety and health in a neoliberal world. *WorkingUSA, 7*(2), 3–6.
NAPA. (2014). LIJ Medical Center introduces one-of-a-kind video monitoring project to enhance patient safety in ORs [Press release]. Retrieved from https://napaanesthesia.com/lij-medical-center-introduces-one-of-a-kind-video-monitoring-project-to-enhance-patient-safety-in-ors/
O'Neill, R. (2003). Criminal neglect: How dangerous employers stay safe from prosecution. *WorkingUSA, 7*(2), 24–42.
Ogus, A. I. (2004). *Regulation: Legal form and economic theory*. London: Hart.
Oppenheimer, M. (1972). The proletarianization of the professional. *The Sociological Review, 20*(1), 213–227.
Orlikowski, W. J. (1991). Integrated information environment or matrix of control? The contradictory implications of information technology. *Accounting, Management and Information Technologies, 1*(1), 9–42.
OSHA. (2000). *Supporting statement for paperwork reduction act 1995 submissions: Ergonomics Program Standard.*
Osmundsen, T. C., & Olsen, M. S. (2017). The imperishable controversy over aquaculture. *Marine Policy, 76*, 136–142.
Otteson, J. (2018). *The essential Adam Smith*. Vancouver: The Fraser Institute.
Paget, M. A. (2004). *The unity of mistakes: A phenomenological interpretation of medical work*. Philadelphia, PA: Temple University Press.

Parrish, M., & Schofield, T. (2005). Injured workers' experiences of the workers' compensation claims process: Institutional disrespect and the neoliberal state. *Health Sociology Review, 14*(1), 33–46.

Paxton, R. O. (1998). The five stages of fascism. *The Journal of Modern History, 70*(1), 1–23.

Peters, J., & Pouw, J. (2004). *Intensieve menshouderij: Hoe kwaliteit oplost in rationaliteit (Intensive people-husbandry: How quality dissolves in rationality)*. Schiedam, the Netherlands: Scriptum.

Peters, J., & Weggeman, M. (2017). *Het Rijnlandveranderboekje: Het gebeurt als je het loslaat*. Amsterdam: Uitgeverij Business Contact.

Petersen, A. H. (2020). *Can't Even: How millennials became the burnout generation*. New York: Houghton Mifflin.

Philipon, T. (2019). *The great reversal: How America gave up on free markets*. Cambridge, MA: Harvard University Press.

Piketty, T. (2017). *Capital in the twenty-first century*. Cambridge, MA: Harvard University Press.

Pink, D. H. (2009). *Drive: The surprising truth about what motivates us*. New York: Riverhead Books.

Polanyi, K. (1944). *The great transformation: The political and economic origins of our time*. Boston, MA: Beacon Press.

Power, M. (1994). *The audit explosion*. London: Demos.

Power, M. (1999). *The audit society: Rituals of verification*. Oxford: Oxford University Press.

Prasad, V., & Mailankody, S. (2017). Research and development spending to bring a single cancer drug to market and revenues after approval. *JAMA Internal Medicine, 177*(11), 1569–1575.

Provan, D. J., Woods, D. D., Dekker, S. W. A., & Rae, A. J. (2020). Safety II professionals: How resilience engineering can transform safety practice. *Safety Science, 195*, 1067–1080.

Rae, A. J., Weber, D. E., Provan, D. J., & Dekker, S. W. A. (2018). Safety clutter: The accumulation and persistance of 'safety' work that does not contribute to operational safety. *Policy and Practice in Health and Safety, 16*(2), 194–211.

Reason, J. T. (1990). *Human error*. New York: Cambridge University Press.

Ritzer, G. (1993). *The McDonaldization of society*. Thousand Oaks, CA: Pine Forge Press.

Roberts, K. A., & Donahue, K. A. (2000). Presidential address—Professing professionalism: Bureaucratization and deprofessionalization in the academy. *Sociological Focus, 33*(4), 365–384.

Rochlin, G. I., LaPorte, T. R., & Roberts, K. H. (1987). The self-designing high reliability organization: Aircraft carrier flight operations at sea. *Naval War College Review, 40*, 76–90.

Rodrik, D. (2017). Rescuing economics from neoliberalism. *Boston Review, 24*(11), 17–26.

Rolston, J. S. (2010). Risky business: Neoliberalism and workplace safety in Wyoming coal mines. *Human Organization*, 69(4), 331–342.

Rosness, R. (2004). *Alt flyter – og hva så? [Everything floats - and so what?]*. Paper presented at the Sikkerhetsdagene 2004, Trondheim, November 2–3, 2004.

Saines, M., Strickland, M., Pieroni, M., Kolding, K., Meacock, J., Nur, N., & Gough, S. (2014). *Get out of your own way: Unleashing productivity*. Retrieved from Sydney, Australia: Deloitte Touche Tohmatsu.

Saloniemi, A., & Oksanen, H. (1998). Accidents and fatal accidents: Some paradoxes. *Safety Science, 29*, 59–66.

Saull, R. (2015). Capitalism, crisis and the far-right in the neoliberal era. *Journal of International Relations and Development, 18*(8), 25–51.

Saunders, T. G. (2001). Bill files 03/20/2001 [S.J.R. 6]. *George W. Bush Presidential Library, FRC ID 778*.

Schofield, T. (2005). The impact of neoliberal policy on workplace health. *Health Sociology Review*, 14(1), 5–7.

Schwarcz, S. L. (2009). The 'principles' paradox. *European Business Organization Law Review, 10*, 175–184.

Schwenk, C. R., & Cosier, R. A. (1980). Effects of the expert, devil's advocate, and dialectical inquiry methods on prediction performance. *Organizational Behavior and Human Performance, 26*(3), 409–409.

Scott, J. C. (1998). *Seeing like a state: How certain schemes to improve the human condition have failed*. New Haven, CT: Yale University Press.

Scott, J. C. (2012). *Two cheers for anarchism*. Princeton, NJ: Princeton University Press.

Sheratt, F., & Dainty, A. R. J. (2017). UK construction safety: A zero paradox. *Policy and Practice in Health and Safety, 15*(2), 1–9.

Shibley, R. (2016). Vindictive protectiveness on campus. *Society, 53*(4), 375–382.

Silbey, S. (2009). Taming Prometheus: Talk about safety and culture. *Annual Review of Sociology, 35*, 341–369.

Simmons, R. (2012, May). The stranglehold of bureaucracy. *The Safety & Health Practitioner, 30*, 20.

Smith, A. (1776/2009). *An Inquiry into the Nature and Causes of the Wealth of Nations*. Blacksburg, VA: Thrifty Books.

Smith, C. (2001). Trust and confidence: Possibilities for social work in 'high modernity', *British Journal of Social Work, 31*, 287–305.

Smith, M. J., Cohen, H. H., Cohen, A., & Cleveland, R. J. (1978). Characteristics of successful safety programs. *Journal of Safety Research, 10*, 5–15.

Springer, S., Birch, K., & MacLeavy, J. (2016). *Handbook of neoliberalism*. London: Routledge.

Starbuck, W. H., & Farjoun, M. (2005). *Organization at the limit: Lessons from the Columbia disaster*. Malden, MA: Blackwell Publishing.

Sterk, C. (2003). *Waterverkenningen: Marktwerking in het watersysteembeheer. Een verkenning van de mogelijkheden van marktwerking (Eindrapport WIM3528 2003.100X)*. Den Haag, the Netherlands: RIZA Rijksinstituut voor integraal Zoetwaterbeheer en Afvalwaterbehandeling.

Stock, C. T., & Sundt, T. (2015). Timeout for checklists? *Annals of Surgery, 261*(5), 841–842.

Storkersen, K., Thorvaldsen, T., Kongsvik, T., & Dekker, S. W. A. (2020). How deregulation can become overregulation: An empirical study into the T growth of internal bureaucracy when governments take a step back. *Safety Science, 128*, 104–113.

Styhre, A. (2014). The influence of neoliberalism and its absence from management research. *International Jounral of Organizational Analysis, 22*(3), 278–300.

Tabuchi, H. (2018, June 19). How the Koch Brothers are killing public transit projects around the country. *New York Times*.

Taylor, F. W. (1911). *The principles of scientific management*. New York: Harper & Brothers.

Taylor, K. (2018). Domino's is repairing roads, and some people say it reveals a 'dystopian' truth about America. *Business Insider, 10*(6), 12–13.

Thelen, T., & Read, R. (2007). Social security and care after socialism: Reconfigurations of public and private. *European Journal of Anthropology, 50*(10), 3–18.

Thorvaldsen, T., Holmen, I. M., & Kongsvik, T. (2017). [HSE survey aquaculture 2016].

Tooma, M. (2017). *Safety, security, health and environment law* (2nd edn.). Annandale, NSW: The Federation Press.

Townsend, A. S. (2013). *Safety can't be measured*. Farnham: Gower Publishing.

Tsoukas, H. (1998). Introduction: Chaos, complexity and organization theory. *Organization, 5*(3), 291–313.

Turner, B. A. (1978). *Man-made disasters*. London: Wykeham Publications.

Ungar, S. (2001). Moral panic versus the risk society: The implications of the changing sites of social anxiety. *British Journal of Sociology, 52*(2), 271–291.

Vaughan, D. (1996). *The challenger launch decision: Risky technology, culture, and deviance at NASA*. Chicago, IL: University of Chicago Press.

Vegter, F., Gijsbers, L., & Voorn, M. (2016). *Verpleeghuiszorg in Nederland: Belevingsonderzoek onder Nederlands publiek, professionals en bestuurders*. Den Haag: Ministerie van Volksgezondheid, Welzijn en Sport.

Vergeer, E. J. M. (2017). *Reguldruk vanuit een ander perspectief: Onderzoek naar de beleving van deregulering bij ondernemers*. Leiden: Leiden University: E. M. Meijers Instituut voor rechtswetenschappelijk onderzoek.

Vilchez, V. F. (2017). The dark side of ISO 14001: The symbolic environmental behavior. *European Research on Management and Business Economics, 23*(1), 33–39.

Watson, I. (2015). Wage inequality and neoliberalism: The Australian experience. *Journal of Industrial Relations, 58*(1), 131–149.

Whalen, C. J. (2017). *Understanding financialization: Standing on the shoulders of Minsky (Working paper No. 892)*. SUNY Buffalo Law School: Levy Economics Institute of Bard College, The Baldy Center for Law and Social Policy.

Woods, D. D. (2006). How to design a safety organization: Test case for resilience engineering. In E. Hollnagel, D. D. Woods, & N. G. Leveson (Eds.), *Resilience engineering: Concepts and precepts* (pp. 296–306). Aldershot: Ashgate Publishing Co.

Woods, D. D., & Dekker, S. W. A. (2001). Anticipating the effects of technology change: A new era of dynamics for human factors. *Theoretical Issues in Ergonomics Science, 1*(1), 272–282.

Woods, D. D., Dekker, S. W. A., Cook, R. I., Johannesen, L. J., & Sarter, N. B. (2010). *Behind human error*. Aldershot: Ashgate Publishing Co.

Zaveri, M. (2020, 4 May). An Amazon Vice President quit over firings of employees who protested. *New York Times*, p. 3.

Zimmerman, R. (1991). Risk bureaucracies in environmental health and safety management. *Journal of Energy Engineering*, *117*(3), 97–114.

Zuboff, S. (2015). Big other: Surveillance capitalism and the prospects of an information civilization. *Journal of Information Technology*, *30*(1), 75–89.

INDEX

Printed in the United States
by Baker & Taylor Publisher Services